Agile Software Development

Torgeir Dingsøyr · Tore Dybå · Nils Brede Moe
Editors

Agile Software Development

Current Research and Future Directions

Springer

Editors
Torgeir Dingsøyr
SINTEF
Dept. Information & Communication
Technology (ICT)
PO BOX 4760 Sluppen
NO-7465 Trondheim
Norway
torgeir.dingsoyr@sintef.no

Tore Dybå
SINTEF
Dept. Information & Communication
Technology (ICT)
PO BOX 4760 Sluppen
NO-7465 Trondheim
Norway
Tore.dyba@sintef.no

Nils Brede Moe
SINTEF
Dept. Information & Communication
Technology (ICT)
PO BOX 4760 Sluppen
NO-7465 Trondheim
Norway
Nils.b.moe@sintef.no

ISBN 978-3-642-43265-1   ISBN 978-3-642-12575-1 (eBook)
DOI 10.1007/978-3-642-12575-1
Springer Heidelberg Dordrecht London New York

ACM Computing Classification (1998): D.2, K.6

Cover design: KünkelLopka GmbH, Heidelberg

Printed on acid-free paper

Springer is part of Springer Science+Business Media (www.springer.com)

Foreword

Agile software development is the most important paradigm that has swept the software development world over the last decade. Even if it does not represent the most popular software development approach in actual use, it has certainly become of the most talked about. Its vocabulary and prime ideas have already started spilling over into other fields, project management in particular.

Agile software development also carries the unique distinction of being the source of continued debate since its inception. The controversy surrounding it simply doesn't want to die out. Few other movements have pitted detractors and advocates against each other so passionately, so religiously.

But why? Shouldn't a decade be enough to settle at least the fundamental arguments? Those arguments should be getting pretty old by now if it were not for two reasons that still fuel the debate.

The first reason is the inherent fuzziness of the topic. Agile software development is multi-faceted and poorly delimited. As such the paradigm doesn't lend itself to a crisp definition, let alone straightforward study. Is agility a general development philosophy? Is it about dealing with change and uncertainty? Is it a project management philosophy? A way of working with software development teams? A way of working inside software development teams? A way of thinking about software? A set of technical practices that target better quality and higher productivity? A set of collaboration practices that cater to the needs of customers and end users? A set of principles and values of professional conduct? A way of life? A rebellion? A religion? A cultural revolution of the software intellectuals? Well, it's all of the above and none of the above at the same time. That the scope of agile software development is nebulous and dependent on personal and contextual interpretation makes it a hard nut to crack in systematic means. Misconceptions both by detractors and advocates find fertile ground to take hold, amplify and multiply in an unproductive cycle. When a topic is that fuzzy, understanding the boundaries and what lies inside those boundaries become almost as important as understanding the intricacies of the individual constituents.

The second reason is poor dissemination and insufficient synthesis of fragmented research results. It's not that our knowledge of the different facets of agile software development has not expanded significantly over the past years. It has, thanks to the still ongoing research efforts that have undertaken the difficult task of dissecting the elastic anatomy of agile software development. Alas, the scattered results of these efforts are neither well publicized nor readily available to the questioning reader. The world simply doesn't know what we collectively know about agile software development. Worse it doesn't know what we still don't know about it.

This book contributes to the agile debate by addressing both sources of the agile confusion: fuzzy, multi-faceted scope and poor, unconsolidated dissemination of efforts representing the collective understanding of an expert community. The book represents a comprehensive snapshot of the knowledge accumulated over many years of research by those working closely with the industry, collecting data, observing practitioners in the field, synthesizing insights, devising theories, trying new methods to investigate core issues, and gathering clues to overcome outstanding challenges. It's your one-stop resource to agile software development research with contributions by the best people in the community, by people who know what they're talking about. Enjoy it. Digest it. Use it.

Ottawa, March 2010

Hakan Erdogmus, Kalemun Research Inc.

Preface

Principles of agile software development have a large impact on how software is developed. Some have characterized the change towards agile development as a paradigm shift, leading the focus to topics that have not been addressed or understood in traditional development.

It is therefore important to address what defines and characterizes agile development, what are the historical roots? How do the different principles, processes and methods work in practice, how does agile development affect various groups who are participating in software development? What new challenges arise when using agile development, and what challenges will the methods be unable to solve?

The transition to agile software development has been driven by practitioners, more or less informed by research results, mainly from fields not traditionally focusing on software development. However, researchers focusing on agile software development have a role in developing an understanding of how agile development methods work. Further, why they do or do not work, and in which situations or environment they work better or worse.

This book seeks to show the current state of research on agile software development through an introduction and ten invited contributions on some of the main research fields and by some of the main researchers. The chapters both show the main results in each subfield, and in addition explain what these results mean to practitioners as well as for future research in the field.

The book is aimed at reflective practitioners and researchers, and we hope the book also can serve for graduate courses at universities.

We are very grateful to the chapter authors who have contributed with important overview articles in their own research areas, and also are presenting their chapters at the 11th International Conference on Agile Software Development (XP2010). The editing of this book was supported by the EVISOFT project, which is partially funded by the Research Council of Norway under Grant 174390/I40.

Trondheim, March 2010

Torgeir Dingsøyr
Tore Dybå
Nils Brede Moe

Contents

List of Contributors

Pekka Abrahamsson
Department of Computer Science
University of Helsinki
PO Box 68
FI-00014 University of Helsinki, Finland
pekka.abrahamsson@cs.helsinki.fi

VenuGopal Balijepally
Department of Accounting, Finance & MIS
Prairie View A&M University
Prairie View, Texas 77446-0519, USA
vebalijepally@pvamu.edu

Kyle Atikus Barnes
Seattle Software Solutions
1969 SW Hillcrest Road
Seattle, WA 98166, USA
kyle@seattle-softwaresolutions.com

Richard Baskerville
Department of Computer Information Systems
Georgia State University
University Plaza, Atlanta
Georgia 30302, USA
baskerville@acm.org

Robert Biddle
School of Computer Science
Carleton University
214C, Social Sciences Research Building
Ottawa, ON K1S 5B6, Canada
robert_biddle@carleton.ca

Barry Boehm
Center for Systems and Software Engineering
University of Southern California
941 W. 37th Place, SAL Room 328
Los Angeles, CA 90089-0781, USA
boehm@usc.edu

Philip L. Bond
Department of Information Systems and Operations Management
University of Texas at Arlington
Arlington, TX 76019, USA
philip.bond@mavs.uta.edu

Alan Cannon
Department of Information Systems and Operations Management
University of Texas at Arlington
Arlington, TX 76019, USA
acannon@uta.edu

Keith C.C.Chan
Department of Computing
The Hong Kong Polytechnic University
Hunghom, Kowloon, Hong Kong
cskcchan@comp.polyu.edu.hk

Kieran Conboy
Department of Accounting and Finance
National University of Ireland, Galway,
Galway, Ireland
kieran.conboy@nuigalway.ie

Torgeir Dingsøyr
SINTEF
NO-7465 Trondheim, Norway
torgeir.dingsoyr@sintef.no

Tore Dybå
SINTEF
NO-7465 Trondheim, Norway
tore.dyba@sintef.no

Theodore D. Hellmann
Department of Computer Science
University of Calgary
ICT 602, 2500 University Drive NW
Calgary, Alberta, T2N 1N4, Canada
tdhellma@ucalgary.ca

Ali Hosseini-Khayat
Department of Computer Science
University of Calgary
CT 602, 2500 University Drive NW
Calgary, Alberta, T2N 1N4, Canada
hosseisa@ucalgary.ca

Juhani Iivari
Department of Information Processing Sciences
University of Oulu
P.O. Box 3000, 90014 Oulun yliopisto, Finland
juhani.iivari@oulu.fi

Netta Iivari
Department of Information Processing Sciences
University of Oulu
P.O. Box 3000, 90014 Oulun yliopisto, Finland
netta.iivari@oulu.fi

Supannika Koolmanojwong
Center for Systems and Software Engineering
University of Southern California
941 W. 37th Place, SAL Room 328
Los Angeles, CA 90089-0781, USA
koolmano@usc.edu

Jo Ann Lane
Center for Systems and Software Engineering
University of Southern California
941 W. 37th Place, SAL Room 328
Los Angeles, CA 90089-0781, USA
jolane@usc.edu

Kim Man Lui
Department of Computing
The Hong Kong Polytechnic University
Hunghom, Kowloon, Hong Kong
cskmlui@comp.polyu.edu.hk

Sabine Madsen
Department of Communication, Business and IT
Roskilde University
Universitetsvej 1
DK- 4000 Roskilde, Denmark
sabinem@ruc.dk

Angela Martin
Department of Computer Science
The University of Waikato
Private Bag 3105
Hamilton, 3240, New Zealand
angela@cs.waikato.ac.nz

Frank Maurer
Department of Computer Science
University of Calgary
2500 University Drive NW
Calgary, Alberta, T2N 1N4, Canada
fmaurer@ucalgary.ca

Nils Brede Moe
SINTEF
NO-7465 Trondheim, Norway
nils.b.moe@sintef.no

Lorraine Morgan
LERO - The Irish Software Engineering Research Centre
University of Limerick
Limerick, Ireland
lorraine.morgan@ul.ie

Sridhar Nerur
Department of Information Systems and Operations Management
University of Texas at Arlington
Arlington, TX 76019, USA
snerur@uta.edu

James Noble
School of Engineering and Computer Science
Victoria University
PO Box 600
Wellington 6140, New Zealand
kjx@ecs.vuw.ac.n

Nilay Oza
VTT Technical Research Centre of Finland
PO Box 1000
FI-02044 VTT, Finland
nilay.oza@vtt.fi

Jan Pries-Heje
Department of Communication, Business and IT
Roskilde University
Universitetsvej 1
DK- 4000 Roskilde, Denmark
janph@ruc.dk

Hugh Robinson
Mathematics, Computing and Technology Faculty
The Open University
Walton Hall
Milton Keynes, MK7 6AA, UK
h.m.robinson@open.ac.uk

Helen Sharp
Mathematics, Computing and Technology Faculty
The Open University
Walton Hall
Milton Keynes, MK7 6AA, UK
h.c.sharp@open.ac.uk

Mikko Siponen
Department of Information Processing Science
University of Oulu
PO Box 3000
FI-90014 University of Oulu, Finland
mikko.siponen@oulu.fi

Richard Turner
Stevens Institute of Technology
Hoboken, NJ 07030, USA
rturner@stevens.edu

1 Agile Software Development: An Introduction and Overview

Torgeir Dingsøyr, Tore Dybå, Nils Brede Moe

Abstract: Agile software development is an important topic in software engineering and information systems. This chapter provides a characterization and definition of agile software development, an overview of research through a summary of existing overview studies, an analysis of the research literature so far, and an introduction to the main themes of this book. The first part of the book provides foundations and background of agile development. The second part describes findings from studies of agile methods in practice. The third part identifies principal challenges and discusses new frontiers that agile development methods will meet in the future.

1.1 Introduction

Agile software development has had a major influence on how software development is conducted. It has become an umbrella term for a number of changes in how software developers plan and coordinate their work, how they communicate with customers and external stakeholders, and how software development is organized in small, medium-sized and large companies from the telecom and healthcare sectors to games and interactive media.

We see the agile development methods as a reaction to plan-based or traditional methods, which emphasize "a rationalized, engineering-based approach" (Dybå 2000) incorporating extensive planning, codified processes, and rigorous reuse (Boehm 2002). By contrast, agile methods address the challenge of an unpredictable world by recognizing the value competent people and their relationships bring to software development (Nerur and Balijepally 2007).

In this chapter, we will first define what we see as agile software development and define other central terms that will be used throughout the book. Further, we give a broad overview of research conducted in this field, and describe the main themes of the book: foundations and background of agile development, agile methods in practice and principal challenges and new frontiers. Finally, we state what we see as some of the main challenges and main future directions for research on agile software development.

T. Dingsøyr et al. (eds.), *Agile Software Development*,
DOI 10.1007/978-3-642-12575-1_1, © Springer-Verlag Berlin Heidelberg 2010

1.2 What is Agile Development?

In an introduction to the special issue on agile methods in IEEE Computer in 2003, Williams and Cockburn (2003) state that agile software development "is about feedback and change", and they emphasize that software development is an empirical or nonlinear process, where short feedback-loops are necessary to achieve a desirable, predictable outcome. Ericksson et al. (2005) further underline the importance of lightweight processes in agile development, defining agility as to "strip away as much of the heaviness, commonly associated with the traditional software-development methodologies, as possible to promote quick response to changing environments, changes in user requirements, accelerated project deadlines and the like." (p. 89).

In an article discussing the concept of agility and leanness in software development, Conboy (2009) argues that agile methods must contribute to one of more of the following: creation of change, proaction in advance of change, reaction to change or learning from change. Further, an agile method must contribute to and not detract from: perceived economy, perceived quality, and perceived simplicity. A third requirement is to be continually ready to prepare the component for use.

Thus, agile software development has been characterized differently than plan-based or traditional development methods, mainly with the focus adapting to change and delivering products of high quality through simple work-processes. Nerur & Balijepally (2005) state that agile and traditional methods diverge on a number of aspects, including their fundamental assumptions, approach to control, management style, knowledge management, role assignment, role of the customer, project cycle, development model and desired organizational structure.

1.3 Research on Agile Software Development

In this section we first give an overview of prior research on agile software development, and then characterize the status of current research through examining the volume of scientific studies on the topic.

1.3.1 An Overview of Prior Research

Introductions to and overviews of agile development are given by Abrahamsson et al. (2002), Cohen et al. (2004), Erickson et al. (2005) and Dybå and Dingsøyr (2008). These four reports describe the state of the art and state of the practice in terms of characteristics of the various agile methods and lessons learned from applying such methods in industry.

The first review of the literature on agile software development was done in a technical report published by Abrahamsson et al. at VTT (2002). The report discusses the concept of agile development, presents processes, roles, practices, and experience with 10 agile development methods, and compares the methods with respect to the phases that they support and the level of competence that they require. Only DSDM and the Rational Unified Process were found to give full coverage to all phases of development, while Scrum mainly covers aspects related to project management. Abrahamsson et al. found anecdotal evidence that agile methods are "effective and suitable for many situations and environments", but state that very few empirically validated studies support these claims. Chapter 3 in this book updates this review.

Cohen et al. (2004) published a review that emphasized the history of agile development, showing some of the roots to other disciplines, and, in particular, discussed relations between agile development and the Capability Maturity Model. The authors believed that agile methods would be consolidated in the future, just as object-oriented methods were consolidated. Further, they did not believe that agile methods would rule out traditional methods. Rather, they believe that agile and traditional methods will have a symbiotic relationship, in which factors such as the number of people working on a project, application domain, criticality, and innovativeness will determine which process to select.

Erickson et al. (2005) described the state of research on extreme programming (XP), agile software development, and agile modelling. With respect to XP, they found a small number of case studies and experience reports that promote the success of XP. The practice of pair programming is supported by a more well-established stream of research, and that there are also some studies on iterative development. Erickson et al. recommend that the other core practices in XP be studied separately in order to identify what practices are working. Further, they saw challenges with matching agile software development methods with standards such as ISO, and they argued that this is an area that needs further research.

What is currently known about the benefits and limitations of agile software development, the strength of the evidence in support of these findings, and the implications of these studies for the software industry and the research community were the focus areas for Dybå and Dingsøyr's (2008) systematic review. The studies fell into four thematic groups: introduction and adoption, human and social factors, perceptions of agile methods, and comparative studies. The authors identified a number of reported benefits and limitations of agile development within each of these themes:

Regarding introduction, XP was difficult to introduce in complex organizations, yet seemingly easy in other types of organizations. Most studies reported that agile development practices are easy to adopt and work well. Benefits were reported in the following areas: customer collaboration, work processes for handling defects, learning in pair programming, thinking ahead for management, focusing on current work for engineers, and estimation.

A recurring theme in studies on agile development was human and social factors. A benefit of XP was that it thrived in radically different environments; in organizations that varied from having a hierarchical structure to little or no central control. Further, conversation, standardization, and tracking progress have been studied and are described as mechanisms for creating awareness within teams and organizations.

Many studies sought to identify how agile methods are perceived by different groups. Customers are satisfied with opportunities for feedback and response to change. However, the role of on-site customer can be stressful and cannot be sustained for a long period. Companies that use XP have more satisfied employees. There were mixed findings regarding the effectiveness of pair programming. University students perceive agile methods as providing them with relevant training.

The last theme was comparative studies. Some studies suggest benefits in projects that use agile methods because changes are incorporated more easily and business value is demonstrated more efficiently. It is possible to combine agile project management with overall traditional principles, such as the stage-gate project management model. With respect to the productivity of agile and traditional teams, three of the four comparative studies that address this issue found that using XP results in increased productivity.

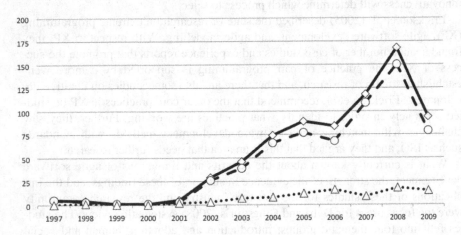

Fig. 1.1 Publications on agile software development, total number (top), conference papers (middle) and journal articles (bottom). Note that the numbers for 2009 do not include all publications from that year

1.3.2 An Analysis of Literature on Agile Development

To describe the status of research on agile software development, we conducted a literature search in the ISI Web of Science[1]. We found 719 scientific publications regarding agile software development, published between 1997 and 2009. Of these, 627 were papers in conference proceedings (87%), and 92 were journal articles (13%, including review articles). Figure 1.1 illustrates the trend in publications for conference papers, journal articles and the total. There seems to be a steady growth in the number of publications in total (until 2009).

Table 1.1 The 20 countries with most publications on agile software development

Rank	Country	Publications
1	USA	153
2	Germany	52
3	Finland	51
4	Canada	46
5	Australia	41
6	England	31
7	Ireland	27
8	Sweden	20
9	Spain	18
10	Italy	17
11	Israel	15
12	Austria	13
13	Denmark	13
14	Norway	13
15	India	12
16	Chile	11
17	Iran	11
18	New Zealand	10
19	Brazil	9
20	Peoples Republic of China	9

Note that all publications from 2009 have not been indexed at the time of the search. For example, papers from the Agile 2009 conference were not indexed, and this conference alone had 28 papers in the search results from 2008.

---

[1] Search conducted on 22 February 2010, using the term "agile AND software AND development" as topics for subject areas computer science: software engineering, theory and methods and information systems. Document types proceedings paper, review or article. Databases: SCI-EXPANDED, SSCI, A&HCI, CPCI-S, CPCI-SSH.

These figures seem to indicate that there is a substantial interest in agile software development amongst research environments.

An examination of the country of origin of the publications, gives the list as in Table 1.1, which states that authors from the USA are by far most frequent in the author lists of publications, followed by Germany and Finland. The total number of articles with authors from Europe among the top 20 countries is 301, about twice that of the USA. Thus, it seems that most agile research is authored in Europe, followed by North America, Oceania and Asia.

Further, we present the institutions that are more frequently occurring in the search, in Table 1.2[2]. The VTT Technical Research Centre of Finland has the highest number of publications, followed by the University of Calgary in Canada, SINTEF in Norway and Technion Israel Institute of Technology. Europe has eleven institutions among the top 20, while North America has four, Oceania three, South America and Asia one each.

Another interesting bibliographic finding in the search is what papers on agile development are most cited, and how much cited they are. In Table 1.3 we list the 20 most cited papers, and we see that the top three have 61, 46 and 33 citations respectively. Further we see that only two of the highly cited articles are published at conferences, papers 2 and 17, which were published at the International Conference on Software Engineering. Of the remaining, nine were published in magazines (IEEE Software, IEEE Computer and Communications of the ACM) and nine were published in primary journals like IEEE Transactions on Software Engineering and the European Journal of Information Systems. 70% of the articles were published in venues we can categorize as mainly software engineering, and 30% we can arguably categorize as mainly information systems.

This analysis shows that journal publications are most important in the field of agile software development, and that the field gathers interest mainly from the software engineering community, but also from the information systems community.

---

[2] Some institutions were registered with several names in ISI Web of Science. For Table 1.2, we aggregated numbers for VTT and SINTEF, which were the only institutions among the top 20 with several names.

Table 1.2 The 20 institutions with most publications on agile software development

Rank	Institution	Publications
1	VTT Technical Research Centre of Finland	22
2	University of Calgary, Canada	21
3	SINTEF, Norway	10
4	Technion Israel Institute of Technology	10
5	Dundalk Institute of Technology, Ireland	9
6	University of Technology Sydney, Australia	9
7	North Carolina State University, USA	8
8	Blekinge Institute of Technology, Sweden	6
9	Carnegie Mellon University, USA	6
10	Helsinki University of Technology, Finland	6
11	Pontificia Universidad Catolica Valparaiso, Chile	6
12	Sharif University of Technology, Iran	6
13	Technical University of Munich, Germany	6
14	University of Alabama, USA	6
15	University of Wollongong, Australia	6
16	Georgia State University, USA	5
17	University of Aalborg, Denmark	5
18	University of Cagliari, Italy	5
19	University of Limerick, Ireland	5
20	University of Oulu, Finland	5

1.4 Main Themes in this Book

The remaining chapters of the book are organized into three parts: Foundations and Background of Agile Development, Agile Methods in Practice and Principal Challenges and New Frontiers.

1.4.1 Foundations and Background of Agile Development

In addition to this chapter, this part includes two chapters: Chapter 2, "Towards an understanding of the Conceptual Underpinnings of Agile Development Methodologies" by Nerur, Cannon, Balijepally and Bond, and Chapter 3, "Agile Software Development Mehods: A Comparative Review" by Abrahamsson, Oza and Sipponen.

Table 1.3 The 20 most cited articles on agile software development

Rank	Reference	Citations
1	Highsmith, J. and Cockburn, A. (2001) Agile software development: The business of innovation, IEEE Computer, vol. 34.	61
2	Abrahamsson, P., Warsta, J., Siponen, M. T. and Ronkainen, J. (2003) New directions on agile methods: A comparative analysis, Proc. ICSE, pp. 244-254.	46
3	Boehm, B. (2002) Get ready for agile methods, with care, IEEE Computer, vol. 35.	33
4	Erickson, J., Lyytinen, K. and Siau, K. (2005) Agile modeling, agile software development, and extreme programming: The state of research, Journal of Database Management, vol. 16.	30
5	Sharp, H. and Robinson, H. (2004) An ethnographic study of XP practice, Empirical Software Engineering, vol. 9.	29
6	George, B. and Williams, L. (2004) A structured experiment of test-driven development, Information and Software Technology, vol. 46.	28
7	Ramesh, B., Cao, L., Mohan, K. and Xu, P. (2006) Can distributed software development be agile?, Communications of the ACM, vol. 49.	26
8	Fitzgerald, B., Hartnett, G. and Conboy, K. (2006) Customising agile methods to software practices at Intel Shannon, European J. of Information Systems, vol. 15.	26
9	Janzen, D. and Saiedian, H. (2005) Test-driven development: Concepts, taxonomy, and future direction, IEEE Computer, vol. 38.	21
10	Dybå, T. and Dingsøyr, T. (2008) Empirical studies of agile software development: A systematic review, Information and Software Technology, vol. 50.	20
11	Aoyama, M. (1998) Web-based agile software development, IEEE Software, vol. 15.	20
12	Turk, D., France, R. and Rumpe, B. (2005) Assumptions underlying agile software software-development processes, Journal of Database Management, vol. 16.	19
13	Boehm, B. and Turner, R. (2005) Management challanges to implementing Agile Processes in traditional development organizations, IEEE Software, vol. 22.	19
14	Alshayeb, M. and Li, W. (2003) An empirical validation of object-oriented metrics in two different iterative software processes, IEEE Trans. on Soft. Eng., vol. 29.	19
15	Henderson- Sellers, B. and Serour, M. K. (2005) Creating a dual-agility method: The value of method engineering, Journal of Database Management, vol. 16.	17
16	Baskerville, R., Ramesh, B., Levine, L., Pries-Heje, I. and Slaughter, S. (2003) Is Internet-speed software development different?, IEEE Software, vol. 20.	17
17	Hulkko, H. and Abrahamsson, P. (2005) A multiple case study on the impact of pair programming on product quality, Proc. ICSE, pp. 495	16
18	Lippert, M., et al. (2003) Developing complex projects using XP with extensions, IEEE Computer, vol. 36.	16
19	Olague, H. M., et al. (2007) Empirical validation of three software metrics suites to predict fault-proneness of object-oriented classes developed using highly iterative or agile software development processes, IEEE Trans. on Soft. Eng., vol. 33.	14
20	Lycett, M., Macredie, R. D., Patel, C. and Paul, R. J. (2003) Migrating agile methods to standardized development practice, IEEE Computer, vol. 36.	14

The intellectual foundation of agile methods is explored in Chapter 2, to understand underlying premises for this new paradigm in software development. This understanding will be valuable both in assessing current practice as well as to advance the field.

An overview and analysis of the agile methods that exist is presented in Chapter 3, to make sense of the approaches. Agile methods are described in an analytical framework covering: project management support, life-cycle coverage, type of practical guidance, adaptability in actual use, type of research objectives and existence of empirical evidence for the method. The analysis shows that agile methods support different phases of development, and most methods lack support for project management.

1.4.2 Agile Methods in Practice

This part includes Chapter 4, "Three 'C's of Agile Practice: Collaboration, Co-ordination and Communication" by Sharp and Robinson, Chapter 5, "From Exotic to Mainstream: A 10-year odyssey from Internet Speed to Boundary Spanning with Scrum" by Baskerville, Pries-Heje and Madsen, Chapter 6, "An Ideal Customer: A Grounded Theory of Requirements Elicitation, Communication and Acceptance on Agile Projects" by Martin, Biddle and Noble and Chapter 7, "Pair Programming: Issues and Challenges" by Lui, Barnes and Chan.

What is crucial in supporting team collaboration, co-ordination and communication is described in Chapter 4, based over on ten eight years of studies of agile development teams. Story cards and walls are crucial to support collaboration and co-ordination related to project progress. To share information on functional dependencies, agile teams rely on communication and social practices.

The evolution of methods is the topic of Chapter 5, deriving from four empirical studies of software development over a ten-year period. From "internet-speed development", methods were affected by dramatic changes in the market for software development, which caused disruption of established practices, experimentation and process adaptations. This was followed by consolidations of lessons learned into more mature software development processes.

The customer has a very important role in agile development projects, and this role is under investigation in Chapter 6. Described as a critical, complex and demanding role, the chapter outlines practices that ensure that the customer role works effectively and sustainably in a way that involve the whole development team.

Pair programming is perhaps still the most known practice in agile development, made popular mainly through extreme programming. But even though pair programming has been one of the most researched topics in agile development, Chapter 7 describe the practice as controversial, despite its growth in popularity both among practitioners and academics. One concern has been the productivity of solo and pair programming, which is still not fully understood. However, the chapter also seeks to explain how and why pair programming can be made productive.

1.4.3 Principal Challenges and New Frontiers

This part includes Chapter 8, "Architected Agile Solutions for Software-Reliant Systems" by Boehm, Lane, Koolmanojwong and Turner, Chapter 9, "Agile Interaction Design and Test-Driven Development of User Interfaces – A Literature Review" by Hellmann, Hosseini-Khayat and Maurer, Chaper 10, "Organizational Culture and the Deployment of Agile Methods: The Competing Values Model View" by Iivari and Iivari, and Chapter 11, "Future Research in Agile Systems Development: Applying Open Innovation Principles Within the Agile Organization" by Conboy and Morgan.

Balancing architecture and agility has been a concern of many, including advocates of plan-driven software development. Chapter 8 describes key principles when scaling up agile development projects that require stronger architectural support. Further, the chapter provides guidance to the key principles, and illustrates these with case studies.

Usability of software solutions is a challenge in any development project. Chapter 9 gives an overview of previous studies on usability engineering which has approaches shown to improve usability and reduce probability of revision. Further, the chapter gives an overview of test-driven development of user interfaces, and explains how these two styles of development can be combined to produce testable GUI-based applications by agile teams.

Agile development seem to be exceptionally well-received by practitioners, what is the explanation for this success? This is the central question in Chapter 10, which describe organizational culture as a factor that affects the deployment of agile software development methods. Among the hypothesis posed is that agile methods are incompatible with a hierarchical organizational culture, although agile development is more disciplined than ad hoc development.

Innovation is the topic of Chapter 11, which argues that the idea of a single customer representative must be abandoned because it leads to a too narrow focus, and to a lack of involvement of important stakeholders. Agile development should adopt current thinking on open innovation, which leads to a much broader perspective, involving other business units, customers and partners.

1.5 Conclusion

In this chapter, we have motivated why agile development is an important topic, and further, we have defined and characterized agile software development. In addition, we have given an overview of research on agile software development in two parts:

First, an overview of prior research in the area through a summary of four overview articles, focusing on describing the agile methods, relations to the capability maturity model, status of research on extreme programming and presenting what is known about the benefits and limitations of agile methods. These articles indicate that the field is still in a nascent phase, and that we need more studies of high quality.

Second, an examination of studies of agile development through a literature analysis. We presented an overview of publications by year for conference papers and journal articles, the 20 countries with most publications, the 20 institutions with most publications, and the 20 most cited articles. The main findings from the literature analysis is that there seems to be a substantial interest in agile software development amongst research environments. Further, we find publications from all over the world: primarily Europe and North America, but also in Oceania, Asia and South America. When we rank the institutions after publications, they follow almost the same pattern. From the presentation of the most cited papers, we see that most highly cited articles are published in journals. Further, we see that the field gathers most interest from the software engineering community, but also from the information systems community.

The overview articles that exist in the field summarize research until 2005. The literature analysis identifies more than 500 articles published on agile software development since then, which justifies the need for a contemporary overview of research in the field, which you will find in the remaining chapters of this book.

References

Abrahamsson, Pekka, Salo, Outi, Ronkainen, Jussi and Warsta, Juhani (2002) Agile software development methods: Review and analysis, VTT Technical report, pp. 107.
Boehm, Barry (2002) Get ready for agile methods, with care, *IEEE Computer*, 35, 64 - 69.
Cohen, David, Lindvall, Mikael and Costa, Patricia (2004) In *Advances in Computers, Advances in Software Engineering*, Vol. 62 (Ed, Zelkowitz, M. V.) Elsevier, Amsterdam.
Conboy, Kieran (2009) Agility From First Principles: Reconstructing the Concept of Agility in Information Systems Development, *Information Systems Research*, 20, 329-354.
Dybå, Tore (2000) Improvisation in Small Software Organizations, *IEEE Software*, 17, 82-87.
Dybå, Tore and Dingsøyr, Torgeir (2008) Empirical Studies of Agile Software Development: A Systematic Review, *Information and Software Technology*, 50, 833-859.
Erickson, John, Lyytinen, Kalle and Siau, Keng (2005) Agile Modeling, Agile Software Development, and Extreme Programming: The State of Research, *Journal of Database Management*, 16, 88 - 100.

Nerur, S., Mahapatra, R. and Mangalaraj, G (2005) Challenges of migrating to agile methodologies, *Communications of the ACM*, 48, 72 - 78.
Nerur, Sridhar and Balijepally, VenuGopal (2007) Theoretical Reflections on Agile Development Methodologies, *Communications of the ACM*, 50, 79-83.
Williams, Laurie and Cockburn, Alistair (2003) Agile Software Development: It's about Feedback and Change, *IEEE Computer*, 36, 39-43.

Author Biographies

Torgeir Dingsøyr works with software process improvement and knowledge management projects as a senior scientist at SINTEF Information and Communication Technology, and as an adjunct associate professor at the Department of Computer and information Science, Norwegian University of Science and Technology. He has published articles in *IEEE Transactions on Software Engineering*, *IEEE Software*, *Communications of the ACM*, *Information and Software Technology* and *Empirical Software Engineering*. He is a co-author of the book "Process Improvement in Practice: A Handbook for IT Companies", which appeared on Kluwer Academic Publishers in 2004. He wrote his doctoral thesis on knowledge management in software engineering. His current research interests include software process improvement, agile software development and knowledge management in software engineering.

Tore Dybå is chief scientist and research manager at SINTEF Information and Communication Technology, and an adjunct full professor at the Department of Informatics, University of Oslo. He received his doctoral degree in computer and information science from the Norwegian University of Science and Technology. Dr. Dybå worked as a consultant for eight years in Norway and Saudi Arabia before he joined SINTEF in 1994. His research interests include empirical and evidence-based software engineering, software process improvement, and organizational learning. Dr. Dybå is the author and co-author of more than 60 refereed publications appearing in international journals, books, and conference proceedings, including *IEEE Transactions on Software Engineering*, *IEEE Software*, *Information and Software Technology*, *Empirical Software Engineering* and *Software Process: Improvement and Practice*. He is the principal author of the book "Process Improvement in Practice: A Handbook for IT Companies," published as part of the Kluwer International Series in Software Engineering. He is a member of the International Software Engineering Research Network, the IEEE, the IEEE Computer Society, and the editorial board of Empirical Software Engineering.

Nils Brede Moe received the MS degree in computer science from the Norwegian University of Science and Technology. He is a research scientist at SINTEF Information and Communication Technology. He has 12 years of experience working as a project manager and researcher within software development. He is a co-author of the book "Process Improvement in Practice: A Handbook for IT Companies". His current research interests include global software development, process improvement, self-management, and agile software development.

2 Towards an Understanding of the Conceptual Underpinnings of Agile Development Methodologies

Sridhar Nerur, Alan Cannon, VenuGopal Balijepally, Philip Bond

Abstract: While the growing popularity of agile development methodologies is undeniable, there has been little systematic exploration of its intellectual foundation. Such an effort would be an important first step in understanding this paradigm's underlying premises. This understanding, in turn, would be invaluable in our assessment of current practices as well as in our efforts to advance the field of software engineering. Drawing on a variety of sources, both within and outside the discipline, we argue that the concepts underpinning agile development methodologies are by no means novel. In the tradition of General Systems Theory this paper advocates a transdisciplinary examination of agile development methodologies to extend the intellectual boundaries of software development. This is particularly important as the field moves beyond instrumental processes aimed at satisfying mere technical considerations.

2.1 Introduction

New approaches to managing software development continue to capture the attention of both practitioners and academic researchers. Across a variety of intellectual traditions, the "conversation" has focused on social, cultural and philosophical underpinnings of problem-solving approaches. Of late this dialogue has begun to be dominated by discussions of the Agile Development Methodology (ADM) (Boehm 2002; Boehm and Turner 2004; Cockburn and Highsmith 2001; Highsmith 2002; Larman 2004), a development approach emphasizing problem-framing and problem-solving techniques that are radical departures from earlier software methods.

While we see the rationale for the fundamental thrusts of the ADM conversation, we are also struck by the similarity of these elements with principles that were articulated long before ADM ever emerged. ADM's emphasis on individuals, for example, seems little removed from Sociotechnical Systems thinking (Cherns 1976; Cherns 1987) and roots that extend as far back as the 1950s. The

T. Dingsøyr et al. (eds.), *Agile Software Development*,
DOI 10.1007/978-3-642-12575-1_2, © Springer-Verlag Berlin Heidelberg 2010

same can be seen in other conceptual foundations of ADM. For example, Larman (2003) mentions several approaches - including some software development practices - that used incremental iterations. In fact, the plan-do-study-act (PDSA), an iterative quality improvement cycle, may be traced back to the 1930s (Larman 2003).

We contend that the underlying assumptions of ADM are not novel in any sense. Concepts such as iterative development, learning, self-organization, reflective practice, self-directed teams and stakeholder participation, to name but a few, have evolved separately in other disciplines, and one or more of them were used in some form in software development as well. As Ludwig von Bertalanffy, the father of General System Theory (GST), points out, "Not only are general aspects and viewpoints alike in different fields of science; we find also formally identical or isomorphic laws in completely different fields." (1950, pg. 136). The goal of this paper is not to unravel the isomorphic principles that ADM shares with other fields, but to explore its conceptual underpinnings from several perspectives. In particular, our work here is an attempt to spell out some of the antecedents of ADM. Such a clarification is an important first step in understanding the underlying assumptions of this paradigm. This, in turn, would be invaluable in our assessment of current practices as well as in our efforts to advance the field of software engineering.

The paper is organized as follows. First, we explore how software development today is: a) more technically complex; b) more strategic; and c) brings to the fore the divergent viewpoints of a wider variety of stakeholders. This leads to the inescapable conclusion that software development, both today and in the future, is and will continue to be undertaken in a much more uncertain context. Second, we highlight the similarity of several ADM principles to long-established intellectual thrusts, both within and beyond the software development field. Third, we provide a brief description of Cherns's (1976; 1987) sociotechnical systems (STS) principles, with a view to focusing attention on their likeness to the core tenets of ADM. Fourth, the paper attempts to position ADM in the system of systems methodology (SOSM) framework presented by Jackson (2003). We then present the implications of our work for research and practice, followed by conclusions.

2.2 The Challenges of Contemporary Software Development

As information technology's role in the modern economy has grown in importance, software developers have found themselves confronted with challenges of unprecedented complexity. Some of this complexity can be attributed simply to technology that has itself grown in both scale and scope. When scholars and software professionals refer to today's software development as the solving of "wicked problems" (Nerur and Balijepally 2007; Poppendieck 2002), they are not simply considering technical issues. Rather, software development today forces developers to interact with and consider the viewpoints of a wide variety of stakeholders, many of whom have conflicting views on the desirability of the software's features and functionality.

Make no mistake: Even when it does not involve navigating through these conflicting viewpoints, software development remains a formidable challenge. As software is developed for ever-more-novel applications, the fact that developers may have limited experience and incomplete information about what can and cannot be done (and what should or should not be tried) makes ADM's principle of iterative learning/adaptation all the more relevant. We argue, however, that two other factors – the "strategic" nature of software development and the increased heterogeneity among software development's stakeholders – interact with technical complexity to make the context of software development more uncertain than ever before. And it is this interaction and its resulting complexity, it stands to reason, that has stimulated the field's rush to adopt the ADM paradigm.

2.2.1 Strategic Nature of Software

The nature of problems addressed by software developers has changed significantly over the past few decades. Early software projects were geared towards increasing efficiencies by automating routine, structured tasks. Examples of these include transaction-processing systems (TPS) and early Management Information Systems (MIS). While the former focused on the collection and storage of data produced by business transactions, the latter used this internal data to generate a variety of reports (e.g., trends, exceptions, summary reports) to facilitate monitoring and control (e.g., Laudon and Laudon 2009). Stakeholders for these projects were few and of a shared mindset, and extensive involvement with them was neither expected nor necessary. Over the years, however, the evolution of development methodologies led to developers spending comparatively less of their time on such projects and more of their time on projects of a more strategic nature.

An Information System (IS) may be viewed as a sociotechnical system in which people, technology, business processes and the organization interact to gather, process, archive, and distribute information for the purposes of control, coordination, and decision making (e.g., Laudon and Laudon 2009, Piccoli 2008; O'Hara et al. 1999). Information Technology (IT) (i.e., hardware, software, telecommunications), a critical component of IS, plays a pivotal role in transforming businesses. O'Hara et al. (1999) provide an excellent conceptualization of three orders of change engendered by the introduction of new IT. Each level of change affects technology, business process/task, people, and organizational structure to varying degrees. First-order change, reminiscent of early IT endeavors, involved the automation of routine tasks, with technology and process being the primary concerns. Second-order change, referred to as "informate", affected the work habits and established roles of people, thus emphasizing the social dimension of change management as well as the need to understand the complex interaction among people, technology, and process. These systems did not merely automate, but provided valuable, timely and accurate information to recognize and leverage opportunities in the market place. Third-order change, called "transform", has far-reaching implications for the organization, not just affecting people, technology, and process, but also the structure of the organization. Clearly, the higher the order of change entailed by IS, the greater its impact on organizational effectiveness and competitiveness, as well as on the strategic orientations of the firm. On the flip side, such high-order changes are fraught with uncertainties and are extraordinarily difficult to execute and manage.

What makes today's projects more "strategic"? Theorists across a variety of disciplines emphasize three critical distinctions between efforts that are "strategic" and those that are not. First, strategic projects tend to be more "unstructured," with no clear means-ends map to guide decision-making (Mintzberg et al. 1976). Second, as projects become more strategic they become more cross-functional, focused on solutions to challenges that cut across traditional functional boundaries such as marketing or operations (Day and Wensley 1983). This, combined with an unstructured setting, makes a "strategic" setting inherently more uncertain and complex. Finally, greater functional breadth raises the likelihood that multiple approaches to a desired end state are available (Galunic and Eisenhardt 1994); a strategic project likely has no "one best solution".

As indicated earlier, in the last few years, development project emphasis has shifted to more unstructured domains. Developers are asked to develop tools that assist decision-making under uncertainty or generate business intelligence for the creation and sustenance of competitive advantage. The scope of projects has broadened from narrow and well-defined domains (e.g., payroll processing) to systems that affect many or even all aspects of an organization, both on an intra-enterprise (e.g., ERP) and extra-enterprise (e.g., virtual integration, supply-chain) basis. These are inherently "strategic" contexts, and they increase the uncertainty and complexity of the software development setting.

Further, software developers must now interact with a broader, more diverse set of stakeholders than ever before. These stakeholders may not be even in rough agreement as to the goals of the software, and their inputs into the software development process may be conflicting. Highly valued systems may not be optimal in a technical sense; rather, they may be attractive simply because they minimize the conflict that results from stakeholders having different wants and needs.

It seems clear, then, that mere technical prowess is no longer sufficient to ensure success in today's software development environment. Further, organizational ideals of democratic workplaces that welcome a variety of viewpoints and encourage continuous learning increase the challenge of structuring software development efforts. Ultimately, today's software developers must balance the often disparate needs of diverse stakeholders, a task far more challenging than merely fulfilling the functional requirements of a system. Thus, it is no surprise that the agile paradigm of development – with its embracing of these emerging realities – is more than welcomed by the field.

2.3 What's New About Agile Development?

A recent article (Nerur and Balijepally 2007) on the theoretical roots of ADM suggests that its principles (Table 2.1) are consistent with problem-framing and problem-solving approaches that have evolved in disciplines such as architecture and strategic management. In this section we reiterate this view in asserting that the ideas and concepts behind the ADM movement have been around for decades. It is possible, we believe, that the field of computing in general – and software practitioners in particular – could have arrived at this level of maturity earlier had there been more openness to intellectual developments in allied fields such as Information Systems. Table 2.1 is by no means exhaustive. It does not, for example, include Iivari's PIOCO Model (Iivari and Koskela 1987), Boehm's Spiral Model (Boehm 1986), or the "collective resource approach" of Ehn and Kyng (1987).

ADM emphasizes the importance of social interaction in software development, stressing the importance of greater autonomy and decision-making discretion for developers. Within the ADM paradigm development is seen not as a means-end process, but rather as ongoing cooperation focused on, among others, the facilitation of learning, flexibility, communication and redundancy of functions. Many of these characteristics were seen in the theoretical schools of systems development that evolved in Europe – particularly in Scandinavia – where development practitioners were challenged early on with the complexity that results from interactions with a wide variety of interests and perspectives (Bansler 1989).

There is also substantial congruence between the field's move toward ADM and the strategic management field's movement from an emphasis on "linear" approaches toward more "adaptive" or "interpretive" understandings (Chaffee 1985). The linear view emphasizes rationality and logic, focusing on purposive planning and action toward clearly defined ends. In contrast, the adaptive view recognizes that an organization, much like an organism, must continually reconfigure and align itself to an ever changing environment (for example, see Morgan 2006). Finally, the interpretive view incorporates a social reality into strategy-making: The strategy chosen likely will reflect the competing worldviews of those who have a stake either in its formulation, implementation or results. Habermas (1984) frames these approaches similarly, pointing to the limitations of social processes grounded in instrumental reasoning. He suggests solutions that incorporate shared understanding and purpose as well as equitable and unconstrained participation of all stakeholders.

Table 2.1 Roots of Agile Principles

Agile Principle	Examples of Previous Developments
Emphasis on individuals	Sociotechnical systems [1976; as early as the 1950s – e.g., Trist(1981)] Soft Systems Methodology [Checkland 1979, 1981, 1988]
Emphasis on job and work design, quality of life, and accomplishing the work	Sociotechnical design [e.g., Cherns 1976; 1987; Olerup 1989]
Learning and adaptation – iterative development	Soft Systems Methodology (Checkland 1981) Interactive Planning (Ackoff 1974) Vickers's Appreciative Systems (1968)
Participative development	Strategic Assumption Surfacing and Testing (SAST) (Mason and Mitroff 1981) Churchman's Systems Approach (1968), Designing participatively (Mumford 1979)
Accepting and leveraging change	Soft Systems Methodology (1981); Interactive Planning (1974)
Self-organization	Complex Adaptive Systems, complexity theory (1970s)
Minimum Critical Specifications	Sociotechnical system design (e.g., Cherns 1976) Holographic principles (Morgan and Ramirez 1983)
Reflection in action (e.g., reflection workshops)	Schon (1983) Collaborative Action Learning (Ngwenyama 1993) Reflective Systems Development (Mathiassen 1998)

Based on the preceding sections, one could easily argue that software development parallels patterns exhibited in a variety of disciplines – from architecture to product design to strategic management. The similarity of software development's trajectory to that of other disciplines can be taken as evidence in support of Jantsch's (1975) assertions that the dynamic process of knowledge acquisition and use remains relatively constant across a variety of diverse domains, particularly when these domains encompass such complexity as is present in social systems. Figure 2.1, based on Jantsch's experience with diverse systems, highlights that inventive rather than purely analytical solutions are necessary to solve problems faced by purposeful human activity systems.

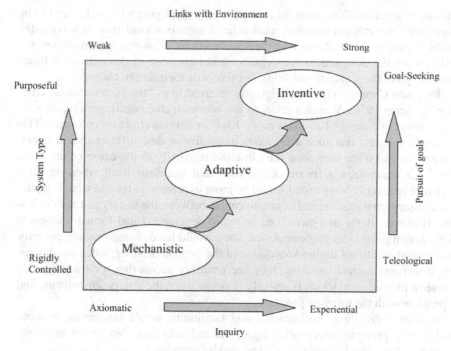

Links with Environment

Fig. 2.1 Changing Dynamics of Systems. Adapted from: Jantsch (1975)

2.4 Principles of Sociotechnical Systems

ADM's principles and assertions also match up well with arguments made by proponents of Sociotechnical Systems (STS) theory. STS theory emphasizes (Cherns 1976; Cherns 1987; Olerup 1989):

Compatibility: Recognizing that design activity is characterized by conflict, Cherns (1987, pg. 154) advocates an approach to design that reconciles the means employed with the design objectives they aim to fulfill. This principle emphasizes a transparent design process that facilitates and encourages participation of all concerned. Concurrence of views is sought in an open organizational climate that is devoid of domination of any sort. Team members must have the latitude to evolve their own ways of solving problems in accordance with the requirements of the design. This is in stark contrast to constraining the actions of designers through rigid processes and rules. Design choices should address technical and social concerns at once rather than giving primacy to the former.

Minimum Critical Specifications: Removing bureaucratic restraints while providing minimal guidelines so that problem-solvers can exercise their ingenuity in solving problems. This principle stresses that only what is absolutely required should be specified. This cautions against overly specifying what tasks need to be done, how they should be done, what roles designers should play in solving the problem, and so forth. Restricting the specifications to an essential minimum not only allows the designers to self-organize and improvise as the solution unfolds, but also gives them greater flexibility in exercising their design choices.

Variance Control: This was originally referred to as "the sociotechnical criterion" (Cherns 1976). Variance refers to any unanticipated occurrence (e.g., a software defect or a design flaw) that might have an adverse effect on outcomes. This principle suggests that such aberrations in quality or design flaws should be addressed as and when they arise (i.e., in close proximity to the cause of the problem). For example, a software design flaw that manifests itself when the final software product is being tested would be more expensive to fix and would require unnecessary coordination and communication between the testers and the designers. However, if the designers (i.e., software developers) had formally assessed their design prior to its implementation, they would have perhaps caught the error and gained additional design knowledge in the process. Further, when the designers detect and correct the error, they are probably accounting for the source or cause of the variance, which is unlikely to occur when the testers downstream find a problem with the software product.

Boundary Location: Encouraging and facilitating ample interaction between and among problem-solvers working on related activities, thereby enabling designers to have free interchange of ideas and information.

Information Flow: Ensuring that problem-solvers have easy and timely access to relevant information/knowledge.

Power and Authority: Designers are provided with resources needed to carry out their tasks. Further, they are given the power and authority to handle their resources. The designers, in turn, assume accountability for their performance and for the responsible use of the resources in their trust.

Multifunctional Perspectives: Developing and nurturing versatile personnel who can incorporate the views of a wider variety of stakeholders, thus enabling problem-solvers to accomplish more with less supervision (Cavaleri and Obloj 1993). Indeed, the goal of having self-organizing software teams that can expeditiously address unanticipated development problems can be realized only if members of such teams are multifaceted and equipped with a broader range of technical and leadership skills. This perspective is akin to the concept of *redundancy of functions* embodied in the holographic principles of management (Morgan 2006; Nerur and Balijepally 2007).

Support Congruence: This principle focuses on providing: a) a "constraint-free design mode" to the extent possible in order to reconcile the tension between control and influence that a team can exercise in its interactions with other related units; and b) a system that rewards and nurtures designers based on their awareness and grasp of the processes in which they are engaged.

Transitional Organization: This principle addresses the myriad challenges that face an organization when it is either starting up or being redesigned. The design team and the process that it employs should not only reflect the new values, but must also disseminate these values to the rest of the organization. Cherns views the transitioning process as an opportunity for learning. Thus, the design team plays a pivotal role in managing and facilitating the change. For example, the extent to which the entire software development team learns, imbibes, and values agile principles would largely determine how successful an organization is in instituting process changes to accommodate agile practices.

Incompletion: Committing to ongoing problem-solving (i.e., planning, doing, reflecting, and acting) to encourage continuous refinement of solutions.

Some of the principles of STS outlined above could inform ADM practices. While ADM principles allude, at least in theory, to many of the STS tenets, their praxis in software development is somewhat limited and a more concerted effort may be required to reify these concepts. For example, agile methods encourage an open and collaborative development environment in which developers have the latitude to make decisions regarding the assignment of individual roles and responsibilities as well as the choice of problem-solving strategy. A closely related concept is the idea of self-organization where members of a software team organize themselves in response to emergent problems (Cockburn and Highsmith 2001). Implicit in this arrangement are the notions of self-management and shared leadership, both of which have considerable value in team-oriented knowledge work (Pearce and Manz 2005). However, these concepts can be implemented only if software developers expand their capabilities (e.g., better understanding of architectural and quality issues) and focus more on adding value to the team's primary objectives rather than to their job functions alone. Further, software developers need to expand their intellectual perspectives to appreciate the relevance of shared understanding, mutual trust, conflict resolution, and self-management leadership behaviors (e.g., self-reinforcement, self-goal-setting, self-evaluation, self-expectation, etc.,) to self-organizing collaborative development (for example, see Manz and Sims 1987 and Pearce and Manz 2005).

It is apparent that STS principles such as *minimum critical specification* and *multifunctional perspectives* have the potential to influence ADM practices. Likewise, the rapidly increasing experience with ADM could be invaluable in extending and/or refining the design ideals of STS.

2.5 ADM and the System of Systems Methodologies (SOSM)

In his book *Systems Thinking: Creative Holism for Managers*, Jackson (2003) articulates the System of System Methodologies (SOSM) framework, which gives a broad classification of problem-solving approaches (akin to Weber's (1969) "ideal types"). The grouping of methods is based on the nature of the system (simple to complex) and the extent of convergence/divergence of the worldview and interests of the participants (a continuum from unitary to pluralistic to coercive). Thus, we have six types – simple/unitary, simple/pluralistic, simple/coercive, complex/unitary, complex/pluralistic and complex/coercive – ranging from very structured problem-solving domains (e.g., payroll processing) to very complex unstructured ones (e.g., addressing global warming). Jackson (2003) subsequently links these approaches to the sociological paradigms of Burrell and Morgan (1979). Our aim in this section is to briefly explore how ADM's ideals relate to the SOSM.

Simple systems in which the participants (such as designers and stakeholders) have compatible worldviews and design goals present problems that are easily solved by hard systems thinking, exemplified by approaches such as Systems Analysis, Systems Engineering, and Operation Research. Efficiency, rather than effectiveness, is the primary aim of such methods. The extreme case involves complex problems involving stakeholders and decision-makers whose values, goals and interests are irreconcilable. Solutions to such situations cannot be evolved through an instrumental rational process, but are often coerced by other means, such as politics, power plays and domination by a majority. Postmodern thinking that strives for achieving diversity by bringing to the fore ignored or suppressed viewpoints is deemed to be influential in tackling such problems.

So, where does ADM figure in the SOSM framework? To answer this, we rely on Jackson's positioning of Soft Systems Methodology (SSM), an approach with which ADM shares similarities, in this framework. SSM involves multiple diverse stakeholders, emphasizes learning, and uses an iterative approach to gain a progressively greater appreciation of the system under development. Further, it may be applied to simple or complex systems. Therefore, it occupies the entire vertical column of the SOSM that corresponds to "Pluralist". ADM emphasizes: a) people and their collaborations; b) iterative development that actively engages customers; c) adaptive planning; d) flexibility of roles; e) self-organizing teams; f) a leadership style that focuses on facilitating and mentoring, rather than on controlling; g) active communication and feedback; h) the need to accept and leverage change; and i) continual reflection on practices. Thus, it leans towards the SOSM location in which Jackson places SSM.

While it would be illuminating to provide an analysis of ADM's assumptions from the perspective of Burrell and Morgan's (1979) sociological paradigms, such an exposition is beyond the scope of this paper. Traditional systems analysis and design approaches (particularly those that are heavily plan- and specification-driven) presume an objective world that is predictable and stable. Such methods further anticipate a specific end and therefore focus on arriving at that end in the most efficient manner as possible. The specifications, as well as the design models and diagrams derived from them, are believed to be objective and consistent with an independent reality in which processes can be directly observed, measured and verified (e.g., Hirschheim and Klein 1989). Thus, traditional approaches are largely functionalist (see Nerur and Balijepally 2007). As mentioned earlier, ADM recognizes that change is inevitable and advocates a "sense-making process" (Berger and Luckmann 1967 as cited in Hirschheim and Klein 1989) that involves adaptive planning, frequent iterations informed by feedback from stakeholders, and reflective learning. Thus, it leans towards "social relativism" (Hirschheim and Klein 1989), or what Burrell and Morgan (1979) refer to as an "interpretive" sociological paradigm. The following observation by Hirschheim and Klein (1989, pg. 1205) seems to bear out this assessment:

"The mechanism of prototyping or evolutionary learning from interaction with partial implementations is the way technology becomes embedded in the social perception and sense-making process."

2.6 Implications for Research and Practice

As information systems development has become more strategic, IT decision-makers and software development leaders have found themselves confronted with ever-more-diverse bases of constituents. This growth in the range or heterogeneity of viewpoints that must be considered increases the complexity of software development efforts independent of the technical challenges that are specific to particular development tasks. Development professionals confronted with such complexity find their task environments increasingly uncertain across multiple dimensions, and in response have seized on the agile paradigm to help overcome this uncertainty.

That this recently "emerged" paradigm can be interpreted as a re-combination of earlier viewpoints is not altogether surprising. Disciplines or sub-disciplines often go through protracted periods of incremental development, in which progress is both orderly and predictable. During such eras, broad agreement exists among discipline members regarding the challenges that should be addressed and the methods that should be used to address them, and the steady progression of knowledge serves to perpetuate this consensus. In many fields, however, there comes a time when the mass of unsolved puzzles or unexplained anomalies reaches some critical point. Then, boundaries that restrict problem-selection and problem-solving to narrow paths are cast aside, ushering in radically new approaches or mindsets.

While ADM has been proffered, in one form or another, for years if not decades, what has made this particular point in time ripe for a Kuhnian revolution with regard to development? We argue that a variety of facets of contemporary IT challenges underscore, more than ever before, the practical value of agility in software development. Further, the nature of software development in a post-industrial global economy is challenging development professionals to take on more roles – or to at least interact with a wider variety of constituents from other intellectual or professional spheres – than they ever have.

These developments have implications for both practice and research in software development. For development professionals, it is becoming increasingly important that their technical skill sets be augmented with social and political tools appropriate for interacting with a wide variety of stakeholders. The ability to respond to and incorporate conflicting viewpoints will come to more readily characterize successful software development professionals.

Professionals also are being challenged to revisit their understanding of how much up-front planning is appropriate. Boehm (2002; also see Boehm and Turner 2004) argues that there is a delicate balance – what he refers to as the "sweet spot" – between being governed by up-front plans and being open to change as the result of new or conflicting information. Clearly, developers schooled in a rational approach will find themselves challenged by the need to find and maintain this balance, particularly as the potential sources of imbalance grow in number or diversity.

Scholars hoping to make sense of and contribute to contemporary software development also must be prepared for changes. The agile paradigm emphasizes the importance of intangibles such as personalities, personal development and reflection. Development efforts that are consistent with the agile paradigm might not conform neatly to "normal science" approaches, raising the risk that what scholars report or suggest is inaccurate or inappropriate. Researchers exploring development must themselves go "back to school" and look to theories or methods that are more consistent with the emerging environment.

2.7 Conclusion

Changes in the milieu of software development are demanding and will continue to challenge professionals for the foreseeable future. In this paper, we have attempted to point out the conceptual underpinnings of ADM. To this end, we outlined the principles of sociotechnical systems, mainly because of their resemblance to some aspects of ADM. There is definitely a potential here to extend this work and carry out a detailed examination of the similarities and differences between STS and ADM, along the lines of the comparative analysis of STS and Lean Production by Niepce and Molleman (1998). In addition, we used Jackson's framework to further our understanding of the assumptions of ADM. One could easily extend the analysis to understand where ADM stands with regard to its ontological and epistemological orientations. The Burrell and Morgan (1979) framework, albeit controversial because of its adherence to Kuhn's notions of paradigms and incommensurability (Deetz 1996), would still be a good starting point for such an analysis.

Not unlike other research studies, our paper has some limitations. First, our social/cultural/technical conditioning likely has influenced our analysis. Second, although there are many intellectual streams from which we could have analyzed the conceptual bases of ADM, we restricted our discussions to but a few. For example, it may be argued that an examination of ADM from some other perspective, say, Lean Production, Complex Evolving Systems (CES), Autopoiesis or Churchman's Inquiring Systems, would have been more fruitful. Despite these shortcomings, we hope our work offers early guidance to both scholars and practitioners alike as they continually seek solutions to contemporary development problems.

References

Ackoff, R.L. (1974). *Redesigning the Future*. New York: John Wiley & Sons.

Bansler, J. (1989). System Development Research, Scandinavia. *Scandinavian Journal of Information Systems*, 1, 3-20.

Berger, P., Luckmann, T. (1967). *The Social Construction of Reality: A Treatise in the Sociology of Knowledge*. New York: Doubleday.

Bertalanffy, von L. (1950). An Outline of General Systems Theory. *British Journal of the Philosophy of Science*, 1, 134-165.

Boehm, B. (1986). A spiral model of software development and enhancement. *ACM Sigsoft Software Engineering Notes*, 11(4), 14-24.

Boehm, B. (2002). Get Ready for Agile methods, with Care. *Computer*, 35(1), 64-69.

Boehm and Turner (2004). *Balancing Agility and Discipline: A Guide for the Perpelexed*. Boston, MA: Addison-Wesley.

Cavaleri, S. and Obloj, K. (1993). *Management Systems – A Global Perspective*. Belmont, CA: Wadsworth Publishing Company.

Chaffee, E.E. (1985). Three Models of Strategy. *Academy of Management Review*, 10(1), 89-98.

Checkland, P.B. (1979). Techniques in 'Soft' Systems Practice Part 1: Systems Diagrams – Some Tentative Guidelines. *Journal of Applied Systems Analysis*, Vol. 6, 33-40.

Checkland, P. (1981). *Systems Thinking, Systems Practice*. Chichester: John Wiley.

Checkland, P.B. (1988). Soft Systems Methodology: An Overview. *Journal of Applied Systems Analysis*, 15, 27-30.

Cherns, A. (1976). The Principles of Socio-Technical Systems Design. *Human Relations*, 29(8), 783–792.

Cherns, A. (1987). Principles of Socio-Technical Design Revisited. *Human Relations*, Volume 40, Number 3, 153-162.

Churchman, C.W. (1968). *The Systems Approach*. New York: Dell.

Cockburn, A., & Highsmith, J. (2001). Agile Software Development: The People Factor. *Computer*, 34(11), 131-133.

Day, G.S., & Wensley, R. (1983). Marketing Theory with a Strategic Orientation. *Journal of Marketing*, 47(4), 79-89.

Deetz, S. (1996). Describing Differences in Approaches to Organization Science: Rethinking Burrell and Morgan and Their Legacy. *Organization Science*, 7(2), 191-207.

Ehn, P. and Kyng, M. (1987). The Collective Resource Approach to Systems Design. In G. Bjerknes, P. Ehn, and M. Kyng (eds.), *Computers and Democracy: A Scandinavian Challenge* (pp. 17-57), Aldershot, United Kingdom: Avebury.

Galunic, D.C., & Eisenhardt, K. M. (1994). Renewing the Strategy-Structure-Performance Paradigm. In L.L. Cummings & B.M. Staw (Eds.), *Research in Organizational Behavior Vol. 16* (pp. 215-255), Greenwich, CT: JAI Press.

Habermas, J. (1984). *The Theory of Communicative Action*. Boston, MA: Beacon Press.

Highsmith, J. (2002). *Agile Software Development Ecosystems*. Boston, MA: Addison-Wesley.

Hirschheim, R. and Klein, H.K. (1989). Four Paradigms of Information Systems Development. *Communications of the ACM*, 32(10), 1199-1216.

Iivari, J. and Koskela, E. (1987). The PIOCO Model for IS Design. *MIS Quarterly*, 11(3), 401-419.

Jackson, M.C. (2003). *Systems Thinking: Creative Holism for Managers*, Chichester: England, John Wiley & Sons, Ltd.

Jantsch, E. (1975). *Design for Evolution*. New York, NY: George Braziller, Inc.

Larman, C. (2004). *Agile & Iterative Development: A Manager's Guide*. Boston, MA: Addison-Wesley.

Laudon, K.C. and Laudon, J.P. (2009). *Essentials of Management Information Systems* (Eighth Edition). Upper Saddle River, NJ: Pearson Prentice Hall.

Manz, C.C. and Sims, H.P. (1987). Leading Workers to Lead Themselves: The External Leadership of Self-Managing Work Teams. *Administrative Science Quarterly*, 32, 106-128.

Mason, R.O., & Mitroff, I.I. (1981). *Challenging Strategic Planning Assumptions : Theory, Cases, and Techniques*. New York: Wiley.

Mathiassen, L. (1998). Reflective Systems Development. *Scandinavian Journal of Information Systems*, 10 (1 & 2), 67-118.

Mintzberg, H., Raisinghani, D., & Theoret, A. (1976). The Structure of "Unstructured" Decision Processes. *Administrative Science Quarterly*, 21(2), 246-275.

Morgan, G., & Ramirez, R. (1983). Action Learning: A Holographic Metaphor for Guiding Social Change. *Human Relations*, 37(1), 1-28.

Morgan, G. (2006). *Images of Organization*. Thousand Oaks, CA: Sage Publications.

Mumford, E., & Henshall, D. (1979). *Participative Approach to Computer Systems Design : A Case Study of the Introduction of a New Computer System*. London: Associated Business Press.

Nerur, S., & Balijepally, V. (2007). Theoretical Reflections on Agile Development Methodologies. *Communications of the ACM*, 50(3), 79-83.

Ngwenyama, O.K. (1993). Developing End-Users' Systems Development Competence. *Information & Management*, 25, 291-302.

Niepce, W. and Molleman, E. (1998). Work Design Issues in Lean Production from a Sociotechnical Systems Perspective: Neo-Taylorism or the Next Step in Sociotechnical Design? *Human Relations*, 51(3), 259-287.

O'Hara, M.T., Watson, R.T., & Kavan, B.C. (1999). Managing the Three Levels of Change. *Information Systems Management Journal*, 16(3), 63-70.

Olerup, A. (1989). Socio-Technical Design of Computer-Assisted Work: A Discussion of the ETHICS and Tavistock Approaches. *Scandinavian Journal of Information Systems*, 1, 43-71.

Pearce, C.L. and Manz, C.C. (2005). The New Silver Bullets of Leadership: The Importance of Self- and Shared Leadership in Knowledge Work. *Organizational Dynamics*, 34(2), 130-140.

Piccoli, G. (2008). *Information Systems for Managers*. John Wiley & Sons, Inc.

Poppendieck, M. (2002). Wicked Projects. *Software Development Magazine* [also available at http://www.poppendieck.com/wicked.htm - accessed on 11/9/2008]

Schon, D. (1983). *The Reflective Practitioner: How Professionals Think in Action*. New York, NY: Basic Books.

Trist, E.L. (1981). The Sociotechnical Perspective. The Evolution of Sociotechnical Systems as a Conceptual Framework and as an Action Research Program. In Van de Ven, A.H., & Joyce, W.F., (Eds.), *Perspectives in Organization Design and Behavior*, Wiley.

Vickers, G. (1968). Science and the Appreciative System. *Human Relations*, 21(2), 99-119.

Weber, M. (1969). *The Methodology of the Social Sciences*. New York, NY: Free Press.

Author Biographies

Sridhar Nerur is an associate professor of Information Systems at the University of Texas at Arlington. He holds an Engineering degree in Electronics from Bangalore University, a PGDM (MBA) from the Indian Institute of Management, Bangalore, India, and a Ph.D. in Business Administration from the University of Texas at Arlington. His publications include articles in leading journals such as *MIS Quarterly, the Strategic Management Journal, Communications of the ACM, Communications of the AIS, the DATA BASE for Advances in Information Systems, European Journal of Information Systems, and Information Systems Management.* He served as an Associate Editor of the *European Journal of Information Systems.* His research and teaching interests are in the areas of software design, adoption of software development methodologies, cognitive aspects of programming, dynamic IT capabilities, and agile software development.

Alan Cannon is an associate professor of operations management and statistics at the University of Texas at Arlington. His research on operations strategy and research methods has appeared in such journals as the *Journal of Operations Management, Organizational Research Methods, the International Journal of Production and Operations Management* and the *International Journal of Production Research.* His current research interests include capacity investment, service operations, performance measurement and hierarchical linear modeling.

VenuGopal Balijepally is an assistant professor of MIS in the College of Business at Prairie View A&M University, Texas. He received his Ph.D. in Information Systems from the University of Texas at Arlington and Post Graduate Diploma in Management (MBA), from the Management Development Institute, Gurgaon, India. His research interests include software development, social capital of IS teams, knowledge management and IT management. His research publications appear in *MIS Quarterly, Communications of the ACM, Communications of the AIS,* and various conference proceedings such as the Americas Conference on Information Systems, the Hawaii International Conference on System Sciences, and the Decision Sciences Institute.

Philip L. Bond holds the BA and MA in Economics from the University of Rhode Island, 1991 and 1993. He received the MS in Information Systems from the University of Texas at Arlington in 2009, and is a doctoral student at the University of Texas at Arlington. He has been an Instructor, Program Chair and Dean at ITT Technical Institute, and a Dean at Everest College.

3 Agile Software Development Methods: A Comparative Review[1]

Pekka Abrahamsson, Nilay Oza and Mikko T. Siponen

Abstract: Although agile software development methods have caught the attention of software engineers and researchers worldwide, scientific research still remains quite scarce. The aim of this study is to order and make sense of the different agile approaches that have been proposed. This comparative review is performed from the standpoint of using the following features as the analytical perspectives: project management support, life-cycle coverage, type of practical guidance, adaptability in actual use, type of research objectives and existence of empirical evidence. The results show that agile software development methods cover, without offering any rationale, different phases of the software development life-cycle and that most of these methods fail to provide adequate project management support. Moreover, quite a few methods continue to offer little concrete guidance on how to use their solutions or how to adapt them in different development situations. Empirical evidence after ten years of application remains quite limited. Based on the results, new directions on agile methods are outlined.

3.1 Introduction

Agile – denoting "the quality of being agile; readiness for motion; nimbleness, activity, dexterity in motion" (http://dictionary.oed.com) – software development methods attempt to offer once again an answer to the eager business community asking for lighter weight along with faster and nimbler software development processes. This is especially the case with the rapidly growing and volatile Internet software industry as well as with the emerging mobile application environment. The new agile methods have evoked a substantial amount of literature (e.g., Cockburn 2002; Highsmith 2002a; Martin 2002) and debates (e.g., Yourdon 2000; Highsmith 2001; Highsmith 2002b). While some authors claim (e.g., Baskerville et al. 2002; Meri-Salo et al. 2005) that agile software development methods do not offer anything new with regard to software development principles, agile advo-

---

[1]An early version of this chapter was presented at International Conference on Software Engineering in 2003 (ICSE 25).

T. Dingsøyr et al. (eds.), *Agile Software Development*,
DOI 10.1007/978-3-642-12575-1_3, © Springer-Verlag Berlin Heidelberg 2010

cates maintain that the agile principles represent a new – radically different – paradigm in software engineering (cf. Rajlich 2006).

Despite of widespread application of agile methods in wide range of different industrial contexts, there is still no clear agreement of what are the focal aspects of agile methods. Some claim that these are simplicity and speed (Beck 1999; Highsmith and Cockburn 2001; McCauley 2001) while others suggest them to be collaboration, co-ordination and communication (see Chapter 4). In development work, accordingly, development groups concentrate only on the functions needed at a given moment, delivering them fast, collecting feedback and reacting rapidly to changes in business and technology (Aoyama 1998; Fowler and Highsmith 2001; Müller and Tichy 2001; Boehm 2002). Since 1998, at least twelve slightly varying definitions of what is agility in software development have been offered (Kettunen 2009). The apparent conceptual confusion has not slowed down the adoption of agile methods in industrial settings. Anecdotal evidence has grown substantially in the 2000's as well as the number of experience reports in conferences and other business driven events.

The number of new agile methods increased rapidly during the first years and this phenomenon is not showing any signs of fading still. This has resulted in a situation where researchers and practitioners are not aware of all the available approaches or of their suitability for varying real-life software development situations. As for researchers and method developers, the lack of unifying research hinders their ability to establish a reliable and cumulative research tradition.

The aim of this study is to order and make sense of the different agile approaches that have been proposed. The result of this analysis will make practitioners better aware of the available agile methods, who will thus be in a better position to understand the features of agile methods, and hence to choose the most appropriate method in a more informed way.

An analytic framework is constructed for scrutinizing and guiding the review of the existing agile methods. The framework encompasses six perspectives: project management support, software development life-cycle coverage, availability of concrete guidance for application, adaptability in actual use, research objective, and empirical evidence. The results show that the existing methods cover various phases of the life-cycle, without, however, offering any rationale. The majority of them do not present adequate support for project management, and only few methods offer concrete guidance to support their solutions or adaptations in different development situations. Furthermore, while method developers' research objective is predominantly means-end oriented (technical), related empirical evidence to date remains very limited. Based on the results, new research directions on agile methods are outlined.

The rest of the chapter is composed as follows. The second section presents a short overview of the existing agile methods. The third section presents the analytical perspectives and the rationale for them. The fourth section presents a comparative review of the referred methods and the fifth section discusses the significance and the limitations of the findings. The sixth section concludes this study, recapitulating the key findings.

3.2 An overview of agile methods

In this section the existing agile methods are identified and introduced. Agile methods (shown as rectangles in Figure 3.1) have been characterized by the following attributes: incremental (small software releases, with rapid development cycles), cooperative (a close customer and developer interaction), straightforward (the method itself is easy to learn and to modify and it is sufficiently documented), and adaptive (the ability to make and react to last moment changes) (Abrahamsson et al. 2002). In addition to showing the various agile methods and their interrelationships, Figure 3.1 also presents the intellectual origins of these agile methods. In other words, these earlier studies have influenced the existing agile methods, or the ideas presented have later been used by agile method developers to build these methods. These lines of influence are represented by arrow lines. These earlier studies intellectually encroaching the existing agile methods are not, however, in the focus of this analysis. The dashed line illustrates which methods (or method developers) contributed to the publication of the agile manifesto. (http://www.agilemanifesto.org). In the following, the objectives of each method are briefly introduced.

Adaptive software development. Adaptive software development (ASD) (Highsmith 2000) attempts to bring about a new way of seeing software development in an organization, promoting an adaptive paradigm. It offers solutions for the development of large and complex systems, in particular. The method encourages incremental and iterative development, with constant prototyping. One ancestor of ASD is "RADical Software Development" (Bayer and Highsmith 1994). ASD claims to provide a framework with enough guidance to prevent projects from falling into chaos, but not too much, which could suppress emergence and creativity.

Agile modeling. Agile modeling (AM) (Ambler 2002) aims to apply the idea of agile, rapid development to modeling. The key focus in AM, therefore, is on modeling practices and cultural issues imposing values required for the application of AM. The underlying idea is to encourage developers to produce sufficiently advanced models to support acute design needs and documentation purposes. At the same time, however, AM is trying to keep the amount of models and documentation as low as possible. Cultural issues are addressed by presenting various ways to encourage communication, and to organize team structures and ways of working.

Agile software process model. The Agile software process (ASP) model (Aoyama 1997; Aoyama 1998) aims at enabling an accelerated development of software while maintaining flexibility to address the changing requirements. Aoyama and his colleagues developed ASP for the purposes of the Fujitsu company. An ancestor to ASP is the concurrent-development process (CPD) model (Aoyama 1987; Aoyama 1993). When CPD was first introduced, it represented a new emerging paradigm in software engineering (Agresti 1986). The philosophy underlying CPD was based on the principles of continuous improvement as found in Japanese production systems (Ohno 1988) for hardware assembly. ASP places emphasis on rapid and flexible adaptation to changes in process, product and environment, and it is characterized by three core processes: incremental and evolutionary process, modular and lean process, and time-based process. In Fujitsu, where ASP has been used for the development of large-scale communication systems, ASP is operationalized through the use of a network-centric tool family designed for the agile software engineering environment.

Crystal family. The Crystal family of methodologies (Cockburn 1998; Cockburn 2000b; Cockburn 2002) includes a number of different methods from which to select the most suitable one for each individual project. Besides the methods, the Crystal approach also includes rules of thumb for tailoring these methods to fit the varying circumstances of different projects. Each member of the Crystal family is marked with a specific color indicating the relative weight of the method. Crystal suggests choosing an appropriate-colored method for a project based on its size and criticality. Larger projects are likely to ask for more coordination and heavier or more formal methods than smaller ones. Crystal methods are open for any development practices, tools or work products, thus allowing the integration of, for example, Extreme Programming and Scrum practices.

Dynamic systems development method. Dynamic systems development method (DSDM) (DSDM Consortium 1997; Stapleton 1997) is a method developed by a dedicated consortium in the UK. DSDM aims at providing a control framework for Rapid Application Development. The fundamental idea behind DSDM is that instead of fixing the amount of functionality in a product, and then adjusting time and resources to reach that functionality, it is preferred to fix time and resources, and then to adjust the amount of functionality accordingly. DSDM can be seen as the first truly agile software development method.

Extreme programming. Extreme programming (XP) (Beck 1999; Beck 2000) is a collection of well-known software engineering practices. XP aims at enabling successful software development despite vague or constantly changing software requirements. The novelty of XP is based on the way individual practices are collected and lined up to function with each other. Some of the main characteristics of XP are short iterations with small releases and rapid feedback, close customer participation, constant communication and coordination, continuous refactoring, continuous integration and testing, collective code ownership, and pair programming. An updated version of Extreme Programming was published in 2004 (Beck and Anders 2004). The revised version divides the practices in two sets: primary practices and corollary practices. The principle ideas remain the same nevertheless. Therefore, in our analysis we are placing the focus on the XP version 1.

Feature-driven development. Feature-driven development (FDD) (Coad et al. 2000; Palmer and Felsing 2002) is a process-oriented software development method for developing business critical systems. The FDD approach focuses on the design and building phases. The FDD approach embodies iterative development with the practices believed to be effective in industry. FDD emphasizes quality aspects throughout the process and includes frequent and tangible deliveries, along with accurate monitoring of the progress of the project.

Internet-speed development. Internet-speed development (ISD) (Cusumano and Yoffie 1999; Baskerville et al. 2001; Baskerville and Pries-Heje 2001; Chapter 5) refers to a development situation where software needs to be released fast, thereby requiring short development cycles. ISD encompasses a descriptive, management-oriented framework for addressing the problem of handling fast releases, and includes three streams of work. In fact, the studies under ISD are considered as more management and business-oriented than other related approaches. As the first stream, Baskerville *et al.* saw that the successful management activities related to agile development framework consist of time drivers, quality dependencies and process adjustments. These are the rules under which companies have survived in ISD. In this context 'process adjustment' means focusing on good people instead of process, i.e., "if people are mature and talented, there is less need for process" (Baskerville et al. 2001, p. 56) Cusumano and Yoffie's (1999) approach to ISD draws from the "*Synch-and-stabilize*" approach by Microsoft, aimed at coping with a fast-moving, or even chaotic, software development business (Cusumano and Selby 1997). The third stream of ISD stems from the viewpoint of an emergent organization. Emergent organizations are organizations having a fast pace of organizational change – thus an opposite to stable organizations, and therefore emergent organizations are argued to need agile development tradition to survive (Truex et al. 1999). The theoretical background of the latter stream stems from Amethodological information systems (IS) development (Baskerville et al. 1992; Truex et al. 2001), which is based on a relativistic philosophy. Amethodological scholars argue that software development is a collection of random, opportunistic processes driven by accident. These processes are simultaneous, overlapping and there are gaps and the development itself occurs in completely unique and idiographic forms. Finally, the development is negotiated, compromised and capricious as opposed to predefined, planned and mutually agreed.

Pragmatic programming. Pragmatic programming (PP) (Hunt 2000) introduces a set of programming "best practices". It puts forward techniques that concretely augment the practices discussed in connection with the other agile methods. PP covers most programming practicalities. The "method" itself comprises a collection of short tips (n=70) that focus on day-to-day problems. These practices take a pragmatic perspective and place focus on incremental, iterative development, rigorous testing and user-centered design.

Scrum. The Scrum (Schwaber 1995; Schwaber and Beedle 2002) approach has been developed for managing the software development process in a volatile environment. It is based on flexibility, adaptability and productivity. Scrum leaves open for the developers to choose the specific software development techniques, methods, and practices for the implementation process. It involves frequent management activities aiming at consistently identifying any deficiencies or impediments in the development process as well as the in the practices that are used.

Other methods. There are several other methods published that claim to be aligned with the agile principles as well. These include lean software development (Poppendieck and Poppendieck 2003), Evo (A method developed by Tom Gilb and summarized in Larman 2004), further developments of Rational Unified Process such as EssUP by Ivar Jacobsen and OpenUP by the Eclipse community among few others. These are left out from the analysis either because they are proprietary (EssUP) or there is a limited amount of published material otherwise

(OpenUP) or they were added to the agile family of methods post-term (Evo). Lean software development's intellectual origins are connected to Toyota Production System and the manufacturing industry. Due to the focusing issues, we excluded lean thinking altogether from the analysis even if similarities may exist.

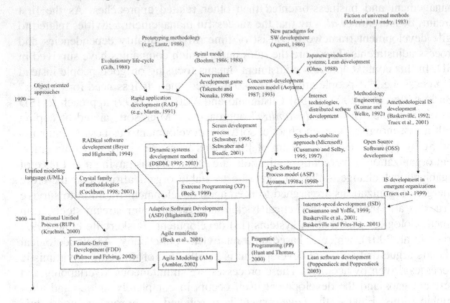

Fig. 3.1 Evolutionary map of agile software development methods

3.3 Comparative review of the existing agile methods

In this section, the existing agile methods are compared using six different analytical perspectives.

3.3.1 Analytical perspectives for the analysis

In order to make sense and scrutinize the existing agile methods, proper analytic tools are needed. The task of comparing any methodology with another is difficult and the result is often based upon the subjective judgment of the authors (Song and Osterweil 1991). Two alternative approaches have been proposed: informal and quasi-formal comparison (Song and Osterweil 1992). Informal comparison indicates a lack of systematic framework to guide the analysis. Quasi-formal comparison attempts to overcome the subjective limitations of the informal comparison technique by offering different strategies for composing the baseline for comparison, i.e. the analytical framework. These strategies involve the following operations (Sol 1983): 1) define an idealized method, 2) select important perspectives or features from each method, 3) derive a framework from empirical evidence, 4) use a defined metalanguage to describe each method and 5) use a contingency approach and relate the features of each method to specific problems. Song and Osterweil (1992) maintain that the second and fourth strategies are the most effective.

Table 3.1 Perspectives for the analysis

Perspective	Description	Key references
Project management support	Does the method support project management activities?	(Gilb 1988; Kumar and Welke 1992)
Software development life-cycle	Which stages of the software development life-cycle does the method cover?	[(Boehm 1988; Cugola and Ghezzi 1998)
Availability of concrete guidance for application	Does the method mainly rely on abstract principles or does it provide concrete guidance: abstract principles vs. concrete guidance?	(Boehm 1988; Nandhakumar and Avison 1999)
Adaptability in actual use	Is the method argued to fit per se in all agile development situations: universally predefined vs. situation appropriate?	(Malouin and Landry 1983; Kumar and Welke 1992; Truex et al. 2001)
Research objective	What is the method developers' research objective: critical, interpretative, means-end oriented?	(Habermas 1984; Chua 1986)
Empirical evidence	Does the method have empirical support for its claims?	(Kumar and Welke 1992; Basili and Lanubile 1999; Fenton 2001)

While many analytical tools have been proposed and used to carry out the quasi-formal comparison (e.g., Olle et al. 1982; Lyytinen 1991; Hirscheim et al. 1995; Hirscheim et al. 1996; Iivari and Hirscheim 1996). The following six analytical perspectives were seen as relevant and complementary to the research purposes of the chapter. They are depicted in Table 3.1 with respective questions for descriptive understanding and the relevant literature references. To further exemplify these analytical perspectives, we analyze each perspective in relation to agile methods.

Methods should be efficient (as opposed to time and resource consuming) (Kumar and Welke 1992). Efficiency requires the existence of *project management* activities to enable an appropriate organization and execution of software development tasks.

A *software development life-cycle* is a sequence of processes that an organization employs to conceive, design, and commercialize a software product (Boehm 1988; Cugola and Ghezzi 1998). The software development life-cycle perspective is needed to observe which phases of the software development process are covered by the agile methods under scrutiny.

Software development methods are often used for other purposes than originally intended by their authors (Nandhakumar and Avison 1999). For example, Wastel (1996) observes that methodologies act as a social defense operating as a set of organizational rituals. Boehm (1988) concludes that the lack of concrete guidance has caused many software projects to fail, due to the fact that they have pursued development and evolution phases in the wrong order. Thus, in order to evaluate how well the methods can be used for the purposes that they have been designed for, a perspective provided by the *availability of concrete guidance for application* is needed.

The perspective of *adaptability in actual use* stems from the works of Kumar and Welke (1992), Malouin and Landry (1983), and Truex *et al.* (2001). This perspective is used for exploring how well agile methods recognize that one ready-made solution does not fit all agile software development situations (i.e., adaptation is allowed), and if guidance is given on how to adapt an agile method in different situations (i.e., adaptation is enabled). A distinction between universally predefined and situation appropriate[2] will be drawn (Kumar and Welke 1992). Adaptability in actual use is particularly relevant in the case of agile methods, since the goal of agile software development is to increase the ability to react and respond to changing business, customer and technological needs at all organizational levels

The analysis of the agile methods in the light of their *research objectives* is used for highlighting the goals of method developers. According to Chua (1986) and Habermas (1984), research objectives include: 1) means-end oriented (technical), 2) interpretative (hermeneutical), and 3) critical (emancipatory). The means-end oriented view holds that the aim of research is to produce knowledge in order to achieve certain concrete goals or ends (Chua 1986) and to increase human control over phenomena or nature (Habermas 1984). Natural science and computer science research are typically means-end oriented, while we can also find means-end oriented research in the social or IS sciences. The goal of critical, or emancipatory, research is to point out the weaknesses of existing theories and practices – particularly dominant ones (Chua 1986).

Empirical support is needed for finding out what kind of empirical evidence the agile methods are grounded upon. It is often noted that while there is a great deal of anecdotal evidence to support the use of agile methods (Lindvall et al. 2002; Melnik et al. 2002), a lot less is known about the empirical evidence obtained through the use of rigorous scientific methods.

Figure 3.2 presents the evaluation for the first three perspectives. Each method is divided into three bars. The uppermost bar indicates the support provided for project management (analyzed in Section 3.3.2). The middle bar indicates how

---

[2]Situation appropriate is also known in IS literature as situational awareness (Tolvanen 1998).

well the software production process is described (pertaining to software development life-cycle analysis). The length of the bar shows which phases of software development are supported by each agile method (analyzed in Section 3.3.3). Finally, the lowest bar shows if a method relies mainly on abstract principles (white color) or if it provides concrete guidance (gray color). This will be analyzed in Section 3.3.4.

In general, gray color in a block indicates that the method covers the perspective analyzed while white indicates lack of such support.

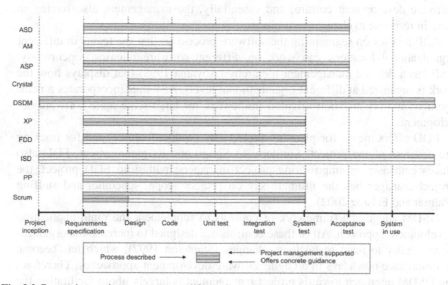

Fig. 3.2 Comparing project management, life-cycle, and concrete guidance support

3.3.2 Project management

Agile software development methods differ to a large degree in the way they cover project management (uppermost bar in Figure 3.2). Currently, AM and PP do not address the managerial perspective at all. XP has been supplemented with some guidelines on project management (Beck and Fowler 2001), but it still does not offer a clear project management view. While some of the existing XP practices – e.g. planning game and small releases – facilitate and feed information to project management activities, the focus is on a single project and on its development. In XP the foundation for efficient project management stems from understanding the flow of user stories (i.e. requirements) from initial ideas to final product. Still, the very concept of user stories remains unclear. Beck and Fowler (2001, p. 46) explain that "[a] user story is nothing more than an agreement that the customer and developers will talk together about a feature". However, in his initial work, Beck (Beck 2000, p. 90) states that "stories are written [...] with a name and short paragraph describing the purpose of the story." The basic concepts in XP, therefore, remain without a clear definition.

Scrum, on the other hand, is explicitly intended for managing agile software development projects. Thus, Schwaber and Beedle (2002) suggest the use of other methods to complement a Scrum based software development approach, naming XP as one alternative.

The approach promoted by ASD is the "adaptive (leadership-collaboration) management model" (Highsmith 2000). The focus of ASD is on changing the software development culture, and essentially, the management also having to bend in response to changes in projects.

ASP focuses on segmenting the software process so that the teams in different organizational locations can work on different software releases concurrently. ASP has a defined management hierarchy (Aoyama 1998) that displays how the work is organized at different organizational levels. ASP thus incorporates a management and organization oriented framework for large-scale agile software development.

FDD offers means for planning projects by product features, and for tracking the progress of the project. Similarly to Scrum and its management, FDD also places emphasis on empowering project managers; within an FDD project, the project manager has the ultimate say on project scope, schedule, and staffing (Palmer and Felsing 2002).

DSDM suggests a framework of controls to supplement the rapid application development approach. All of these controls are designed to increase the organizational ability to react to business changes (Stapleton 1997), which has become commonplace nowadays in all agile software development approaches. Therefore, the DSDM approach towards project management is largely about facilitating the work of the development teams, with daily tracking of the project's progress. Finally, Crystal's solution to project management focuses on increasing the ability to choose the correct method for each individual purpose (Cockburn 2002).

3.3.3 Software development life-cycle

In Figure 3.2, the overall length of the bar demonstrates which software development life-cycle phases are supported by the different agile methods. Figure 3.2 shows that agile methods are focused on different aspects of the software development life-cycle. DSDM is an independent method in the sense that it attempts to provide complete support over all life-cycle phases. Similarly Internet-speed development approaches also address all the phases of the software development life-cycle, but only from management and organization perspective. The others are more focused. ASD and ASP cover all the phases expect for project inception, acceptance test and system in use. AM aims at providing modeling support for requirements specification and design phases.

The Crystal family covers the phases from design to integration test. XP, PP, FDD and Scrum are focused on requirements specification, design, implementation (except for Scrum) and testing up until the system test.

From the process perspective, AM, ISD, Scrum (for the implementation part) and PP do not emphasize (or have not described) the process through which the software development proceeds. AM and PP are supplements to other methods. Thus, in the case of AM and PP the lack of process perspective seems reasonable. However, the ISD approach lacks clarity in this regard. In the other agile software development methods (i.e. ASD, ASP, Crystal, DSDM, XP, FDD and Scrum), the development process has been described.

3.3.4 Availability of concrete guidance for application

The lowest bar in Figure 3.2 indicates whether the method relies on concrete guidance (gray color) or on abstract principles (white color).

FDD lays down eight practices that "must" be used if compliance with the FDD development rules is to be valued (Palmer and Felsing 2002). The authors state that the "team is allowed to adapt them according to their experience level". Especially, in the case of these "must" practices, concrete guidance should be provided on how, in practice, this adaptation can be executed. If such guidance is missing (as it is, in this case), it is interpreted in our evaluation as reliance to abstract principles.

Based on this distinction, it was found that six out of ten agile software development methods included in the analysis placed emphasis on abstract principles over concrete guidance. ASD, again, is more about concepts and leadership-collaboration management culture than software practice. ASP (Aoyama 1998, pp. 59-65) provides the design rationale for agile software engineering environment, which describes to some extent how ASP is operationalized in Fujitsu, including the principal lessons-learned. However, ASP is a tool-centric solution for distributed agile software development. Hence, high level principles in guiding how to implement the ASP method can not be considered sufficient for other practitioners if they wish to adopt a similar working environment.

Crystal, depending on the system criticality and project size, mandates certain practices but provides little guidance on how to execute them. DSDM states that due to the fact that each organization is different no practices are detailed (Stapleton 1997). Instead, organizations should develop their practices themselves. Concrete guidance on how this should be done is not provided. Internet-speed development approaches establish certain practices or principles that should be in place. However, they do not offer any concrete guidance on how one should actually carry out the ideas of, e.g. "always analysis" or "dynamic requirements negotiation".

AM, XP and PP have been directly derived from practical settings. Their purpose and goal is to feed the collected "best practices" back into the actual practice of software development. Scrum defines the practices and offers guidance for the requirements specification phase and the integration testing phase. Implementation phases, as stated earlier, are not a part of the method.

3.3.5 Adaptability in actual use

Majority of agile software methods allow adaptability in actual use but refrain from offering guidance on how to perform the adaptation (Table 3.2).

Table 3.2 Adaptability in actual use

Perspective	Universally predefined	Situation appropriateness	
		Allow adaptation	Enable adaptation
Adaptive software development		X	-
Agile modeling		X	X
Agile software process		X	-
Crystal family of methodologies	X		-
Dynamic Systems Development Model		X	-
Extreme Programming		X	-
Feature-Driven Development	X		-
Internet Speed development		X	-
Pragmatic programming		X	X
Scrum		X	-

Cockburn's (2002) Crystal family of methodologies explicitly provides criteria on how to select the methodology for a project. The selection is made based on project size, criticality and priority (Cockburn 2000a). On the basis of these factors a decision is made about which methodology should be used. However, when the project is underway the situation appropriateness is decreased. This interpretation is based on the fact that Crystal methods offer prescriptive guidance. This means that Crystal, e.g., enforces certain rules such as "the projects always use incremental development cycles with a maximum increment length of four months". Thus, the adjustment is made by choosing one of the several "universal solutions", such as Crystal Clear.

FDD has goals that are grounded on imperatives or prescriptive guidance similar to Crystal. Palmer and Felsing (Palmer and Felsing 2002, p. 35) explain that FDD is "built around a core set of 'best practices'." All of these practices must be used in order to "get the full benefit that occurs by using the whole FDD process". FDD is claimed to suit "any software development organization that needs to deliver quality, business-critical software systems on time." (Palmer and Felsing 2002, p. xxiii). Thus, FDD and Crystal represent universal prescriptions that claim to have the suitability for all agile software development situations, scopes and projects.

The DSDM Consortium (1997) has published a method suitability filter in which three areas are covered: business, systems and technical (Stapleton 1997). The filter involves a series of questions such as "Are the requirements flexible and only specified at a high level?" or "Is functionality going to be reasonably visible at the user interface?" and some rationalization about which type of answer would yield greater benefits if DSDM were to be applied. While the method filter is predominantly about deciding whether the method itself is applicable or not, a recent study (Aydin and Harmsen 2002) has explicated how DSDM was adjusted to fit the purposes of an individual project, implying the necessary situation appropriate characteristics. Still, the lack of guidance on adapting DSDM in a particular software development situation indicates that the method does not *enable* adjustments on the fly.

Further, the ASD, ASP, AM, XP, ISD, PP and Scrum approaches allow situation appropriate modifications. For example, regarding XP Beck (1999, p. 77) suggests: "If you want to try XP, [...] don't try to swallow it all at once. Pick the worst problem in your current process and try solving it the XP way." Beck maintains that there is no process that fits every project as such, but rather the practices should be tailored to suit the needs of individual projects. We interpret this in such a way that the number of adjustments is not limited. One of the XP practices, namely "just rules", implies that while the rules are followed, they can be changed if a mutual understanding among the development team is achieved. This implies that XP supports situation appropriateness. Again, the lack of guidance on how to perform tailoring and adaptation during the development indicates that XP lacks the adjustment enabling characteristics.

AM and PP offer supplemental practices and concrete guidance on how and when to apply these methods in actual software development work. Authors describe the situations and rationale for applying the practices suggested but refrain from offering any prescriptive guidance.

3.3.6 Primary research objectives

The principal research objective of agile software method developers is means-end oriented (Table 3.3). Their primary goal is to provide technical solutions for the practitioners in the field.

Adaptive software development aims at offering concrete practical guidelines for helping practitioners in agile software development problems: "the book is written for project teams [using] a high-speed, high-change project to support a critical new business initiative." (Highsmith 2002a, p. xxix). This means-end oriented research objective can be observed in several places. Highsmith (2002a, p. xxv) argues that a "goal [of the book] is to offer a series of frameworks or models to help an organization employ adaptive principles." and "a goal of Adaptive Software Development is to provide a path for organizations needing to use an adaptive approach on larger projects." These extracts are further examples of the means-end oriented research objective - to offer practical solutions for solving real-life problems. Highsmith points out two major software development traditions in the history of software development: "Bureaucracy" and "adhocracy". This historical outlook can be seen as an interpretive research objective, aimed at increasing our understanding of the principles and background of these two traditions. The author also offers critiques of these approaches (Highsmith 2002a, pp. 6-8) thus engaging in critical (emancipatory) research.

The primary research objective of agile modeling (Ambler 2002) is means-end oriented, i.e. designed to present practical guidelines and examples on how "agile modelers" should do "agile modeling". There also seems to be a further critical research objective: "Current modeling approaches can often prove dysfunctional. In the one extreme, modeling is non-existent, often resulting in significant rework when the software proves to be poorly thought through. The other extreme is when excessive models and documents are produced, which slows your development efforts down to a snail's pace. AM helps you find the modeling sweet spot, where you have modeled enough to explore and document your system effectively, but not so much that it becomes a burden that slows the project down." Given that the above evidence is understood as a critique of existing modeling approaches, Ambler (2002) engages in critical research.

Aoyama's (1997; 1998) research objective falls also into the means-end oriented category, as he "proposes a new software process model, ASP (Agile Software Process) and discusses its experience" (Aoyama 1998, p. 3). In other words, Aoyama shows how ASP can be used for developing software in an agile manner.

The research objective of Cockburn (2002) is means-end oriented, as well: "These pages [Cockburn's book] contain the guidelines I use in my use case writing and in coaching: how a person may think, what he or she might observe, to end up with a better use case and use case set". Cockburn (2002), therefore, aims at presenting the best practices for use cases. Cockburn (2002) presents practical guidelines on how to increase the level of agility in software development – a means-end oriented research objective. Cockburn (2002) also engages in interpretive research by carrying out a meta-level analysis of certain concepts. He, for example, attempts to explain the meaning of a methodology thus aiming at increasing our understanding of the basic concepts, which is a sign of interpretive research objective.

Table 3.3 Primary research objectives

Research objective	Means-end oriented (technical)	Interpretative (hermeneutical)	Critical (emancipatory)
Adaptive software development	X	X	X
Agile modeling	X		
Agile software process	X		
Crystal family of methodologies	X		
Dynamic Systems Development Model	X		
Extreme Programming	X		
Feature-Driven Development			
Internet Speed development		X	X
Pragmatic programming	X		
Scrum	X		X

Stapleton (1997, p. xi) argues: "DSDM provides a framework of controls and best practice for the rapid application development [...] there is no book on the market that provides practical guidance on the use of the method [DSDM] or one that provides case studies from real DSDM projects." Stapleton (1997) presents the DSDM life-cycle and a nine step process, and explains how to apply these concepts in solving practical problems. This clearly refers to a means-end oriented research objective.

Beck's (1999; 2000) research objective is both means-end oriented and critical. He puts forth a set of XP practices, and explains how to apply these in industrial settings. Beck (2000) also provides guidelines for using XP principles at different levels of abstraction.

The research objective by Palmer and Felsing (2002) is means-end oriented: "spell out day-to-day details of using FDD on a real project, giving development team leaders all the information they need to apply FDD successfully to their situations." (Palmer and Felsing 2002, p. xix) This shows that their aim is to offer practical solutions to real-life problems. Palmer and Felsing also review the problems of the so-called waterfall process, but this cannot be classified as critical research, as Palmer and Felsing do not themselves explore the problems of existing methods.

Internet-speed development approaches show a degree of critical (emancipatory) research. This can be perceived from the following statement: "If emergence, rather than stability, is taken as the dominant character of organizations, at least in some periods, there is a need to radically rethink the way in which IS are developed." (Truex et al. 1999, p.118) and "[Traditional information systems development] goals were highly valued by IS managers and developers, but are inappropriate for emergent organizations". Here Truex et al. (1999) criticize the traditional text-book IS/software development practices as inadequate for agile development. Baskerville et al. (2001) engage in interpretive research, since they are aiming to reveal the agile-development practice of small companies. Truex et al. (1999, p.118) reveal their interpretive research objective by explaining the background of emergence (or agile development): "In order to understand how IT can promote organizational emergence, we need to understand some of the forces behind organizational emergence."

Hunt and Thomas' (2000) research objective is primarily means-end oriented. The aim of pragmatic programming is to provide practitioners with a knowledge to "become a better programmer" (Hunt 2000, p. xvii). The authors introduce a set of programming "best practices" that cover most programming practicalities including hints and tips on how to utilize their suggestions in real-life situations. There is also a sense of interpretative analysis to be found in Hunt and Thomas' work as they attempt to describe in practical terms what the pragmatic philosophy encompasses.

The primary research objective of Schwaber and Beedle (2002) is means-end oriented: "This is a practical book that describes the experience we have had using Scrum to build systems. In this book, we use case studies to give you a feel for Scrum-based projects and management. We then lay out the underlying practices for your use in projects." (Schwaber and Beedle 2002, p.1). As seen in these extracts, the authors aim to provide practical guidance for solving real-life problems, thus placing emphasis on their means-oriented research objective. Scrum can also be regarded as critical research as it makes an attempt to show "why current system development methodologies don't work" (Schwaber and Beedle 2002, pp. 94-100). Scrum (Schwaber and Beedle 2002, pp.105-122) also touches interpretive research in attempting to explain its theoretical underpinnings in the light of Kuhn's concept of paradigm and in terms of knowledge creation as suggested by Takeuchi and Nonaka (1986).

3.3.7 Empirical evidence

The development of agile software development approaches are not based on systematic research (Dybå and Dingsøyr 2008). The only meta-analysis performed up-to-date in the area is done by Dybå and Dingsøyr (2008) where the authors perform a systematic review on empirical studies of agile software development. They conclude that the field is still nascent and the quality of the research falls evidently short. In what follows, each of the agile methods and the empirical research connected to these methods are summarized briefly. The list is not exhaustive but rather an illustration of the type of research conducted.

The most scientific efforts can be identified within the realm of XP practices, i.e. pair programming (Williams et al. 2000; Nawrocki and Wojciechowski 2001; Succi et al. 2002; Heiberg et al. 2003; Janes et al. 2003; Lui and Chan 2003; Williams and Kessler 2003) and test-first approach to software development (Müller and Hagner 2002), or their combination (Rostaher and Hericko 2002; George and Williams 2003).

Experiences from using XP, and its variations, can be identified in university (Müller and Tichy 2001; Nawrocki et al. 2002), research institute (Abrahamsson 2003; Wood and Kleb 2003; Sfetsos et al. 2006), and commercial settings (Anderson et al. 1998; Grenning 2001; Schuh 2001; Murru et al. 2003; Rasmusson 2003). While these studies and reports provide necessary insight into the possibilities and restrictions of extreme programming, concrete data is, however, more difficult to find. Maurer and Martel's study (Maurer and Martel 2002b; Maurer and Martel 2002a) provides some data regarding the productivity gains using XP in a web development project. Wood and Kleb (2003), Abrahamsson (2003) and Hulkko and Abrahamsson (2005) have published the empirical data from their projects, which can be seen as building up the empirical body of evidence. Based on these studies, empirical hypotheses can be drawn, which are subject to further validation. For example, pair programming has been shown to reduce up to 40-50% calendar time required for job completion (Williams et al. 2000), improving job satisfaction (Williams et al. 2000; Succi et al. 2002) and producing consistently higher quality code than solo programmers (Williams et al. 2000). As an another example, Capiluppi et al. (2007) investigates evolution patterns over two and a half years for a system developed using XP. The study reports that the system shows a smooth pattern of growth overall, that (McCabe) code complexity is low, and that the relative amount of complexity control work (e.g. refactoring) is higher than in other systems authors had studied.

Contradictory findings are prominent as well. George and Williams (2003) have found that test-driven development takes, on average, 16% more time for development but that the resulting code quality is better. Müller and Hagner (2002) have concluded that in general test-first does not accelerate the implementation and that the results are not more reliable. Müller and Hagner (2002) base their findings on 19 students (10 in the test group and 9 in the control group) while George and Williams' (2003) subjects were 24 professional pair programmers. Based on the systematic review of 15 studies, Dybå et al. (2007) presented the meta-analysis to examine the effectiveness of pair programming. The analysis is reported on different angles of pair programming including its effect on quality, duration, effort, task complexity and expertise. The meta-analysis concluded that the pair programming's effectiveness "depends"— on both the programmer's expertise and the complexity of the system and tasks to be solved. Pair programming is better for achieving correctness on highly complex programming tasks. They might also have a time gain on simpler tasks. Furthermore, on qualitative aspects on pair programming, Sfetsos (2008) investigates developer personalities and temperaments and how they affect pair effectiveness. It concludes that pairs with heterogeneous personalities and temperaments may indicate better communication, pair performance and pair collaboration-viability.

AM, ASD, Crystal, FDD, PP and Scrum have been derived from the subjective practical experience of their authors, as opposite to rigorous research. Thus, their solutions can be seen as lacking reliable empirical support. Regarding Scrum, Schwaber and Beedle (2002, p.31) claim, e.g., that "[Scrum] practices have been established through *thousands* of Scrum projects", (italics added). None of these projects are cited, however, it invites skepticism regarding the validity of the empirical evidence. Although Sutherland (2001), who is one of the originators of the method, describes how the Scrum method has evolved over years in practical setting, the details of these settings and the data are not disclosed. More recently, however, real life empirical studies on Scrum have increased substantially (Rising and Janoff 2000; Jensen and Zilmer 2003; Dingsøyr et al. 2006; Hosbond et al. 2008; Marchenko and Abrahamsson, 2008).

Agile software process and Internet-speed development were both found to have a degree of empirical support. ASP has been used for the development of large scale communication systems in Fujitsu (Aoyama 1997; Aoyama 1998). ISD, for its part, is based on interpretive (qualitative) case studies in several companies (Cusumano and Yoffie 1999; Baskerville et al. 2001; Baskerville and Pries-Heje 2001, 2004). Baskerville et al.'s case study findings have also received further empirical support (Alatalo et al. 2002). We furthermore see that these studies are aimed at increasing our understanding of how Internet-speed companies have survived, not proposing "laws" for making successful agile software development.

DSDM has been developed by a dedicated Consortium. While the aim of the Consortium has been to develop a public-domain method (Millington and Stapleton 1995), the empirical results are not openly shared with the scientific and user communities. Stapleton (1997) claims that there exists empirical evidence in the form of reports (i.e., white papers), but these are only shared with the members of the Consortium. However, since these reports have not been made publicly available, we can only conclude that the claims of DSDM are not empirically supported. Recently, Coyle and Conboy (2009) report a case study of risk management in DSDM. However, in general the empirical evidences supporting DSDM in the agile literature are almost inexistent.

The studies substantiating empirical evidences in agile methods at meta-level have been emerging recently. Dybå and Dingsøyr (2008) present a systematic review on empirical studies of agile software development. They filter thirty three agile empirical studies for analysis, in different settings, from professional projects to university courses. Dybå and Dingsøyr (2008) identify that there is a need to increase both the number and the quality of studies on agile software development. The analysis also suggests that most of the empirical studies analyzed were using XP. Scrum, one of the most popular agile methods of recent times, and having rather very low volume of empirical studies, needs further attention.

The results of the analysis confirm the initial conjectures. Empirically validated agile software engineering studies are scarce. The existing empirical studies are mostly focused on XP and its practices as well as Internet-speed development. The other methods have received considerably less attention.

3.4 Discussion

In this section, the results of the comparative review are discussed. The purpose is to identify the principal implications for research and practice. Table 3.4 summarizes these implications.

Project management support: software engineering is a practice-oriented field. Yet, while most (i.e. seven out of ten) agile methods do in fact incorporate some support for project management, real support is scarce. If this perspective is considered from a method feasibility point of view, efficient project management is of the utmost importance in following agile principles, such as daily builds, short release-cycles etc. Moreover, the concepts of, e.g., release and daily builds differ from one method to another. This is likely to lead to confusion rather than clarity. It appears that method developers are aiming at a niche market by deliberately using differing terminology. Practitioners, especially project managers, find themselves in a difficult position when a decision as to the most suitable approach has to be made. The operational success of any method lies in its ability to be incorporated in the daily rhythm of the software project. On this basis, we maintain that project management considerations need to be addressed explicitly to ensure alignment between developers and those managing the project.

Table 3.4 Results and implications of the study

Perspective	Results	Implications
Project management support	While most methods appear to cover project management, real support is missing	Conceptual harmonization is needed. Project management can not be neglected
Software development life-cycle coverage	Current agile methods are variously focused. Reasons or rationale for their life-cycle coverage is not provided	Life-cycle coverage needs to be explained and interfaces with phases not covered need to be clarified
Availability of concrete guidance for application	Abstract principles dominate the method literature	Emphasis should be placed on enabling practitioners to utilize the suggestions made
Adaptability in actual use	Majority of the agile methods recognize that they need to be adapted to different development situations. Yet, methods lack the mechanism to enable this adaptation	More work needs to be done on how to adapt or adjust agile methods in different development situations
Research objective	The most common research objective is means-end oriented	Critical studies are particularly needed
Empirical evidence	Empirical evidence is very limited	More empirical, situation-specific, experimental work is needed; the results need to be publicly available

Software development life-cycle coverage: Different agile methods cover different phases of the software development life-cycle. One possible reason for this is that most of the methods have been developed independently by different practitioners (Highsmith 2002a; Lindvall et al. 2002). Therefore, the rationale for the method focus is currently largely lacking. This hinders the possibility of effectively comparing the existing methods when trying to determine which of them is the most suitable for a given purpose. As the rationale for the life-cycle coverage is omitted, the interfaces with the phases not covered also remain unspecified, which further makes the method more difficult to apply. It is therefore suggested that the developers of agile methods pay more attention in the future to explaining their reasons for their choice of coverage, including the interfaces with the remaining phases. Information about these interfaces should include at the very least the necessary inputs for the method as well as the outputs that are generated through the application of the method.

Availability of concrete guidance for application: Only three out of ten agile methods offer concrete guidance. Thus, the current agile method literature is dominated by abstract and generic principles that offer little concrete guidance. Apparently, the agile community is more concerned about gaining acceptance of its proposed principles than offering guidance on how to use the operative versions of these principles. Currently, concrete guidance exists mostly in methods that are very limited in their life-cycle coverage (i.e. AM) or the level of detail beyond practices (i.e. pair programming). More work is needed to determine how the claimed practices, activities and work products can be made to operate in different organizations and situations, so as to provide practitioners with a solid base on which to formulate their decisions.

Adaptability in actual use: Some of the known agile methods (FDD and Crystal) were found to be universally predefined. Nevertheless, the methods that recognize the fact that "one size does not fit all situations", still do not offer any guidance on how this fitting process can be achieved. This being the case, forthcoming methods and studies should pay particular attention to adaptability in actual use, and offer guidance on how these methods should be used in different agile software development situations. This also requires the ability to identify the particular situations in which these fitting or adjustment activities need to be done.

The most common research objective found is means-end oriented. Of the agile methods, only a few approaches (i.e. ASD, ISD, Scrum) also have a critical research objective. Owing to the paucity of critical studies, these are particularly needed. Critical studies help us to perceive the weaknesses in the existing, perhaps dominant, agile methods and practices, while they also underline the fact that nothing should be accepted "blindly".

Empirical evidence grounded in rigorous research is scarce. The results of the analysis confirmed the initial conjectures. Only four of the ten methods studied present some empirical support for their claims. However, some methods (e.g. XP) are increasingly producing more and more empirical studies, which are bound to make the methodological base more mature. The lack of empirical evidence results in practitioners not having reliable evidence on the real usability and the effectiveness of the different agile methods. Therefore the practitioners cannot determine whether the existing methods really make sense or not, wondering if the methods describe proven wisdom or if they are merely just appealing development stories. As for researchers and method developers, the lack of empirical evidence does not help in establishing a reliable and cumulative research tradition; in fact researchers do not have access to reliable evidence on existing work. Such information is, however, vital. For example, it is essential to have the knowledge of which parts of the existing work have solid foundation, and thus in deciding the extent to which we can base our future research on the existing wisdom. Thus, more empirical work is needed on the applicability of the different agile methods in different organizations and situations. Moreover, any empirical evidence should be publicly accessible. Unfortunately, the empirical studies carried out on DSDM – if such do exist – have been made available only to the members of the development consortium. What is especially needed is empirical work exploring the effects of particular methods, their ease of use, costs, and possible negative implications for different sizes and lines of business. Such empirical work should make use of both qualitative and quantitative research methods along with data collection devices. As shown in the analysis, there exists an empirical body of evidence on the application of certain sets of agile practices. This enables the development of empirically based hypotheses with regard to the use of, e.g., pair programming and test-driven development. However, despite a great deal of literature (e.g., Grady 1992; Kitchenham 1996; Fenton and Pfleeger 1997; Hughes 2000) dealing with software metrics, what is currently lacking is a framework for measuring and validating agile software development in practical settings. This framework should define the metrics suitable for agile software development as well as provide guidance on data collection and analysis issues.

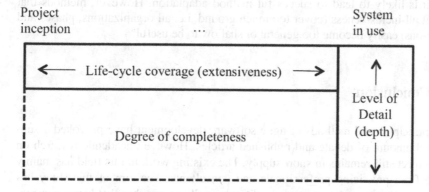

Fig. 3.3 The fundamental problem of agile methods; combining extensiveness with depth in a sensible way

The perspectives addressed raise an important question that needs to be answered by the agile software community. Specifically, would it be more profitable to opt for extensiveness and cover more phases, or to cover fewer and aim at greater precision. In Figure 3.3 depth refers to the level of detail in each phase of the life-cycle. Concrete guidance supplements the level of detail by describing how the goals are achieved. Adaptability-in-use aims to make the solutions applicable to different situations.

The fundamental problem here is that if a method covers all phases in great detail, it may become a methodological dinosaur, which is likely to make tailoring solutions to specific needs difficult in practice. One promising avenue of approach to this problem is method engineering (Kumar and Welke 1992), which has been applied in tailoring the DSDM in a recent case study reported by Aydin and Harmsen (2002). Completeness, a notion introduced by Kumar and Welke (1992), requires that a useful method is complete as opposed to partial. Figure 3.3 shows that "completeness" is an element that must be associated with both the vertical (i.e. depth of a method) and horizontal (i.e. life-cycle coverage) dimensions. None of the methods evaluated were either extensive or precise. Practitioners, currently, have only partial solutions to problems that cover a wider area than that covered by the methods. At least two possibilities can be identified. On one hand, method developers can concentrate more on specialization than generalization in their areas of expertise. Specialization refers to the development of methods or techniques to fit a particular setting or a specific development phase. An example of such a specialized approach is the Rapid7 specification technique (Kylmäkoski 2003), which focuses on efficient document authoring in software development projects. The problem here is that when methods cover too little (e.g., one phase of software development, such as requirements analysis or coding), they may become too restricted for practical purposes. Another way to approach this problem is to incorporate built-in mechanisms in to the methods to enable learning-in-use, which is likely to lead to successful method adaptation. However, methods that aim at all-inclusiveness (cover too much ground, i.e. all organizations, phases and situations) easily become too general or shallow to be useful.

3.5 Conclusion

The principles and methods of agile software development have provoked a substantial amount of debate and published articles. However, academic research on the subject still remains in short supply. The existing work in this field has mainly come from practicing professionals and consultants. The aim of this study has been to order and make sense of the different agile approaches that have been proposed. The existing methods were reviewed from six perspectives to determine the current situation and to suggest what directions the future agile methods should take.

In principal, it was found that the existing methods, without offering any rationale, covered various phases of the life-cycle. The majority of them do not present adequate support for project management, and only a few methods offered concrete guidance to support their solutions or adaptations in different development situations. While the method developers' research objective has been predominantly means-end oriented (technical), related empirical evidence is to date very limited.

On the basis of the above findings, new research directions were proposed. To begin with, the future agile methods need to clarify their range of applicability and to explain the interfaces to the software development life-cycle which are not part of the focus of these methods. The project management perspective cannot be neglected, either, if a method is to be welcomed in day-to-day software development practice. Emphasis should also be placed on enabling practitioners to utilize the suggestions made by the method developers. This requires more empirical work to be done on how agile methods can be adapted to different software development situations as well as studies exploring the real strengths and weaknesses of the alternative agile methods in different real-life situations. Finally, a fundamental problem was raised regarding the relationship between the coverage and depth of an agile method. If a method covers all phases in great detail, it may become a methodological dinosaur, making it difficult to apply in practice. Method engineering was proposed as a promising avenue of approach to this problem.

The current thinking on agile methods focuses on constructing a pile of conceptual methods. Instead of making haste to introduce yet more agile methods, developers should pay particular attention to the problems raised above. The field is crying out for sound methods, i.e. for methodological quality, not quantity.

Acknowledgements

The authors are grateful for the authors participating to the authoring of the well-known VTT technical report – Agile Software Development Methods: Review and Analysis, which inspired us to take the analysis further. These are Dr. Outi Salo, Jussi Ronkainen and Dr. Juhani Warsta.

References

Abrahamsson, P. (2003). Extreme programming: First results from a controlled case study. Euromicro 2003, Antalya, Turkey.
Abrahamsson, P., O. Salo, J. Ronkainen and J. Warsta (2002). Agile software development methods: Review and Analysis. Espoo, Finland, Technical Research Centre of Finland, VTT Publications 478, Online: http://www.inf.vtt.fi/pdf/publications/2002/P478.pdf.

Agresti, W. W. (1986). New paradigms for software development. Los Alamitos, CA, IEEE CS Press.

Alatalo, T., H. Oinas-Kukkonen, V. Kurkela and M. Siponen (2002). Information Systems Development in Emergent Organizations: Empirical Findings. Eleventh International Conference on Information Systems Development (ISD '02), Riga, Latvia.

Ambler, S. W. (2002). Agile modeling. New York, John Wiley & Sons, Inc.

Anderson, A., R. Beattie, K. Beck, D. Bryant, M. DeArment, M. Fowler, M. Fronczak, R. Garzaniti, D. Gore, B. Hacker, C. Handrickson, R. Jeffries, D. Joppie, D. Kim, P. Kowalsky, D. Mueller, T. Murasky, R. Nutter, A. Pantea and D. Thomas (1998). "Chrysler Goes to "Extremes". Case Study." Distributed Computing(October): 24-28.

Aoyama, M. (1987). "Concurrent development of software systems: A new development paradigm." ACM Software Engineering Notes: 20-24.

Aoyama, M. (1993). "Concurrent-development process model." IEEE Software 10: 46-55.

Aoyama, M. (1997). Agile Software Process Model. The Twenty-First Annual International Computer Software and Applications Conference 1997. COMPSAC '97., Washington, DC, USA.

Aoyama, M. (1998). "Web-based Agile Software Development." IEEE Software 15(6): 56-65.

Aydin, M. N. and F. Harmsen (2002). Making a method work for a project situation in the context of CMM. Product Focused Software Process Improvement (Profes 2002), Rovaniemi, Finland, Springer.

Basili, V. R. and F. Lanubile (1999). "Building knowledge through families of experiments." IEEE Transactions on Software Engineering 25: 456-473.

Baskerville, R., L. Levine, J. Pries-Heje, B. Ramesh and S. Slaughter (2001). "How Internet companies negotiate quality." IEEE Computer 34(5): 51-57.

Baskerville, R., L. Levine, J. Pries-Heje, B. Ramesh and S. Slaughter (2002). Balancing quality and agility in Internet speed software development. 23rd International Conference on Information Systems, Barcelona, Spain.

Baskerville, R. and J. Pries-Heje (2001). Racing the E-bomb: How the Internet is redefining information systems development methodology. Realigning research and practice in IS development. B. Fitzgerald, N. Russo and J. DeGross. New York, Kluwer: 49-68.

Baskerville, R. and J. Pries-Heje (2004). Short cycle time systems development. Info Systems J. 14: 237 - 264.

Baskerville, R., J. Travis and D. P. Truex (1992). Systems without method: The impact of new technologies on information systems development projects. Transactions on the impact of computer supported technologies in information systems development. K. E. Kendall, K. Lyytinen and J. I. DeGross. Amsterdam, Elsevier Science Publications: 241-260.

Bayer, S. and J. Highsmith (1994). "RADical software development." American Programmer 7(6): 35-42.

Beck, K. (1999). "Embracing change with extreme programming." IEEE Computer: 70-77.

Beck, K. (2000). Extreme programming explained: Embrace change. Reading, MA., Addison Wesley Longman, Inc.

Beck, K. and M. Fowler (2001). Planning extreme programming. New York, Addison-Wesley.

Beck, K., Anders, C. (2004). Extreme programming explained: embrace change (2nd. ed): Addision-Wesley

Boehm, B. (1988). "A Spiral Model of Software Development and Enhancement." IEEE Computer 21: 61-72.

Boehm, B. (2002). "Get Ready For The Agile Methods, With Care." Computer 35(1): 64-69.

Capiluppi, A., J. Fernandez-Ramil, J. Higman, H. C. Sharp, and N. Smith (2007). "An Empirical Study of the Evolution of an Agile-Developed Software System." In Proceedings of the 29th international Conference on Software Engineering (May 20 - 26, 2007). ICSE. IEEE Computer Society, Washington, DC, pp 511-518.

Chua, W. F. (1986). "Radical developments in accounting thought." The Accounting Review 61(5): 583-598.

Coad, P., E. LeFebvre and J. De Luca (2000). Java Modeling In Color With UML: Enterprise Components and Process. Englewood Cliffs, NJ, Prentice Hall.

Cockburn, A. (1998). Surviving Object-Oriented Projects: A Manager's Guide, Addison Wesley Longman.

Cockburn, A. (2000a). "Selecting a project's methodology." IEEE Software 17: 64-71.

Cockburn, A. (2000b). Writing Effective Use Cases, The Crystal Collection for Software Professionals, Addison-Wesley Professional.

Cockburn, A. (2002). Agile software development. Boston, MA., Pearson Education.

Coyle, S. and K. Conboy (2009). A Study of Risk Management in DSDM. Presented at 10th International Conference, XP 2009, Pula, Sardinia, Italy. Proceedings in P. Abrahamsson, M. Marchesi, and F. Maurer (Eds.): XP2009, LNBIP 31, pp. 142 - 148

Cugola, G. and C. Ghezzi (1998). "Software Processes: a Retrospective and a Path to the Future." Software Process Improvement and Practice 4: 101-123.

Cusumano, M. A. and R. W. Selby (1997). "How Microsoft builds software." Communications of the ACM 40(6): 53-61.

Cusumano, M. A. and D. B. Yoffie (1999). "Software development on Internet time." IEEE Computer 32(10): 60-69.

Dybå, T. and T. Dingsøyr (2008). "Empirical studies of agile software development: A systematic review." Information and Software Technology, 50(9-10): 833-859

Dybå, T., E. Arisholm, D.I.K. Sjoberg, J.E. Hannay, and F. Shull (2007). "Are Two Heads Better than One? On the Effectiveness of Pair Programming". IEEE Software 24(6): 12-15

DSDM Consortium (1997). Dynamic Systems Development Method, version 3. Ashford, Eng., DSDM Consortium.

Fenton, N. (2001). "Viewpoint Article: Conducting and presenting empirical software engineering." Empirical Software Engineering 6: 195-200.

Fenton, N. and S. L. Pfleeger (1997). Software metrics: A rigorous and practical approach. Boston, PWS Publishing Company.

Fowler, M. and J. Highsmith (2001). "Agile methodologists agree on something." Software Development 9(8): 28-32.

George, B. and L. Williams (2003). An initial investigation of test driven development in industry. ACM Symposium on Applied Computing, Melbourne, Florida, USA.

Gilb, T. (1988). Principles of Software Engineering Management. Wokingham, Addison-Wesley.

Grady, R. B. (1992). Practical software metrics for project management and process improvement. Upper Saddle River, NJ, Prentice-Hall.

Grenning, J. (2001). "Launching XP at a Process-Intensive Company." IEEE Software 18: 3-9.

Habermas, J. (1984). The Theory of Communicative Action. Boston, MA, Beacom Press.

Heiberg, S., U. Puus, P. Salumaa and A. Seeba (2003). Pair-programming effect on developers productivity. XP 2003, Genoa, Italy, Springer-Verlag.

Highsmith, J. (2001). "The great methodologies debate: Part 1." Cutter IT Journal 14(12).

Highsmith, J. (2002a). Agile software development ecosystems. Boston, MA., Pearson Education.

Highsmith, J. (2002b). "The great methodologies debate: Part 2." Cutter IT Journal 15(1).

Highsmith, J. and A. Cockburn (2001). "Agile Software Development: The Business of Innovation." Computer 34(9): 120-122.

Highsmith, J. A. (2000). Adaptive Software Development: A Collaborative Approach to Managing Complex Systems. New York, NY, Dorset House Publishing.

Hirscheim, R., H. K. Klein and K. Lyytinen (1995). "Exploring the intellectual structures of information systems development." Australian Journal of Information Systems 5: 3-29.

Hirscheim, R., H. K. Klein and K. Lyytinen (1996). "Exploring the intellectual structures of information systems development: A social action theoretic analysis." Accounting, Management and Information Technology 6: 1-64.

Hirschheim, R. (1985). Information systems epistemology: An historical perspective. Proceedings of the IFIP WG 8.2., Amsterdam, Elsevier Science Publisher.

Hosbond, J.H. and P. A. Nielsen (2008). Misfit or Misuse? Lessons from Implementation of Scrum in Radical Product Innovation. In P. Abrahamsson et al. (Eds.) : XP2008, LNBIP9, pp 21 - 31

Hughes, A. (2000). Practical software measurement. Cambridge, McGraw-Hill Publishing Company.

Hulkko, H. and P. Abrahamsson (2005). A multiple case study on the impact of pair programming on product quality. In Proceedings of the 27th international Conference on Software Engineering (St. Louis, MO, USA, May 15 - 21, 2005). ICSE '05. ACM, New York, NY, 495-504.

Hunt, A., Thomas, D. (2000). The Pragmatic Programmer, Addison Wesley.

Iivari, J. and R. Hirscheim (1996). "Analyzing information systems development: A comparison and analysis of eight IS development approaches." Information Systems 21: 551-575.

Janes, A., B. Russo, P. Zuliani and G. Succi (2003). An empirical analysis on the discontinuous use of pair programming. XP 2003, Genoa, Italy, Springer-Verlag.

Jensen, B. and A. Zilmer (2003). Cross-continent development using Scrum and XP. XP 2003, Genoa, Italy, Springer-Verlag.

Kettunen, P. (2009). Agile software development in large-scale new product development organization: team-level perspective, doctoral dissertation, Helsinki University of Technology, http://lib.tkk.fi/Diss/2009/isbn9789522481146

Kitchenham, B. A. (1996). Software metrics: measurement for software process improvement. Cambridge, Mass., Blackwell Publishers.

Kumar, K. and R. J. Welke (1992). Methodology engineering: A proposal for situation-specific methodology construction. Challenges and strategies for research in systems development. W. W. Cotterman and J. A. Senn. New York, John Wiley & Sons: 257-269.

Kylmäkoski, R. (2003). Efficient Authoring of Software Documentation Using RaPiD7. 25th International Conference on Software Engineering, Portland, Oregon, IEEE Computer Society Press.

Larman, G. (2004). Agile and iterative development - A manager's guide, Boston, MA: Pearson Education

Lindvall, M., V. Basili, B. Boehm, P. Costa, K. Dangle, F. Shull, R. Tesoriero, L. Williams and M. Zelkowitz (2002). Empirical findings in agile methods. XP/Agile Universe 2002, Chicago, USA.

Lui, K. M. and K. C. C. Chan (2003). When does a pair outperform two individuals. XP 2003, Genoa, Italy, Springer-Verlag.

Lyytinen, K. (1991). A taxonomic perspective of information systems development: Theoretical constructs and recommendations. Critical issues in information systems research. R. J. Boland and R. A. Hirschheim. Chichester, UK, John Wiley and Sons.

Malouin, J. L. and M. Landry (1983). "The miracle of universal methods in systems design." Journal of Applied Systems Analysis 10: 47-62.

Marchenko, A. and P. Abrahamsson (2008). "Scrum in a Multiproject Environment: An Ethnographically-Inspired Case Study on the Adoption Challenges," AGILE 2008 Conference, pp. 15-26,

Martin, R. C. (2002). Agile Software Development, Principles, Patterns, and Practices. Englewood Cliffs, NJ, Prentice Hall.

Maurer, F. and S. Martel (2002a). "Extreme programming: Rapid development for Web-based applications." IEEE Internet Computing 6(1): 86-90.

Maurer, F. and S. Martel (2002b). "On the Productivity of Agile Software Practices: An Industrial Case Study." (page accessed May 15, 2003) http://sern.ucalgary.ca/~milos/papers/2002/MaurerMartel2002c.pdf.

Mautner, T. (1996). A dictionary of philosophy. Oxford, UK., Blackwell Publishers ltd.

McCauley, R. (2001). "Agile Development Methods Poised to Upset Status Quo." SIGCSE Bulletin 33(4): 14 - 15.

Merisalo-Rantanen H., T. Tuunanen and M. Rossi (2005) Is Extreme Programming Just Old Wine in New Bottles: A Comparison of Two Cases. Journal of Database Management 16 (4), 41-61.

Millington, D. and J. Stapleton (1995). "Developing a RAD standard." IEEE Software 12: 54-55.

Murru, O., R. Deias and G. Mugheddu (2003). "Assessing XP at a European Internet company." IEEE Software 20(3): 37-43.

Müller, M. M. and O. Hagner (2002). Experiment about test-first programming. Conference on Empirical Assessment In Software Engineering (EASE), Keele, UK.

Müller, M. M. and W. F. Tichy (2001). Case study: Extreme programming in university environment. International Conference on Software Engineering (ICSE23), Toronto, Canada.

Nandhakumar, J. and J. Avison (1999). "The fiction of methodological development: a field study of information systems development." Information Technology & People 12(2): 176-191.

Nawrocki, J. and A. Wojciechowski (2001). Experimental evaluation of pair programming. ESCOM 2001, London, UK, Shaker Publishing.

Nawrocki, J. R., B. Walter and A. Wojciechowski (2002). Comparison of CMM level 2 and eXtreme programming. 7th European Conference on Software Quality, Helsinki, Finland, Springer.

Ohno, T. (1988). Toyota production system. Cambridge, Mass., Productivity Press.

Olle, T. W., H. G. Sol and A. Verrijn-Stuart (1982). Information systems design methodologies: A comparative review. Amsterdam, North-Holland.

Palmer, S. R. and J. M. Felsing (2002). A practical guide to feature-driven development. Upper Saddle River, NJ, Prentice-Hall Inc.

Poppendieck, M. and T. Poppendieck (2003). Lean software development - An agile tolkit for software development managers. Boston: Addison-Wesley.

Rajlich, V. (2006). Changing the paradigm of software engineering: Communications of the ACM, 8(49):67-70

Rasmusson, J. (2003). "Introducing XP into Greenfield projects: Lessons learned." IEEE Software 20(3): 21-28.

Rising, L. and N. S. Janoff (2000). "The Scrum software development process for small teams." IEEE Software 17(4): 26-32.

Melnik, G., L. Williams and A. Geras (2002). Empirical Evaluation of Agile Processes. XP/Agile Universe 2002, Chicago, USA, Springer-Verlag.

Rostaher, m. and M. Hericko (2002). Tracking test first pair programming - an experiment. XP/Agile Universe 2002, Chicago, Illinois, USA, Springer-Verlag.

Schuh, P. (2001). "Recovery, Redemption, and Extreme Programming." IEEE Software 18(6): 34-41.

Schwaber, K. (1995). Scrum Development Process. OOPSLA'95 Workshop on Business Object Design and Implementation, Springer-Verlag.

Schwaber, K. and M. Beedle (2002). Agile Software Development With Scrum. Upper Saddle River, NJ, Prentice-Hall.

Sfetsos, P., L. Angelis, and I. Stamelos (2006). "Investigating the extreme programming system–An empirical study." Empirical Software Engineering 11(2): 269 - 301.

Sfetsos, P. (2008). "An experimental investigation of personality types impact on pair effectiveness in pair programming." Empirical Software Engineering 14(2): 187 - 226.

Sol, H. G. (1983). A feature analysis of information systems design methodologies: Methodological considerations. Information systems design methodologies: A feature analysis. T. W. Olle, H. G. Sol and C. J. Tully. Amsterdam, Elsevier: 1-8.

Song, X. and L. J. Osterweil (1991). Comparing design methodologies through process modeling. 1st International Conference on Software Process, Los Alamitos, Calif., IEEE CS Press.

Stapleton, J. (1997). Dynamic systems development method - The method in practice, Addison Wesley.

Succi, G., W. Pedrycz, M. Marchesi and L. Williams (2002). Preliminary analysis of the effects of pair programming on job satisfaction. XP 2002, Alghero, Sardinia, Italy.

Sutherland, J. (2001). "Agile Can Scale: Inventing and Reinventing SCRUM in Five Companies." Cutter IT Journal 14(12): 5-11.

Takeuchi, H. and I. Nonaka (1986). "The new product development game." Harvard Business Review(1): 137-146.

Tolvanen, J. P. (1998). Incremental method engineering with modeling tools. PhD dissertation. Jyväskylä University Printing House and ER-Paino Ky, University of Jyväskylä, Finland.

Truex, D. P., R. Baskerville and H. Klein (1999). "Growing systems in emergent organizations." Communications of the ACM 42(8): 117-123.

Truex, D. P., R. Baskerville and J. Travis (2001). "Amethodological systems development: The deferred meaning of systems development methods." Accounting, Management and Information Technology 10: 53-79.

Wastell, D. G. (1996). "The fetish of technique: methodology as a social defense." Information Systems Journal 6: 25-49.

Williams, L. and R. Kessler (2003). Pair programming illuminated. New York, Addison-Wesley.

Williams, L., R. R. Kessler, W. Cunningham and R. Jeffries (2000). "Strengthening the case for pair programming." IEEE Software 17(4): 19-25.

Wood, W. A. and W. L. Kleb (2003). "Exploring XP for scientific research." IEEE Software 20(3): 30-36.

Yourdon, E. (2000). "Light methodologies." Cutter IT Journal 13(11).

Author Biographies

Pekka Abrahamsson is a professor in the Department of Computer Science at University of Helsinki. His research interests are centred on lean thinking, agile software development and empirical software engineering in the complex systems design space. He leads large European research projects on these topics. He is in the editorial board of *Software Process Improvement and Practice* and in the advisory board of *IEEE Software*. He is member of the ISERN, ACM and IEEE.

Nilay Oza holds a PhD is software business and he is a senior research scientist at VTT Technical research centre of Finland. He conducts research, develops and manages R&D projects and offers consultation to companies as a member of VTT. His current areas of research interest include agile adoption and transformation, lean thinking, Green IT business models, and global software business. He has been providing consultation in large-scale agile transformation, innovation enablement, and global software business coordination. He is actively connected in international software and information systems communities.

Mikko Siponen is a Professor and Director of the IS Security Research Centre in the Department of Information Processing Science at the University of Oulu, Finland. His research interests include IS security, IS development, computer ethics, and philosophical aspects of IS. He has 33 published or forthcoming papers in journals such as *MIS Quarterly*, *Journal of the Association for Information Sys-*

tems, *European Journal of Information Systems*, *Information & Organization*, *Information Systems Journal*, *Information & Management*, *ACM Database*, *Communications of the ACM*, *IEEE Computer*, *IEEE IT Professional* and *ACM Computers & Society*. He has served as a senior and associate editor for ICIS and ECIS, and special issue SE for the *MIS Quarterly*. He sits on the editorial boards of the *European Journal of Information Systems*, *Journal of Organizational and End User Computing*, and *Journal of Information Systems Security*.

4 Three 'C's of Agile Practice: Collaboration, Co-ordination and Communication

Helen Sharp, Hugh Robinson

Abstract: The importance of collaboration, co-ordination and communication in agile teams is often discussed and rarely disputed. These activities are supported through various practices including pairing, customer collaboration, stand-ups and the planning game. However the mechanisms used to support these activities are sometimes more difficult to pin down. We have been studying agile teams for over a decade, and have found that story cards and the Wall are central to an agile team's activity, and the information they hold and convey is crucial for supporting the team's collaboration and co-ordination activity. However the information captured by these usually physical artefacts pertains mainly to progress rather than to functional dependencies. This latter information is fundamental to any software development, and in a non-agile environment is usually contained in detailed documentation not generally produced in an agile team. Instead, this information resides in their communication and social practices. In this chapter we discuss these three 'C's of agile development and what we know about how they are supported through story cards and the Wall.

4.1 Introduction

The tight social and technical cohesion found in agile teams is not disputed, but understanding the detailed mechanisms, activities and patterns that support this cohesion is less well-understood. This chapter distills the results of several field studies investigating agile teams to describe a set of collaborative mechanisms, co-ordination activities and communication patterns of agile practice.

For the purpose of this chapter, we define collaboration, co-ordination and communication as follows: *collaboration* takes place when two or more people are working together on a task; *co-ordination* is the process of managing dependencies among activities; *communication* takes place when two or more people exchange information or knowledge through verbal or non-verbal means.

The need for agile developers to work collaboratively is repeated in several agile seminal works (e.g. Cockburn and Highsmith, 2001; Highsmith, 2002; Beck, 2005), but there has been limited research in the area. Bryant et al (2006a) investi-

T. Dingsøyr et al. (eds.), *Agile Software Development*,
DOI 10.1007/978-3-642-12575-1_4, © Springer-Verlag Berlin Heidelberg 2010

gated collaboration in pair programming and concluded that pairing is highly collaborative with both partners contributing new information to almost every subtask. In other work, the same authors (2006b) show how programming pairs will actively work towards enhancing collaboration, e.g. by re-appropriating tools designed for individual use and instead use them to assist collaboration.

Co-ordination of work is necessary whenever group working is involved – managing dependencies between tasks is fundamental to project progress.

Intuitively, collaboration and co-ordination depend on communication, and communication – in one form or another – is central to successful software development (Cockburn, 2002; Coplien and Harrison, 2005). Understanding the nature and role of communication in agile software development however is challenging given agile's discounting of comprehensive documentation and its valorization of interactions. Communication in agile development is both crucial but also tacit, informal and predominantly verbal.

The rest of this chapter is structured as follows. In the next section we summarise the fieldwork that forms the basis of this chapter, including data collection and analysis approaches. Section 4.3 is the core of the chapter, and summarises the key results obtained through our analyses. In section 4.4 we discuss our findings, limitations and future directions, and suggest some implications for theory and practice. The chapter ends with some a brief conclusion.

4.2 Fieldwork

The findings presented in this chapter are distilled from a series of qualitative studies of XP teams conducted during the period 2002 to 2009. All teams comprised practitioners working in a commercial setting (in contrast, to say, students role playing) and had been practicing the 12 original practices of XP (Beck, 2000) for at least a year; an overview of these teams is provided in Table 4.1.

4.2.1 Data collection

Our research took an ethnographically-informed approach in which the nature of practice is not know *a priori*, and the researchers avoid any form of control, intrusion or experimentation (Robinson et al, 2007). In keeping with this approach, the researchers did not intervene in the teams' day-to-day working, but instead joined the team mostly as a passive observer – attending meetings, sitting with developers and other team members, going for lunch, having informal discussions and so on. In some teams, we conducted more formal semi-structured interviews in order to elicit participants' perceptions of agility and the way it was working. A summary of the data collected in each study is included in Table 4.1; note that fieldnotes and photographs were collected in each study. The exact nature of the data collected was influenced by the team's own situation and what seemed to be important to them. For example, we did not collect wiki pages for Team C as we did not see team members using any or referring to them in conversation (although they may have existed); we did collect video recordings of Team G as they had recently been filmed for internal training purposes, had become accustomed to the cameras, and we needed detailed data for the planned analysis.

For each team, the study usually coincided with one development iteration. Where the iteration spanned a longer period, extra days were added to the observation period to cover significant meetings or events. For teams A to E both authors were involved in data collection and analysis; for teams F and G the second author was involved in analysis only.

4.2.2 Analysis

The initial analysis of data from teams A to F followed a rigorous thematic approach in an ethnographic tradition, seeking counter examples to validate and/or refine any suggested finding. From this analysis it became clear that all of the teams put significant effort into maintaining an environment that supports intense collaboration, continual communication and ongoing co-ordination. At the centre of this effort appeared to be the simple artefacts of the story card and the Wall. To pursue this initial conclusion, we conducted further analysis: first using distributed cognition, then applying cognitive dimensions and most recently drawing on communication and learning theory. In this chapter, we distill findings from all of these analyses that relate to collaboration, co-ordination and communication. In the rest of this section we summarise the analysis frameworks used in reaching our results.

Thematic analysis

Analysis in the ethnographic tradition seeks to identify insights into the activity from the observational data collected, and these insights take the form of meaningful themes that occur and re-occur and whose utility and validity can be sustained from the empirical data. The researcher(s) will use all of the data collected to reflect on and reconsider the situation observed. When a theme appears to be emerging – that is, its recurrent nature is evident from the data – the data is rigorously searched for 'disconfirming instances', i.e. data that contradicts and therefore does not sustain the theme. This is done so that the utility and validity of the emergent theme can be confirmed or so that it can be refined and then tested again against disconfirming instances. So, analysis proceeds in an iterative fashion where themes are identified, then validated or refined for further validation.

Table 4.1. Agile teams studied in the course of this work

Team	Team size (Number of developers)	Domain	Type of organisation	Co-located?	Iteration length	Study length	Data collected (apart from field notes and photographs)
A	12(8)	Web-based intelligent adverts	Start-up	Yes, including graphic designer and customer proxies	Three weeks	One week and a day	Wiki pages, story cards, audio
B	23(16)	Multi-author document use	SME	Yes, including testers and customer proxies	One week	One week and a day	Wiki pages, artefacts
C	15(12)	Financial risk assessment	Large international bank	Yes. Customer was on the same floor	One week	One week and a day	
D	10(5)	Database consolidation and migration	Large international bank	Yes, including customers, project manager and analysts. 'Live' database control was abroad	One week	One week and a day	Database schema, architecture diagrams
E	26(23)	Travel information web pages and alerts	SME	Yes, including graphic designer, database administrator and customer proxies	One week, collated into three week cycles	Eight working days	Wiki pages, story cards
F	7 (5)	Network monitoring	Large telecomms company	Largely. Customer in a different city; testers were in India	One week	Two days	Wiki pages, interview audio
G	6(4)	Cloud computing services	Large telecomms company	Yes, including customer.	Iterationless	Three days	Audio and video of standups and pairing sessions

For example, where analysis suggests that stand ups in front of the Wall, are significant and meaningful as the agreed place and time where developers jointly take decisions on which stories to implement next, we rigorously search the data for cases that contradict this theme. That is, we look for cases where decisions on which stories to implement next are taken by the team outside stand ups, and away from the Wall. If no such cases can be found then our data sustains and confirms the validity of the theme.

As an example of the refinement of a theme via disconfirming instances, suppose our analysis suggests a recurring theme that pairing is a particular sort of conversation between two people as they use a machine. We then ask "Do they ever have that sort of conversation when they are *not* using a machine?" If the answer from the data is "no", then we can refine our theme to incorporate the notion that the machine is significant to, and influences, the conversation in some way. In turn, this refinement is sustained by the observation that the machine influences and changes talk. For example, we observe that a "red bar"[1] from the machine changes the talk. Hence, the theme that pairing is dominantly a three-way conversation that must always involve the machine is produced by refinement.

As well as the central position of story cards and the Wall, we have developed, refined and confirmed a range of emergent themes such as the role of culture (e.g. Robinson and Sharp, 2003), team characteristics (e.g. Robinson and Sharp, 2004) and the social nature of technical practices (Robinson and Sharp, 2005).

Distributed cognition
Distributed cognition (Hutchins, 1995) is a theoretical framework for analysing collaborative activity that regards collaborative work as one cognitive system. It is quite a complex framework, and although some application to software development has been reported (e.g. Flor and Hutchins, 1992), its use in this domain has been limited. It is more widely used in CSCW (e.g. Halverson, 2002) and HCI (Hollan et al, 2000; Wright et al, 2000). In our analysis we applied DiCOT (Distributed Cognition for Teamwork (Furniss and Blandford, 2005)), a methodology developed to support the application of distributed cognition. DiCOT highlights 22 principles of the framework and relates them to the diagrams and perspectives associated with Contextual Design (Beyer and Holzblatt, 1998) through groupings called 'themes'. Our analysis focused on teams A to E and particularly concentrated on the following three themes:

1. The *physical theme* focuses on the physical environment such as office layout and adjacencies of co-workers, within which the cognitive system operates.

2. The *artefact theme* focuses on the detail of artefacts that are created and used in carrying out the activity under study.

3. The *information flow theme* identifies what information flows through the cognitive system, the media which facilitate that flow and how the information is transformed.

We did not concentrate on the story cards and the Wall during this analysis, but our results provided confirmation and further insight into their focal role and details of their underlying structure (Sharp et al, 2006; Sharp and Robinson, 2008). Specifically, it became clear that co-ordination and collaboration are supported by these two key artefacts. In addition, when used with discipline the artefacts work in a sophisticated and complementary manner that is significant in underpinning

---

[1] Indicating a failed test.

the highly collaborative and self-organising style of agile teams. Current texts on agile methods, such as Beck (2005) and Cockburn (2002) discuss the importance of information radiators and informative workspaces in terms of 'visitors' or 'passersby' being able to see clearly the state of progress within a team, but our analysis showed that these properties are crucial to the work of the team themselves.

From the distributed cognition analysis, the following observations emerged:

1. There are few mediating artefacts in the cognitive system and hence there is little transformation between different media. The story cards and the Wall were identified as key artefacts.
2. The information captured by these artefacts is largely restricted to process issues, for example plans, goals and progress.
3. Information flows are simple and open, thus promoting situational awareness amongst the team (e.g. see Figure 4.1). Information was available to all team members from a number of sources including other members of the team, the customer, text books, intranet wikis and internet developer sites.
4. An agile team works in an information-rich environment. This is particularly evident through our modelling when considering the information flows around pair programmers. Information is both easily accessible and immediately relevant and applicable.

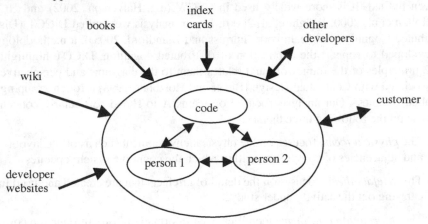

Fig. 4.1. Information flows around a pair in team E

Cognitive dimensions

Through the distributed cognition analysis it became clear that the purpose of the story cards and the Wall can be viewed from two contrasting perspectives: one which is largely notational, and one which is largely focused on communication and social practices. The cognitive dimensions framework (Green, 1989; 1991) was devised to analyse information artefacts, representations, and notational systems, and hence allowed us to investigate the notational perspective in more detail. As the original framework was devised for general use, in order to apply it to specific representations it is necessary to modify the dimension definitions. This has been done in the past to apply the framework to visual programming languages (Green and Petre, 1996), GUIs (Blackwell and Green 2003), and tangible user interfaces (Edge and Blackwell, 2006). Table 4.2 lists the cognitive dimension definitions applied to the agile team data.

To apply this analysis framework, we revisited and reviewed the data and findings from teams A to F and considered each dimension in turn (Sharp et al, 2009). This analysis revealed that the cognitive dimensions emphasised by the story cards and the Wall in terms of notation are: abstraction, closeness of mapping, terseness, provisionality, ease of change, and process visibility. It also revealed dimensions that are de-emphasised by the notation: functional dependencies, role expressiveness, progressive evaluation, and error-proneness. These latter properties are important for successful software development (particularly functional dependencies) and hence must be provided through other means, i.e. not from the notation.

Our thematic analysis suggests that these information requirements are fulfilled through disciplined social practices and teamwork, i.e. they are developed and shared through communication. For example, the considerable flexibility in abstraction (i.e. the use of story cards) is shaped and disciplined by the social practice that agrees and maintains those abstractions (i.e. the stories). Social practice also maintains the consistency of the cards. In order to investigate this aspect further, we have turned to communication and learning theory, as described below.

Communication and learning
The significance of communication within an agile team was highlighted through our thematic analysis and confirmed through distributed cognition and cognitive dimensions. However these analyses do not allow us to investigate in detail what is being achieved through communication within the team, nor what influences this communication. To do so we need more detailed data than we have collected for teams A to F, and alternative theoretical analyses. Our work in this area is so far limited to one team (team G) and is preliminary, but we include it here for completeness.

Table 4.2. Summary of the cognitive dimensions framework used in our analysis

Cognitive dimension	Definition
abstraction	Can elements be encapsulated? If so, to what extent?
closeness of mapping	How directly can the entities in the domain be expressed in the notation? Docs the notation include entities that match the key concepts or components of the domain?
consistency	When some of the language has been learned, how much of the rest can be inferred? Are similar features of structure and syntax used in the same way throughout?
diffuseness	How many symbols or graphic entities are required to express a meaning?
error-proneness	Does the design of the notation induce 'careless mistakes'?
hard mental operations	Does the notation use mechanisms such as nesting and indirection that require mental unpacking or 'decoding'? For example, are there places where the user needs to resort to fingers or additional annotation to keep track of what's happening?
hidden dependencies	Is every dependency overtly indicated in both directions? Is the indication perceptual or only symbolic?
premature commitment	Do developers have to make decisions before they have the information they need?
progressive evaluation	Can a partially-complete representation be executed or evaluated to obtain feedback on 'how am I doing?'
provisionality	Can indecision or options be expressed?
role-expressiveness	Can the reader see how each component relates to the whole, and what the relationships between notational elements are?
secondary notation	Can developers use layout, colour and other cues to convey extra meaning, above and beyond the 'official' semantics of the language?
viscosity	How much effort is required to perform a single change? How much effort is required to perform multiple changes of the same type? Does making one change then have the 'knock on' effect of requiring other changes?
visibility	Is every part of the notation simultaneously visible – or is it at least possible to juxtapose any two parts side-by-side at will? If the notation is dispersed, is it at least possible to know in what order to read it?

The analysis conducted for this stage of the research uses pragmatics and discourse analysis (Levinson, 1983) and is based on two theories of cognition: learning and communication theory (Bateson, 1972); and situated cognition (Clancey, 1977). Bateson's theory tells us that an individual's stimulus and response is tied to learning in context. Clancey's theory tells us that an individual's activity is a dynamic construction between perception and memory in which the process of memory is interdependent on context. The combination of these two theories helps us to explain how the context and environmental setting affect a team's communication and hence how story cards and the Wall influence communication. The analysis approach adopted is described in Binti et al (2010b).

Results so far indicate that the repeated articulation and re-articulation that an agile way of working encourages results in the team having a common conceptualisation of system requirements and joint activity, and that the story cards and the Wall play a mediation role to helped members form and sustain that common conceptualization.

4.3 Results

From the fieldwork described above, several significant aspects of agile teams have emerged: the central role played by story cards and the Wall; the rhythms of agile development; collaboration mechanisms; co-ordination activities; and communication patterns. The last three of these are headlined in this chapter, but they are dependent on the first two aspects, and are heavily intertwined, as we shall illustrate in this section where we summarise our main findings.

4.3.1 Story cards and the Wall: simple yet sophisticated

From our very first study (Sharp and Robinson, 2004), the importance of story cards and the Wall were evident and striking. The story card is a 3x5 inch index card on which a short abstraction of partial system requirements is captured. Our first study revealed that story cards were used in a number of roles including:

- Customer stories were written on cards.

- Estimates were written on story cards.

- Tests were written on the back of story cards.

- Rough designs and notes were drawn on the cards and used to communicate or explain ideas.

- Coloured stickers were placed on cards to denote progress, and so they were used as progress trackers.

- When pairs choose the story to work on in the morning, they take the card from the Wall. This means that no-one else can be working on the same story at the same time, so they are a means of controlling work.

- During the Planning Game the cards were moved about and clustered to show related work.

Story cards are ubiquitous in agile teams and are a central focus of activity. Different coloured cards are used to capture different kinds of story. In team E, story cards were green, task cards (stories were at times decomposed into several tasks) were white and bug cards were pink; indeed this team kept a whole Wall for bug cards (see Figure 4.2). In team D, business analysts designing the database were an integral part of the development team and so on this Wall (see Figure 4.3), green cards were used to capture the next analysis tasks, pink cards were used to label categories of story cards, and story cards were white. A story card that is being implemented is often highly annotated with different (coloured) symbols, stickers and images. Each of these annotations represents some kind of progress. For example, in team A a red star indicated an unfinished card, yellow a card that has been finished by developers and is ready for acceptance test, and green indicated that the change has been accepted by the customer. In addition, a blue star indicated that the card was a task card. In team G, photographs of the developers currently working on the story were stuck to the card. Whatever the conventions chosen by the team, in terms of how the stories were written, how current 'ownership' was recognized, or what annotations were allowed, the team applied these conventions through agreement within the team, and strict discipline. An example story card and its underlying conventional structure are shown in Figure 4.4.

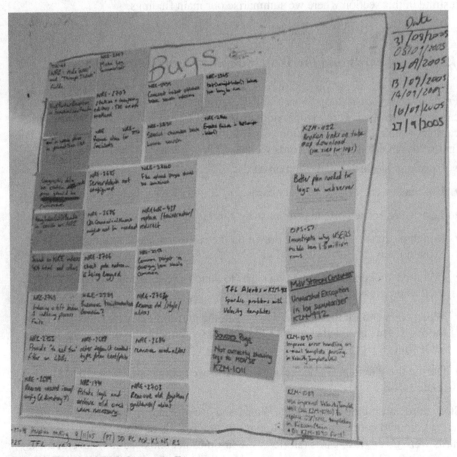

Fig. 4.2. The 'bug' Wall from team E

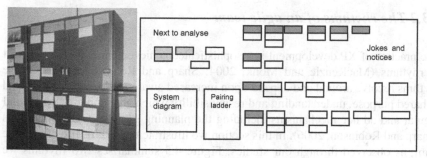

Fig. 4.3. A set of filing cabinets used as a Wall, and the underlying structure of the Wall from Team D

Fig. 4.4. An example story card and its underlying structure from team E

The Wall is usually[2] a visible, vertical space on which the story cards being worked on in the current iteration were placed (in practice, this might be a wall, a window, a flip chart, filing cabinets or other convenient vertical location). Similarly to the cards, the Wall followed strict conventions for its content and structure. At the start of an iteration, the story cards to be implemented are placed in a particular location on the Wall, and as they are developed, refined, tested and accepted they are annotated and moved around the Wall to reflect progress. Hence the location of the card on the Wall conveys information regarding the card's progress, as well as the kind and level of annotation. The Wall is the focus of daily activity including the stand-up meetings and discussions between team members and customers. Figure 4.3 shows the Wall from team D and its underlying structure.

At one level, story cards and the Wall are very simple artefacts, but the situation is much more complex. Used in a disciplined and consistent fashion they support sophisticated teamwork. Their power lies in their simplicity, easy accessibility and the way in which they support each other.

---

[2] In team C it was a folding portfolio.

4.3.2 The rhythms of an agile team

The practice of XP development is a sophisticated achievement with a distinct set of rhythms (MacKenzie and Monk, 2004; Sharp and Robinson, 2004). These rhythms revolve around and depend upon increased awareness (Chong, 2005), and a shared purpose, understanding and responsibility which are supported by several regular and ad hoc mechanisms including the planning game and daily stand-ups (Sharp and Robinson, 2006). In this section we illustrate the routine life of an agile team, as observed through our studies. Figure 4.5 summarises two rhythms we have observed (daily and iteration), plus a further rhythm that has been reported to us through *ad hoc* conversations (the release rhythm). For all teams, our data shows the daily rhythm as described below, for teams A to E our data illustrates the iteration rhythm, and for team F the rhythm was reported to us in conversation. Team G was iteration-less in that there was no fixed time between planning games; during our observations the team had identified a set of stories to be implemented that were estimated to fill three days of elapsed time, and the iteration rhythm was reported to us. We have not observed the release rhythm in our studies, but team members from teams A, B, and E have described this pattern to us – for teams A and E the length of the releases rhythm was dictated by their clients' requirements, in team B releases were dictated by perceptions of market need and were described in terms of a rhythm rather than a deadline. We do not provide an account of this rhythm but include it for completeness.

Daily rhythm
> Start of day > stand-up > pairing conversations > end of day

Rhythm of the iteration
> Pre-planning > planning game > daily rhythm > retrospective

Release rhythm
> Release planning game > iteration rhythm > release retrospective

Fig. 4.5. The rhythms of agile development

Daily rhythm
Each team we have studied works to a recognizable and pervasive daily rhythm. While the details of this rhythm vary between teams, there were key similarities that are summarized in Figure 4.5, and we describe here. These rhythms were marked by events that signalled the opening and closing of activities, i.e. were temporal markers, and were punctuated by other events which signalled progress, i.e. signalled significant achievements in work.

For example, the daily rhythm begins slowly as people arrive, but the 'real' day does not begin until the stand-up meeting. The following is an extract from our fieldnotes:

When developers arrived in the morning (any time up to about 9.30), they engaged in various activities such as eating breakfast, checking email, and reading the newspaper. When most people
were present, there was a stand-up meeting to start the day. It felt as though this meeting her-
alded the real start of the day. After the stand-up everyone went off to start the agreed tasks.

During the stand-up meeting, issues from yesterday's work are reported and discussed, tasks for the day are identified and pairs are chosen. Following the stand-
up, the main business of developing code from stories is accomplished through
pair programming, which continues until the end of the day. This concentrated en-
deavour is punctuated by regular breaks, lunch and the bustle of intense activity.
Although mostly what you observe in an agile team appears to be mundane there
is considerable activity happening, if you only know what to look for. Not only are
paired developers sitting side-by-side, they are surrounded by other pairs all of
whom are talking about their own story; this environment encourages peripheral
awareness, and it is common for one pair to break off their own discussion and
join another's when issues of mutual interest are being addressed. In addition,
pairs are often accessing information from developer wikis, through instant mes-
saging to other developers and commercial developer websites. All teams we have
studied also have some way of signalling who is working on specific stories, and
who is integrating new code into the current build, thus quietly communicating a
sense of progress and achievement. The closing of the day is marked by people
gradually leaving over a period of 30 minutes or so, rather than an explicit event.

In our agile teams, daily working life has plenty of 'busy-ness' but that 'busy-
ness' is distinctly not hectic or frenetic haste. For example, the end of the day simply comes (as night follows day, so to speak) without any sense of frustration,
such as might be associated with missed targets in a rigid schedule. Within this
busy-but-relaxed atmosphere, tasks are completed in a rhythmic pattern which has
been referred to as the 'heartbeat' of an agile team. It was striking that no-one told
the teams to behave this way; the rhythm was understood and followed by developers as a matter of course.

Rhythm of the iteration
As each day of an iteration passes, the story cards progress through their life history of different coloured stickers, annotations and re-location around the Wall,
with the ultimate aim of having all the iteration story cards moved from the 'to be
done' area to the 'done' area (which in teams A, C and D was off the Wall altogether). The daily rhythm thus forms the core of the iteration rhythm but the iteration rhythm starts earlier than this, with planning activities: a pre-planning meeting in which the previous iteration is reviewed and future direction is set, and the
planning game in which story cards for the upcoming iteration are chosen. The organisational structure within which teams D and E were located meant that a pre-
planning meeting was required. In the case of team D a project manager liaised
between the team and the rest of the organization, and he prioritized activity in
consultation with the technical team and the customer. These priorities were
communicated and discussed during a pre-planning meeting. In the case of team E

the pre-planning meeting was held to co-ordinate development activity with the requirements of the company's range of clients. In both cases this meeting was chaired by a project manager and attended by lead technical developers; it usually took place one working day before the planning game.

The Planning Game embodies a number of interwoven activities: designing, estimating and planning. Here is an edited extract from the field notes on one Planning Game.

The business of the Planning Game was to examine stories, to estimate how long it will take to implement each story, and to decide which story cards can be satisfied in the next iteration. This was achieved by talking with each other and with <customer representatives> when necessary. Some of the stories for this iteration were developer-generated; i.e., they were concerned with infrastructure issues or changes of architecture. <Customer representatives> were asked to make trade-offs between customer story cards, but if the developers said that a technical card had to take priority then the <customer representatives> did not argue. <Customer representatives> were not asked for their opinion about prioritising these technical cards. Everyone calmly attempted to find ways around any conflicts.

Towards the end of the Planning Game, there was a clear sense of 'wanting to get on with the real work'. This was not frustration. It was a reflection of the fact that everyone understood what was agreed and needed – and was ready to get on with it.

During this process the story cards are usually spread out on a flat surface where they are shuffled and grouped. Figure 4.6 illustrates the state of play part way through a planning game.

Fig. 4.6. A planning game table from team A

One of the agile mantras to be found in the literature is 'inspect and adapt', specifically in a Scrum context. One mechanism for ensuring that this happens is the retrospective (Derby et al, 2006). All of the teams we studied performed retrospectives, and most of them ran one at the end of each iteration. During a retrospective, three key questions are asked: What worked well? What can be improved? What are the barriers to improvement? Although this can be a source of conflict, it is a useful springboard for the next iteration, with new changes in place if appropriate. It is common for the results of the retrospective to be on show throughout the following iteration. The whiteboard from team G is shown in Figure 4.7. On the top left is a smiley face (indicating that these areas are working well) against issues including 'co-located team', 'pairing better' and 'M is a better customer'. Top right is a sad face against 'delivery of stories', 'acceptance confusion' and 'acceptance criteria could be better'. Bottom right against a question mark are some technical queries and 'story decomposition, smaller stories'. The bottom left quadrant shows an electric light bulb and the comment 'iteration-less'.

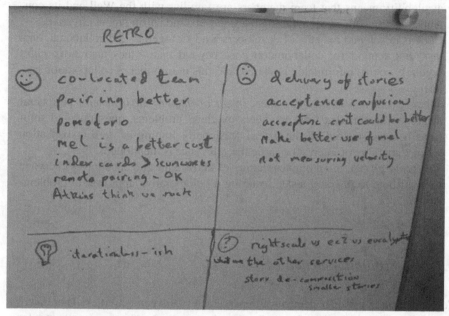

Fig. 4.7. Record of an iteration retrospective from team G

4.3.3 Collaboration mechanisms

Collaboration happens where two or more team members work together on a task, each of whom contributes information to that task. Members of an agile team collaborate on a wide range of activities: estimating stories, implementing stories, developing and running tests, planning an iteration, talking to customers, solving problems, and so on. In fact, many agile practices promote a collaborative environment.

Our studies highlight a range of collaboration mechanisms in use:

- *Story cards* promote collaboration between developers and customers. As the card can hold only a limited amount of information, they need to talk to each other in order to clarify what needs to be done.
- The level of discussion promoted by the *card as a token* generates much activity and information exchange that is accessible, and hence supports the sharing

of knowledge. This in turn helps team members to collaborate effectively on tasks.

- The *Wall* is available to view all the time, and is *regularly being updated*. This means that the information it displays is immediately relevant, and this ready availability means that team members are familiar with the Wall and its contents, making collaboration during the stand-up, and pairing more effective.
- Code is developed by pairs of developers who sit together and collaborate on a task, but support for collaboration goes beyond that – they also *swap pairs* regularly so that information is shared, and this in turn makes collaboration easier.
- Where *pairs are located together, in an open plan environment*, peripheral awareness means that team members overhear problems, questions and solutions being discussed all the time, occasionally 'tuning in' to a conversation when something of interest or particular relevance is mentioned.
- The *stand-up meeting* promotes sharing of knowledge and encourages everyone to contribute to ongoing tasks, fostering a collaborative approach to problem-solving.

4.3.4 Co-ordination activities

Co-ordination is the management of dependencies between activities. There were broadly two different types of co-ordination that we observed in our teams: regular and *ad hoc*. The key regular co-ordinating activities were the annotation and manipulation of story cards, the maintenance of card status on the Wall, the planning game, the daily stand-ups, and the pre-planning meeting (for teams D and E). Supporting these was the wide spectrum of *ad hoc* meetings, peripheral awareness, and fluid pairing situations. These supporting activities were essential; for example stand-up meetings would be less effective if these other activities did not ensure a continual updating of shared knowledge.

Teams A, F and G relied entirely on these regular and *ad hoc* activities, but others employed some higher level activities that helped the teams interface with the rest of the business. Teams C and D also relied on an overall project plan from which story cards were generated. In team E an overall project plan for the whole company (spanning 3 teams) was maintained by a project manager who sat outside the development teams. Team B did not have physical story cards, but kept their stories within the supporting software environment. This meant that the detailed manipulation of stories was not clearly visible, although they employed summary flip charts which showed which stories were being worked on and who was in which team.

All the teams were fundamentally self-organising and hence there was little or no co-ordination imposed from higher management. Teams C and D included a project manager role who was accountable to the management outside the team, but this did not seem to substantially alter the self-organising approach.

In summary, the regular activities provided:

- The *daily stand-ups* are a key co-ordination point in the day. These take place around the Wall which is the focus of discussion regarding what's been done and what needs to be done. The ease with which the information on the Wall can be digested and immediately applied facilitates the stand-up.
- The *planning game* sets the scene for the iteration and involves a negotiation with customers (or customer proxies) both to identify which customer-generated cards to address but also which technical cards need attention.
- *Taking a card down* from the Wall when it is being worked on means that no-one else can be working on it at the same time. In Teams E and G we saw cards stuck to the monitor of the pair who were working on it, and a 'ghost' of the card was drawn onto the (glass) Wall. Sticking the card on a monitor like this shows clearly who is responsible for the story at that time, increases awareness of activity, and prevents others from working on the same card by mistake.
- The *structure of the Wall* provides an easily digested overview of the iteration's current status. This is usually indicated by the physical location of the story cards, and is also shown by annotations and different coloured cards and stickers. Usually, the structure of cards, e.g. story versus task cards, is maintained on the Wall.
- The use of *different coloured cards* and the *disciplined annotation* of cards provides detailed progress-tracking information. This in turn indicates what needs to be done next and how much is left before that story is complete.

4.3.5 Communication patterns

Our findings relating to communication come from two types of analysis. First, the thematic analysis provides an overview of the agile teams' communication; second, the application of the cognition theories described above hints at a more detailed explanation of how story cards and the Wall support everyday communication (the results in the last subsection require further investigation).

Communication themes

All teams relied heavily on verbal communication. They were very sensitive to the need to talk with each other within the team and with customers or with others who had the right expertise. One of the consequences of agile practices such as stand-ups and pairing with regular swapping, and the open flow of information identified through our distributed cognition analysis is that much of the knowledge and expertise required to solve any problems is available quickly and easily in a form that can be immediately applied to the existing situation. 'Collective ownership' is one of the XP practices, and our data includes several examples confirming that our teams practiced this principle. For example, at team C there was considerable preoccupation with technical debt, indicating that all team members cared about the health of all of the code. In team A the maintenance arrangements included an 'exposed pair' who took turns to handle queries on all of their code. Collective ownership also had its exceptions in some contexts though. For example, at B there was no collective ownership on certain portions of the code base: the 'systems' concerns and the 'database' implementation, but largely collective ownership was sustained. Because of the existence of collective ownership, all team members have a good understanding of the context of any problem that arises. This means that the time needed to explain the problem is minimised, and the applicability of potential solutions can be assessed rapidly.

Individuals vary in how they communicate ideas and thoughts. For example we came across three different types of individual: those who liked to write down notes, draw diagrams and generally doodle while exploring an issue; those who wrote only short notes on index cards; and those who were not observed writing any notes at all. Any pairing session involving the first kind of individual produced and relied on a large collection of notes and diagrams. When the latter two types were pairing they spoke infrequently.

Although the purpose of pairing is to produce code, the process of pairing is fundamentally about communication – both verbal and non-verbal. This interaction is much like a three-way conversation with developers occasionally talking directly with each other, sometimes interacting through the code and sometimes interacting directly with the code while the other developer watches. This intense three-way relationship introduces different ways of communicating; both developers typically engage in talking, typing, and gesturing - using the cursor and highlighting techniques to focus attention. In addition, the ability for pairs to overhear and be overheard appears to support the distributed nature of problem-solving where relevant expertise is offered when it is needed.

Communicative pathways in our agile teams were simple, with the story card as a key focus. For example, cards act as tokens giving the holder speaker's rights, making it clear to others that they have something to say. This theme is picked up in the cognition analysis below.

A cognition perspective on communication
Using the combination of cognitive theories introduced above, focusing on how individuals react to the external world, we have analysed team G's detailed communication. Through this analysis we have identified patterns that begin to reveal how agile practices support the articulation and re-articulation of software requirements which leads to the development and refinement of understanding within the team. The external event system for an agile team is made up of the story cards, the Wall and other team members. The story cards and the Wall provide team members with a stimulus for remembering (Ericsson et al, 1980) and a tool for inquiry (Clancey 2005). The articulation, and re-articulation to each other

of the functional requirements that the story cards represent creates a dynamic and interactive construct of speaking and doing. According to situated cognition, speaking, or articulation, is viewed as creating knowledge, and the process of speaking is a complex coordination process, both as neurobiological circuits and as a conscious behaviour.

This process of dynamic articulation and re-articulation among members, coupled with gesturing and supported by the story cards allows team members to co-ordinate and rebuild common descriptions which are perceived, interpreted, and reformulated through new conceptions (Clancey 2005). When descriptions convey deeper meaning, it has been reported in Baddeley et al, (2009; 79) that they affect memory, and how well individuals can recall their memory. This appears to be the case for team G: team members are able to recall the requirements of a system, despite the fact that only abstractions are captured on the cards. Further detail on the findings from this analysis are in Binti et al (2010a).

4.4 Discussion

Collaboration, communication and co-ordination arose as significant themes in our ethnographically-informed studies of teams A to F listed in Table 4.1. Although these aspects of agile development are discussed in the literature, we did not set out to investigate them – our initial analysis identified them. We subsequently chose analytical frameworks to view the findings from different perspectives. Distributed cognition, cognitive dimensions and communication theory are based on different epistemological and methodological assumptions, yet each has provided insight into the collaboration, co-ordination and communication practices of agile teams. Each analysis has also explicated the role that story cards and the Wall play in these practices.

The teams we have studied vary according to several dimensions including application domain, size and organisational context, yet our data provides evidence of themes, collaboration mechanisms, co-ordination activities and communication patterns that are common to these teams, albeit adapted to specific contexts. Our findings are therefore supported through triangulation of data and of method.

In this section, we consider the implications these results have for theory and practice, what limitations exist and directions for further research.

4.4.1 Implications for theory

The work reported here informs theory in two respects. Firstly it illustrates the application of theoretical frameworks to a new domain: the use of DiCOT to analyse our data provides evidence of its applicability within software development; the cognitive dimensions framework was refined for this analysis; and the combination of communication theories has led to a new method for analyzing the relationship between artefacts and communication (Binti et al, 2010b). Application of existing analysis frameworks to new domains can help to extend their explanatory power, and feed back into theoretical developments.

Secondly, our findings will be useful to anyone wishing to construct a theoretical account of agile practice. As yet, a good theoretical model for successful agile development has not been reported, but any such model will need to incorporate the role and influence of the three 'c's described here. Building on these and other studies of practice is a first step towards creating such a model.

4.4.2 Implications for practice

The immediate implication for agile teams and their management is that the mechanisms identified here should not be hindered. Longer term implications also exist for the design of software development environments and electronic management tools.

A key message is to understand the role of story cards and the Wall: in collaboration, in co-ordination and in communication. Story cards and the Wall are central to all three, and all three are intertwined and mutually supportive. Disciplined use and teamwork are important. 'Simplicity' is supported explicitly by agile development, so it is not surprising that the notion of simplicity underlies the activities described above. For example, the artefacts are easy to see and understand, the artefacts hold minimal information, and they are flexible, i.e. the structures can be easily and visibly changed if appropriate, cards can be moved around, are easy to carry and easily accessible, if necessary they can be ripped up and thrown away. Importantly, this simplicity works because the teams follow an agreed and disciplined approach to use.

In all but one of our teams, the story cards and Wall were physical artefacts, since the teams were co-located (in team B where an electronic system was used, they reverted to physical cards following a communication breakdown that caused significant wasted work). Our findings show that a visible, easily accessible Wall affects all three 'c's of agile practice described here. The physical nature of these artefacts is important, and has been recognised in other domains outside software development. For example, Nomura et al (2006) found that the paper-use practices of pilots serve a set of important cognitive functions, and that these practices have a range of implications for the design of computer-based media to support pilots as they work in collaboration. In team F, where the customer was located several miles away from the development team, a wiki had been implemented to support team interaction. A set of pages in the wiki recorded the stories to be developed during the current iteration, and their status was denoted by different colours. The wiki was in addition to the physical cards and Wall and did not replace them. In-

terestingly, a photograph of the physical Wall was taken at the end of each iteration and uploaded into the wiki!

The affordances of physical artefacts and the reliance on them that we have
seen in co-located agile teams are significant factors for all teams, but especially
for distributed teams where sharing physical artefacts is not so straightforward.
Before committing cards and the Wall to the electronic medium to enable distributed working, it is important to consider what is gained and what is lost in this
translation.

Story cards and the Wall don't operate in isolation, as we have shown, and
other agile practices such as stand-ups, pairing, open plan environment, suitable
furniture and room for the Wall all need to be attended to. The notational effectiveness of these artefacts is limited, and effective use relies on the establishment
and maintenance of a suitable social environment where information can be freely
exchanged and understood. To achieve their goals, agile teams tend to work in information-rich environments with easily accessible, easily applicable knowledge.
Individual team members put effort into making sure the cognitive system performs as it should. The regular co-ordination mechanisms used, for example,
would not be as effective if the more *ad hoc* system were to be removed or pre-
vented from working effectively.

4.4.3 Limitations

The results presented here are based on detailed and rigorous investigations of the
seven teams summarised in Table 4.1, and hence cover a variety of domains and
organizational settings. In addition, our key findings have been met with general
recognition and agreement when presented to other practitioners at conferences,
workshops and in conversation, and are supported by the practices of other agile
teams we have studied.

However our investigations represent only a snapshot of each situation, and all
of our teams were largely co-located. Our data is therefore not necessarily representative of the wider community of agile developers, and in particular does not
include distributed teams.

4.4.4 Further research directions

We see three main areas for further work that arise from our investigations here:
the consequences of having physical or virtual versions of the story cards and the
Wall; a more detailed investigation of communication; and the role of a fourth 'c':
co-operation.

Although we are convinced that in our teams, the physical nature of the arte-facts supporting the three 'c's is significant, we don't yet understand in detail what are the benefits of physicality and hence what support would be lost if these arte-facts were instead virtual. This is particularly pertinent for distributed teams where sharing physical artefacts between team members is not possible. Using different interaction styles such as table-tops and large displays may be beneficial (and some work in this area has been reported, e.g. Liu et al (2005)), but this is still a profitable area of research.

A detailed understanding of the communication within and around an agile team will help to ensure that practice is adequately supported through organisa-tional, technical and social means. Investigations here are at an early stage and there is much left to be done.

Our findings have illustrated the pervasive nature of collaboration, co-ordination and communication. There is a fourth 'c' that is often discussed along-side collaboration and co-ordination and that is co-operation. Co-operation hap-pens when two or more people are working independently on parallel but depend-ent tasks and come together for co-ordination. Whilst recognizing that some aspects of agile working are co-operative, this has not featured significantly in our fieldwork results – teams seem to aim for tightly-coupled collaboration rather than looser co-operative work. However where tightly-knit agile teams need to interact with roles outside the team (e.g. user experience designers, database administra-tors, system testers), co-operation becomes more significant and may cause con-flict and friction. In practice, it is infeasible for all individuals with relevant exper-tise to be part of the team, and it is inevitable that agile teams will have to find ways to manage this interaction. Work in this area is at an early stage (e.g. Ferreira et al, 2010) and further investigation is required.

4.5 Conclusion

Agile teams rely on story cards and the Wall, and their ability to collaborate, co-ordinate and communicate effectively is dependent on them. A combination of ag-ile practices such as stand-ups, pairing and collective ownership underpin these activities and are equally important in supporting teamwork. Changing or remov-ing any of these practices or artefacts needs to be done in the full knowledge of the consequences of such changes.

Acknowledgements

We are grateful to all our collaborators and study participants for their time and patience, and for sharing their practice with us. Others who have influenced this work are Jennifer Ferreira, Dominic Furniss, Johanna Kollman, Marian Petre and Judith Segal. The communication analysis was performed largely by Nik Nailah Binti Abdullah and was supported by NII, Japan. The Agile Alliance provided financial support for some of the work presented here.

References

Baddeley, A., Eysenck, M., Anderson, M.C. (2009) *Memory*, Psychology Press.
Bateson, G. (1972) *Steps towards Ecology of Mind. Collected Essays in Anthropology, Psychiatry, Evolution, and Epistemology.* University Of Chicago Press.
Beck, K. (2000) *eXtreme Programming Explained: embrace change*, Addison-Wesley, San Francisco.
Beck, K. (2005) *Extreme Programming Explained: Embrace Change* (2nd edition), Addison-Wesley, San Francisco.
Beyer, H. and Holtzblatt, K. (1998) *Contextual Design: Defining Customer-Centered Systems*, Morgan Kauffman, San Francisco
Binti Abdullah, N.N., Sharp, H. and Honiden, S. (2010a) 'Communications in context: a stimulus-response account of Agile team interactions' to appear in *Proceedings of XP2010.*
Binti Abdullah, N.N., Sharp, H. and Honiden, S. (2010b) 'A Method of Analysis to Uncover Physical Artifact-Communication Relationship'. to appear in *Proceedings of the 23rd FLAIRS conference.* Special track: Cognition and AI: Capturing Cognitive Plausibility and Informing Psychological Processes. AAI Press
Blackwell, A.F., Green, T.R.G. (2003) 'Notational systems – the cognitive dimensions of notations framework', in J.M. Carroll (ed), *HCI Models, Theories and Frameworks: Toward a Multidisciplinary Science*, Morgan Kaufmann, San Francisco, CA, pp 103-134.
Bryant, S., Romero, P., and du Boulay, B. (2006a) 'The Collaborative Nature fo Pair Programming' in *Proceedings of XP2006*, LNCS 4044, pp 53–64.
Bryant, S., Romero, P., and du Boulay, B. (2006b) 'Pair programming and the re-appropriation of individual tools for collaborative software development' in *Proceedings of COOP 2006*
Chong, J. (2005) Social Behaviors on XP and non-XP teams: a comparative study, in *Proceedings of Agile 2005*, 39-48.
Clancey. W.J. (1997) *Situated Cognition on human knowledge and computer representation*, Cambridge University Press.
Clancey, W.J. (2005) 'A transactional perspective on the practice-based science of teaching and learning' in T. Koschmann (Ed.), *Theorizing learning practice*. Mahwah, NJ: Erlbaum.
Cockburn, A. (2002) *Agile Software Development*, Addison-Wesley, Boston.
Cockburn, A. and Highsmith, J. (2001) 'Agile software development: the people factor', *IEEE Computer*, **34**(11), 131-133.
Coplien, J.O. and Harrison, N.B. (2005) *Organisational Patterns of Agile Software Development*, Pearson Prentice Hall, New Jersey.
Derby, E., Larson, D. and Schwaber, K. (2006) *Agile Retrospectives: Making Good Teams Great*, Pragmatic Bookshelf.

Edge, D. and Blackwell, A. (2006) 'Correlates of the cognitive dimensions for tangible user interface', *Journal of Visual Languages and Computing*, **17**, 366-394

Ericsson, K.A., Chase, W.G., Faloon, S. (1980) 'Acquisition of a Memory Skill', *Science*, New Series, **208**(4448), June 6, 1181-1182.

Ferreira, J., Sharp, H. and Robinson, H.M. (2010) 'Values and assumptions Shaping Agile Development and User Experience Design in Practice' to appear in *Proceedings of XP2010*.

Flor, N.V. and Hutchins, E.L. (1992) 'Analyzing distributed cognition in software teams: a case study of team programming during perfective maintenance', *Proceedings of Empirical Studies of Programmers*.

Furniss, D. and Blandford, A. (2005) Understanding Emergency Medical Dispatch in terms of Distributed Cognition: a case study, *Ergonomics Journal* Special Issue on Command and Control.

Green, T.R.G. (1989) 'Cognitive dimensions of notations', in *People and Computers V*, A. Sutcliffe and L. Macaulay (eds), Cambridge University Press, pp 443-460.

Green, T.R.G. (1991) 'Describing information artifacts with cognitive dimensions and structure maps', in *Proceedings of HCI'91: Usability Now*, D. Diaper and N.V. Hammond (eds), Cambridge University Press, Cambridge, pp297-315.

Green, T.R.G. and Petre, M. (1996) 'Usability analysis of visual programming environments: a 'cognitive dimensions' framework', *Journal of Visual Languages and Computing*, **7**, 131-174.

Halverson, C. A., (2002) 'Activity theory and distributed cognition: Or what does CSCW need to DO with theories?' *Computer Supported Cooperative Work*, 11:243-267.

Highsmith, J. (2002) *Agile Software Development Ecosystems*, Addison Wesley, Boston.

Hollan, J. Hutchins, E., Kirsch, D. (2000) 'Distributed Cognition: Toward a new foundation for human-computer interaction research', *ACM Transactions on Computer-Human Interaction*, **7**(2), 174-196.

Hutchins, E. (1995) *Cognition in the Wild*, Cambridge MA: MIT Press.

Levinson, S. C. (1983) *Pragmatics, Cambridge Textbook in Linguistics*, Cambridge University Press.

Liu, L. Erdogmus, H. and Maurer, F. (2005) An Environment for Collaborative Iteration Planning in *Proceedings of Agile 2005*, IEEE Computer Society Press.

MacKenzie, A. and Monk, S. (2004) From Cards to Code: How Extreme Programming Re-Embodies Programming as a Collective Practice, *Computer-Supported Co-operative Work*, **13**, 91-117.

Nomura, S., Hutchins, E. and Holder, B.E. (2006) The Uses of Paper in Commercial Airline Flight Operations, in *Proceedings of CSCW 06*, pp249-258

Robinson, H.M., J. Segal, and H. Sharp (2007) Ethnographically-informed Empirical Studies of Software Practice. *Information and Software Technology*, 2007. **49**(6): pp. 540-551.

Robinson, H. and Sharp, H. (2003) 'XP culture: why the twelve practices both are and are not the most significant thing' in *Proceedings of Agile Development Conference*, IEEE Computer Society Press, pp12-21.

Robinson, H., and Sharp, H. (2004) 'The characteristics of XP teams' in *Proceedings of XP2004*, LNCS 3092, Springer, pp139-147.

Robinson, H. and Sharp, H. (2005) 'The social side of technical practices', in *Proceedings of XP2005*, LNCS 3556, Springer, pp 100-108.

Sharp, H. and Robinson, H.M. (2004) 'An ethnographic study of XP practices', *Empirical Software Engineering*, **9**(4) 353-375.

Sharp, H. and Robinson, H.M. (2006) A distributed cognition account of mature XP teams, in *Proceedings of XP2006*, LNCS 4044, pp 1-10.

Sharp, H. and Robinson, H.M. (2008) 'Collaboration and Co-ordination in mature eXtreme Programming teams' *International Journal of Human-Computer Studies*, **66,** 506-518

Sharp, H., Robinson, H.M. and Petre, M. (2009) 'The Role of Physical Artefacts in Agile Software Development: two complementary perspectives', *Interacting with Computers* **21**(1-2) 108-116.

Sharp, H., Robinson, H.M., Segal, J. and Furniss, D. (2006) 'The Role of Story Cards and the Wall in XP teams: a distributed cognition perspective', *Proceedings of Agile 2006*, IEEE Computer Society Press, pp65-75

Wright, P.C., Fields, R.E. and Harrison, M.D. (2000) 'Analyzing Human-Computer Interaction as Distributed Cognition: the resources model', *Human-Computer Interaction*, **15**, 1-41

Author Biographies

Helen Sharp is Professor of Software Engineering at The Open University, UK. Her main research interest focuses on understanding the social nature of software development, and she has been conducting qualitative studies of software development teams since the early 1990s. More recently, her focus has been on agile software development. She is a regular presenter at industrial and academic conferences on software engineering and agile software development and is a joint author of a leading textbook on Interaction Design.

Hugh Robinson is Professor of Computing at The Open University, UK. His research centres on the social and practice-oriented nature of software development, principally on the social dimensions of software development. His research emphasises software development as a social construction, drawing on ethnography as an underpinning research methodology. His research has given insight into the role of programming language paradigms and the emergence of object-oriented technology. His recent work has provided a detailed analysis, based on fieldwork, of the reflexive relationship between the social and the technical in the reality of agile practice.

5 From Exotic to Mainstream: A 10-year Odyssey from Internet Speed to Boundary Spanning with Scrum

Richard Baskerville, Jan Pries-Heje, Sabine Madsen

Abstract: Based on four empirical studies conducted over a 10-year time period from 1999 to 2008 we investigate how local software processes interact with global changes in the software development context. In 1999 companies were developing software at high speed in a desperate rush to be first-to-market. In 2001 a new high speed/quick results development process had become established practice. In 2003 changes in the market created the need for a more balanced view on speed and quality, and in 2008 companies were successfully combining agile and plan driven approaches to achieve the benefits of both. The studies reveal a two-stage pattern in which dramatic changes in the market causes disruption of established practices, experimentation, and process adaptations followed by consolidation of lessons learnt into a new (and once again mature) software development process. Limitations, implications, and areas for future research are discussed.

5.1 Introduction

Over the course of the last ten years, agile software development has received much attention from both the practitioner and research community, first as a novelty and later as a development approach that has become widely used in practice (Dybå and Dingsøyr 2008). In this chapter we look at how software development in practice has changed over this ten year time period. More specifically we compare and contrast the practices of Internet speed and agile software development at four different points in time: When the internet was booming in 1999; during the peak of the "dot.com" boom in 2000-2001; just after this economy collapsed in 2002-2003; and most recently in 2008. For simplicity, the four studies and points in time are here after referred to as study one from 1999, study two from 2001, study three from 2003, and study four from 2008.

Right before the beginning of the millennium the Internet was being adopted faster than nearly any other technology. It took 30 years (1920-1950) for the telephone to reach a 60% penetration in USA. It took 15 years for computers to reach a 60% penetration. But it only took 2 years for the Internet to reach 60% penetra-

T. Dingsøyr et al. (eds.), *Agile Software Development*,
DOI 10.1007/978-3-642-12575-1_5, © Springer-Verlag Berlin Heidelberg 2010

tion (Atlanta_Constitution 2001). In 1999 we therefore compared the growth of the Internet to an exploding bomb, and we called this phenomenon the "e-bomb" (Baskerville and Pries-Heje 2001).

At this point in time, in 1999, we carried out an interview study in three Danish companies. The study revealed that the then present notion of software development methodology was changing. In fact we found that the lack of methodology in its traditional form was characteristic. Instead of methodology, time pressure and requirements ambiguity was found to be at the core.

Two years later, in 2001, we did a comprehensive study in US. Ten companies that themselves claimed to be working at Internet speed were interviewed. Data analysis identified three major factors that influenced Internet software development processes: demand for rush to market, a different kind of market environment, and the lack of experience developing software for the Internet. Further we identified a new software development process used within a unique and enthusiastic development culture.

In 2003, after the dot.com bubble had burst we interviewed in the same companies. Fundamental changes in the economic conditions now affected the resources available for Internet software development and expectations had changed dramatically, resulting in three outcomes. First, the IT economy underwent a major upheaval as revenue fell, productivity rose, and budgets were slashed. Second, business expectations changed. Rather than an unbridled obsession with fast software delivery, customers demanded both speed *and* quality. Third, the economy drove an emphasis on the business case for software projects, and the concerns of the project managers changed to encompass the value to the enterprise, including development of more complex, mission critical software systems.

After the publication of our internet studies agile methods, and especially Scrum (Rising and Janoff 2000) and eXtreme Programming (XP) (Beck 2000; Beck and Fowler 2001; Jeffries et al. 2001), became popular in practice. However, the ideal settings for the use of agile methods versus more traditional methods were much discussed. Boehm (2002) has for example speculated on what constitutes the agile 'home ground', defined as the application area in which agile ISD has its special strengths and performs best given the project characteristics. Boehm and Turner (2004) have also suggested a radar diagram to characterize software projects and thereby obtain a recommendation on whether to use agile or 'disciplined' methods. Cockburn (2002) suggested a framework where one axis was number of people and the other was criticality (life at risk) of defects. He described an ideal setting (with up to 20 people and no serious money or life at risk) as the 'sweet spot' in which agile methods were preferable.

Some years later, in 2008, more and more companies were adopting Scrum in both Denmark and US (the two places where we live and work and thus have the closest contact to). It also looked as if Scrum was being used outside the 'sweet spot'. Therefore we identified and conducted interviews in three Danish companies that were using Scrum near the edge of its suggested application area. This usage was occurring in larger, sometimes geographically distributed teams and with essential money at risk. All three companies studied were successful in organizing the use of both Scrum and a plan-driven approach to achieve the benefits of both, namely the ability to respond quickly to change *and* the alignment of long-term plans and on-going activities.

In this chapter we provide a historical overview over the changes that the practical phenomenon of agile software development has gone through with regard to the aspects of time, application area, scope, and organization from 1999 to 2008. The research methodology and results address questions of *how local software processes interacts with global changes in the software development context.*

We have organized the remainder of this chapter in the following way. First we describe our research methodology, which is anchored in grounded theory techniques. Then we summarize the individual story line that proceeds from each of the four study periods. Lastly we conclude with a discussion of the overall story line that covers the 10-year time span.

5.2 Research Methodology

We have undertaken four phases of research, using Grounded Theory (GT) as our research methodology. GT is a qualitative research methodology that takes its name from the practice of discovering theory that is grounded in data. This research methodology does not begin with a theory, and then seek proof; rather it starts with an area of study and allows the relevant theory to emerge from that area (Strauss and Corbin 1998). The research outcome is grounded theories that are inductively discovered by careful collection and analysis of qualitative, empirical data. Use of GT in IT research is exemplified by a landmark paper by Orlikowski (1993) on CASE tools and organizational change, as well as explorations on software requirements (Urquhart 1997, 2000). GT is best used in research where one has relatively "uncharted land", which for example was the case with the notion of 'Internet speed'.

Our research questions in the 1999 and 2001 studies revolved around the concept of Internet speed: What does it mean? Is there something one could distinguish as "Internet speed development"? How is it different from or similar to traditional development? In 2003, we continued to ask about Internet speed, but were more focused on what had changed from the boom to the bust. In 2008 agile development had become widely diffused and successfully used, also beyond the application area initially recommended by the agile method authors. Our research interest therefore centered on the question of how agile development, and more specifically the agile method, Scrum, was used in projects at or well beyond the edge of its original sweet spot and why this seemed to work.

For all four phases of research, we have collected our data via semi-structured interviews. The interview guide was structured around the following topics:

1. The firm, and its' products and services
2. The interviewee
3. Projects in the organization – from start to end
4. Development model used?
5. Internet time / Agile development – What docs it mean to you?
6. The development process itself
7. Talent, training, learning, and knowledge
8. Transfer of knowledge
9. The biggest problem / Greatest challenge?

Each interview lasted approx. 1-1½ hour, relevant documents were collected, and observation notes were recorded (e.g., about the use of open- or closed space offices; and the general impression of the pace, atmosphere, and 'tone' of the work place).

For data analysis we have applied the three coding procedures of GT (Strauss and Corbin 1998) called open, axial and selective coding.

The goal of open coding is to reveal the core ideas found in the data. Open coding involves two tasks. The first task is labeling phenomena. This task involves decomposing observations into discrete incidents or ideas. Each discrete incident or idea receives a name or label that represents the phenomenon. These names represent a concept inherent in the observation. The second task is discovering categories. Categorizing is the process of finding related phenomena or common concepts and themes in the accumulated data in order to group them under joint headings, thus identifying categories and sub-categories of data.

The purpose of axial coding is to develop a deeper understanding of how the identified categories are related. Axial coding also involves two tasks. The first task connects categories in terms of a sequence of relationships. For example, a causal condition or a consequence can connect two categories, or a category and a sub-category. The second task turns back to the data for validation of the relationships. This return gives rise to the discovery and specification of the differences and similarities among and within the categories.

Selective coding involves the integration of the categories that have been developed to form the initial theoretical framework. First, a story line is generated or made explicit. A story is simply a descriptive narrative about the central phenomenon of study; the story line is the conceptualization of this story (abstracting). The story line becomes the core category, which is related to all the categories found during axial coding, thereby validating these relationships, and elaborating the categories into a theoretical expression that explains the phenomena observed.

5.2.1 Study One: Interview Study in Denmark

The first phase of our research aimed at exploring the influence of working on Internet time (Cusumano and Yoffie 2000). One could say that we were testing the hypothesis that working on Internet time would have to cause some changes in the way software development work was organized. But beyond this no hypotheses were pre-formulated and tested.

We interviewed in three Danish companies. Two of the companies were new to the authors and the third was a company we had visited over a period of time for a longitudinal study. The main facts about the three companies are given in Table 5.1, and further details can be found in Baskerville and Pries-Heje (2001).

Table 5.1 Facts about the three companies (study one)

Name (Pseudonym)	What offered?, When founded?, Which size?	Number of people interviewed and their organizational roles
NewWays	Develops custom-tailored Internet products for major customers internationally. Founded in the mid 1990s. 50 employees when interviewed.	4 people interviewed: One project manager, a development manager and two developers.
ProfWeb	Develops custom-tailored Internet and Intranet products interfacing with large existing databases. Founded in the early 1990s. 40 employees when interviewed.	2 people interviewed: A development manager and a developer.
AlfaWeb	A general web-based product sold on the market as a standard product for e-commerce. Founded in the late 1990s. 12 employees when interviewed.	2 people interviewed: The CEO and a development manager.

5.2.2 Study Two: Interview Study in USA

The second phase of our research involved ten detailed case studies of Internet software development companies in two major U.S. metropolitan areas. The firms ranged in size from 10 employees to more than 300,000 employees and covered different industries in the private and public sectors including: financial services, insurance, business and consulting services, courier services, travel, media, utilities, and government services. Some of the firms were Internet start-ups while others were "brick and mortar" companies with newly established Internet development units.

Table 5.2 Facts about the ten companies (study two and three)

Name (Pseudonym)	What offered?, When founded?, Which size?	Number of people interviewed in each round and their organizational roles
Calliope	Offers forecasting tools for energy and communications industry. Founded in the mid 1990s. 20 employees when interviewed.	2001: 3 people interviewed: VP Operations, Project Manager, Software Developer. 2003: Not interviewed.
Clio	Low-price health care and utilities for groups of customers. Founded in the late 1990s. 35 employees when interviewed.	2001: Six people interviewed: President & CEO, VP Technology Operations, Director of Marketing Research, Chief Information Officer, two developers. 2003: Not interviewed.
Deca	Develops and markets a platform of E-business software modules that allow users more control when doing business online. Founded in the late 1990s. Approx. 10 employees when interviewed.	2001: Not interviewed. 2003: Four people interviewed: CEO, developer, QA specialist and marketing manager.
Erato	Offers to help Brick & Mortar companies get online. Founded in the late 1990s. 55 employees when interviewed.	2001: Four people interviewed: Director, Chief Financial Officer, Chief Operations Officer, and developer. 2003: Not interviewed
Euterpe	Film and Television Industry. Offers high-tech tools online. Founded in the mid 1990s. 80 employees when interviewed.	2001: Four people interviewed: Project managers, marketing specialists, senior web developers. 2003: Not interviewed
Melpomene	Carries out personnel administration for other companies online. Founded in the mid 1990s. More than 100 employees when interviewed.	2001: Seven people interviewed: Project managers, process improvers, architects, user interface designers, web developers. 2003: 6 of 7 people interviewed. Process improvement person had left company.
Polyhymnia	Offers online services for transport and tourist industry. Founded in the early 1990s. More than 1000 employees when interviewed.	2001: Six people interviewed: Senior managers, Project managers, QA manager, lead developers, web developer. 2003: Seven people interviewed: Same distribution of roles as in 2001.
Terpsichore	Offers industrial insurance online. Founded in the 1930s. More than 10000 employees when interviewed.	2001: Three people interviewed: Human Resources Manager, Internet site manager and Internet site developer. 2003: Not interviewed.
Thalia	Online service for transport and logistics industry. Founded in the 1930s. More than 100000 employees when inter-	2001: Six people interviewed: CIO, Senior manager, project managers, architects, senior developers, web developers.

		viewed.	2003: Three of the six people interviewed: CIO, senior and project manager.
Urania		Business-to-business communication. Founded in the 1980s. More than 100,000 employees when interviewed.	2001: Six people interviewed: Senior manager, Project managers, quality assurance manager, QA specialist, Web developers. 2003: Six people interviewed. Same roles. But only three were the same people.

The objective was to understand whether software development for the Internet differs from traditional software development. This phase identified the practices used for Internet software development and explored the role of quality in fast-cycle development environments (Baskerville and Pries-Heje 2002). Further details on this study are given in Baskerville et al. (2003).

5.2.3 Study Three: A Follow-up Study

Another round of interviews in the same companies as in phase 2 was conducted two years later. Only five of the original ten companies (from 2001) remained in business or were available to participate in the study. A brief description of each firm is provided in Table 5.2, and further details are available in Pries-Heje et al. (2005).

5.2.4 Study Four: Scrum Interview Study in Denmark

The fourth round of interviews was conducted for the purpose of exploring how Scrum was used in projects characterized by larger and geographically distributed teams concerned with the development of business and life critical software. Three Danish companies were selected as relevant sites for data collection as their IT projects exhibited these characteristics (See Table 5.3). The case companies had from one year to two and a half years of experience with the use of Scrum, with SuperSystem being the most experienced.

The results of the four phases of research are presented below in the form of four grounded theories. The theories cover several levels of analysis, namely the market, the portfolio, the project, and the team level. However, many of our respondents were operating at the project and team level (project managers and developers). We have therefore been able to collect more detailed data, conduct more thorough analyses, and develop more robust theories about these two levels.

Table 5.3 Facts about the three companies (study four)

Name (Pseudonym)	What offered?, When founded?, Which size?	Number of people interviewed in each round and their organizational roles
GlobeRiver	Develops engineering products with built-in intelligence (software). Founded in 1940s. 500 employees in R&D function worldwide when interviewed; of this 25 in a company-owned development house in India (Developers and Scrum masters).	3 people interviewed: a Danish Scrum master, a Danish Facilitator, and an Indian Scrum master.
SuperSystem	Develops software for the military, the banking industry, hospitals, etc. Founded in 1980s. Approx. 400 employees when interviewed.	4 people interviewed: a Lead Developer, a Scrum master, the manager of the internal software process improvement (SPI) department, and the person officially in charge of implementing Scrum in the company.
DareYou	An off- and online gaming company; works with several suppliers located in different places and countries to develop the online games. Founded in 1940s. Approx. 250 employees when interviewed.	2 people interviewed: The Project manager and the Product owner.

5.3 Study One Results: Racing the E-bomb

In the first study we noted ten properties of a new methodology for "e" development (Baskerville and Pries-Heje 2001). Each of these properties is briefly described below, along with examples of how these properties are manifested in the cases. We also describe the chain of causal links that we discovered among these properties, which helps explain why this particular set of properties has come to characterize Internet time development (an early manifestation of agility). These properties and the causal chain are depicted graphically in Figure 5.1.

Time pressure. We found time pressure to be a condition permeating software development in the three companies we studied. First-to-market is the central, defining high-priority goal of Internet time development. Minimizing time-to-market from concept to customer is an all-consuming activity and achievement of this goal drives almost all other elements of the methodology. This goal is not new in business (Smith and Reinertsen 1995) nor in software development (Cusumano and Selby 1995; Iansiti and McCormack 1997). However, the degree to which it influenced systems development had not yet been recognized when we conducted this study.

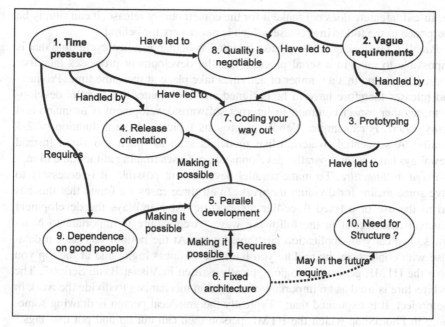

Fig. 5.1 Results from the first study

Vague requirements. An inability to pre-define system requirements is the central, defining constraint of Internet time development. The requirements specification has traditionally been the heart of systems development. However, Internet time development accepts a starting point in which the requirements are permitted to persist in near or full ambiguity. For example a project manager at NewWays said, "Often a project starts without a requirements specification. ...companies come to us and say: We believe there is a treasure buried in the World Wide Web. ... we want something new."

Prototyping. The idea of using prototypes seems to be widespread and permeating both early and late work in development projects. For example ProfWeb describes their use of prototypes as being part of their core competence. The R&D manager said: "We live from being technologically in front of our competitors, and from being able to visualise more far-reaching and wide-ranging solutions for our customers than our competitors are able to."

Release orientation. The vague requirements are not just something we see in the beginning of a project. In fact it continues throughout the development process. One consequence is what we have named a "release orientation". Software systems are produced in a series of ever more refined and extensive versions of the product; and each release contains bug-fixes and new features. These maturing product cycles characterize Internet software development in which competition demands significant product and feature changes every few months (Cusumano and Selby 1995). This release orientation helps relieve some of the time pressure because if a feature does not make it for the contemporary release, it can simply be postponed to the following release, which is never very far behind.

Parallel development. The release orientation demands a fast cycle time that is impossible to meet in a serial process. Parallel development processes therefore flourish, meaning that a number of activities take place at the same time. Products and releases therefore have to be designed and coordinated for parallel development, another aspect common to Internet software development (Cusumano and Selby 1995). For example, NewWays projects typically have a duration of 2-3 months. A sequential, waterfall-like model is seen as much too slow. Instead NewWays have several parallel development processes running at the same time.

Fixed architecture. To make parallel development possible, it is necessary to have some means for dividing the work. In all three cases we found that this has led to the use of a fixed three-tier architecture. At NewWays the development manager describes it in the following way: "Architecture is important to New-Ways. Typically an application has three layers: At the bottom you have a database with content; in the middle you have the business logic; and at the top you have the HTML generating logic, typically written in Visual Basic Scripts". The architecture is used as an important coordination mechanism to divide the work in the project. It is explained that: "Typically the graphical person is drawing something in PhotoShop which the HTML person then can cut up and put into tags," says one developer and another continues, "Which means that we are released from worrying about presentation and can concentrate on the heavy things" [i.e. the business logic and the database].

Coding your way out. The short time frame allowed for developing applications also introduces a coding focus or even hacking: "You have to accept that hacks are being made, that you don't have time to think systematically, and that you don't reuse because of the time pressure" (NewWays).

Quality is negotiable. Three different ways of looking and talking about quality have appeared over the last 20 years (Crosby 1980). One school of thought focuses on fulfilment of customer expectations. Another way of thinking emphasizes measurable product attributes and conformance to requirements. The third approach is process oriented and assumes that a good development process will lead to quality. The three resulting kinds of quality can be named expectation-based, product-based, and process-based quality.

As a consequence of both time pressure and vague requirements we found that both product-based and process-based seemed to be ignored. Moreover, customers and users seemed to expect low quality. We decided to call this phenomena negotiable quality.

ProfWeb was for example struggling with quality. They knew it was not good enough and they had started thinking about what to do: "We collect a Test Group for every project. At least that is the plan for the future, but right now we are running the pumps, not financially, but we are very busy ... I have a capacity planning system and the UNIX department is booked 4 months ahead" (ProfWeb). Thus time pressure is a cause of the negotiable quality.

Dependence on good people. Time pressure is also the primary reason why good people are in high demand. As one of the founders of ProfWeb phrased it: "I believe the largest bottleneck we have is to get enough qualified employees". However, not all kinds of IT people were in high demand. Traditional analysts were not in as high demand as the technical people who were close to the code: "I also realised that the job market is such that I could find 25 new consultants to-morrow but I wouldn't be able to find two new programmers" (ProfWeb).

Need for new kinds of structure. An issue that is closely related to methodology and to a number of issues we have addressed above is structure. We have not been able to establish a solid causal relationship, but we have indications that seem to reveal that the older and larger the organization and/or the customers the larger the need for structure. For example, AlfaWeb, which only had existed for half a year when we interviewed them, was not feeling any need for structure. The CEO explained: "I believe it is the informality but also the lack of formal structures. If people have to close-knit a framework to work in they might cut down on creativity" (AlfaWeb). In contrast, NewWays, which had existed for two years and had 50 employees, had started creating some structures, and had started using a number of object-oriented techniques.

5.4 Study Two Results: A New Software Development Process

In the second study we identified three major categories of observations that were causing a change, and three major categories that were resulting from the changing causes (Baskerville et al. 2003). Key findings are that Internet software development is different from traditional development and that the case companies are getting good at developing software at Internet speed by using an increasingly established set of practices that facilitate quick results, i.e. by using a new (agile) software process.

A different kind of market environment. The Internet created a unique platform and marketplace for software products - one that was flexible in terms of requirements and quality. Requirements and quality were negotiable from release-to-release in a market-oriented process where competition and pragmatics were allowed to intervene to limit the scope of features in each release.

Lack of experience. The interviewees reported that there were too few knowledgeable and experienced developers who understood the new technology, changing market conditions, and who could meet the need for speed. A manager from Melpomene told us that "lots of people [in our organisation] came from more corporate environments where it took forever to get things out the door." Much of this prior experience was a hindrance rather than a benefit in the new environment. The shortage of experienced professionals made the marketplace for developers tight and expensive, and created development organisations that lacked sufficient experience and expertise.

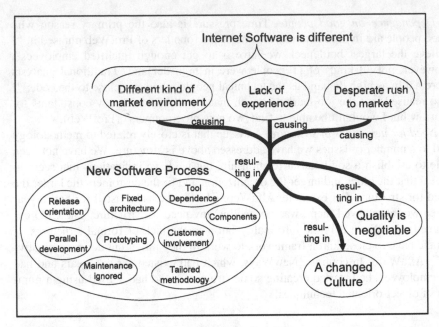

Fig. 5.2 Results from the second study

Desperate rush to market. In all the case companies they explained that Internet software development was driven by a desperate rush to market. "Time-to-market...Bigger, faster, better. Everything is very rush, rush, rush" (Polyhymnia).

Quality is negotiable. Many quality factors were not as critical in Internet speed development as they were in traditional software development. Customers and users appreciated quick results and were willing to defer a certain amount of reliability and performance until later releases. And developers were willing to rebuild badly designed or coded features later when the deferment ran out. "It is different working at Internet speed. Compressed cycles mean that quality suffers. With speed we are sending poorer quality out the door" (Polyhymnia).

A changed culture. We found that Internet software development organizations had a distinct culture that appreciated informal structure, smaller teams, and diverse team compositions. Moreover, there seemed to be a tight bond among Internet software developers, a sense of belonging with others who shared the same values. "We are not 9 to 5 people down here. We are more dynamic ... There is a lot more excitement and enthusiasm here" (Thalia).

A new software process. At the project level, we identified nine distinct characteristics (see Table 5.4). Although no single characteristic was unique to the new development process, the collection of characteristics was distinctive, aimed at producing quick results, and remarkably common in the case companies.

Table 5.4 Nine characteristics of the new software process (study two)

Characteristic of the new software process	Description and examples
Parallel development	To achieve high speed we found that companies compressed development into a time frame where only overlapping, parallel development could meet the demands.
Release orientation	"People have a perception of Internet speed. They expect it. So we've had to scope our delivery or deliver a smaller set of features. Thereby releasing more often", said a manager from Euterpe. Clio said: "Development cycles last from 2 to 15 days... timing is important. Features that cannot be completed in time can slip from one release to the next. The fast cycle time softens the penalty from slipping a feature."
Tool dependence	Urania estimated that "fifty percent of development is already taken care of by tools we use such as iplanet or websphere. The APIs to these tools gives a lot of functionality." Many Internet software development organizations made heavy use of development tools and environments that could speed up the design and coding process. New tools also helped to create well modularized and architected systems.
Customer involvement	When requirements are fuzzy it helps having close access to customers. Thus intimately involving customers to cope with evolving and unstable requirements was typical. We also found that customers were often co-located with the development team, and participated closely in all phases of development. Most projects relied on such involvement rather than a formalized requirements management process.
Prototyping	Instead of using formal requirements documents, most projects used prototyping as a way to communicate with their customers to validate and refine requirements. Customers would describe the basic functionality for new or changed features and these were quickly prototyped for demonstration and experimentation. "We are supposed to have a full [requirements and design document] but a lot of programmers use the prototype and go back and forth to check, or go back and ask: what was this supposed to do" (Melpomene).
Criticality of architecture	A well-planned architecture enable releases with some similarity. A three-layer architecture was common: (1) Database layer, (2) Business logic layer, the detailed processing code, and (3) User interface layer.
Components based development and reuse	Internet speed can be achieved by software assembled with as many reusable components as possible, rather than crafted from scratch. "Internet speed needs reuse. We need to take components and to know how to put them together" (Thalia).
Maintenance ignored	The short life span of Internet software meant that maintenance often was not given serious consideration. "Products are not documented. No design document, no requirements specification. The person who did it is gone. It takes much longer time. Often we can start from scratch. It leads to a throw away mentality"(Polyhymnia).
Tailored methodology	The processes and methods used in Internet software development varied considerably depending on the composition of the project team and the nature of the product. "We have an overall methodology. But we have to tailor processes for individual teams"(Urania). Just "enough process to be effective", added Euterpe.

5.5 Study Three Results: Balancing Speed and Quality

Three major changes took place from our second to our third study, i.e. in just two years (Pries-Heje et al. 2005). First, quality was no longer being treated as a disadvantaged stepchild. Speed and quality had to be balanced for companies to survive. Second, the unending supply of money that characterized the dot com boom had dried up. Third, good people were no longer in such short supply.

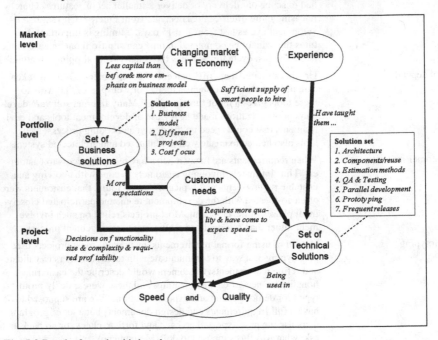

Fig. 5.3 Results from the third study

5.5.1 The Market Level

At the market level two things had changed. *The changing market and IT economy* were having visible impact on the firms that we visited. The companies were still under pressure to develop and deliver software at Internet speed, but they were operating with significantly lower capital than before, and were no longer finding it difficult to hire or retain the talent they needed. Most of the companies described their states as either holding back or cutting down on their employees. Thus, changes in the IT economy were especially noticeable with respect to personnel and staffing. Moreover, disappearing venture capital as well as tight budgets forced the companies to focus on business value and costs. What is new is the employment of a set of business solutions at the portfolio level, carefully coordinated with use of a set of technical solutions at the project level.

Also contributing to the state of Internet software development at this point in time is the hard-won *experience* gained during both the dot com boom and bust. Whereas development staff at the companies we visited in our second study expressed boundless energy, excitement, and some confusion about what they were supposed to do and how, in our third study a more mature and reflective perspective was evident. One member at Melpomene suggests that caution contributed to the company's survival: "I am critical of the phrase 'Internet speed', of the dotcom craze and demise. At that time, there was excitement. But all the successful practices were successful because they were good practices. We made conservative decisions and are still here." Thus, significant learning has taken place in these companies, across a wide range of business and technical topics. A member of Thalia sums up the learning in the following way: "Products are getting better due to more experienced developers."

5.5.2 The Portfolio Level

Sets of business solutions. The changing market and IT economy resulted in increased attention to the need for business models and a new, or increased focus on costs. "What has changed? We don't waste time on things that don't generate revenue" (Thalia).

As opposed to the days of abundant resources where risky projects even with faint hopes of success were undertaken, organizations were now much less willing to fund projects that did not have a clear business case. "We have to balance the need to do things fast and [the] desire to do it right – you need to have a business case." (Urania). A manager at Thalia also explains that his "Product is expected to generate revenue. That is different than before. Now we need to make a business case for each project". This situation encouraged project managers to clearly articulate the rationale for their projects, position them appropriately in alignment with organizational needs and requirements and in addition, market them to relevant decision makers.

All of the companies were refining their identities and offerings, but the challenges were being tackled in different ways. Some companies harkened back to more conventional business models, recognizing that "Success from now on depends on being a software and service company rather than an Internet company" (Melpomene), while others were forming partnerships with external (development) organizations.

Customer needs. The voice of the customer was still very much present, expressed through product strategy concerns, relationships, and ongoing contact. "The speed hasn't changed. If anything it gets faster and faster as customer expectations grow…[the biggest challenge] is meeting your customer's expectations" (Urania).

Customer needs remained a challenge to discern and satisfy and at the same time customer expectations - for speed *and* quality - were significantly higher than in the second study.

5.5.3 The Project Level

The project level categories manifested themselves as a set of technical solutions. Of the seven categories in this solution set, five were somewhat similar to the process elements in study two. These five similar elements are: a standard architecture, the (re)use of components, parallel development, prototyping, and frequent releases. Two new elements appeared: estimation and the improvement and involvement of quality assurance (QA) and testing. The two new elements are described in Table 5.5.

Table 5.5. Two distinctive characteristics of the technical solution set (third study)

Characteristics of the technical solution set	Description and Examples
Estimation	A major difference between our second and third study was the recognition of the need for good estimation methods to track and improve performance. The organizations that had been involved in internet software development for a few years declared that they were more mature in their estimation of effort and schedule -"we know what it is like to develop in this environment" (Polyhymnia).
Improve and involve QA and Testing	With markets and products maturing, quality was getting more important. QA and testing was now seen as important aspects of software development. Due to the time-constrained environment, the need for more efficient QA was stressed. "If I look at a project time line, a lot of it is in QA testing. We need to improve and automate and create scripts to drive that down" (Thalia).

Speed and Quality. Individuals in all the case companies commented explicitly on the struggle to balance speed and quality. "E-speed and e-haste are just normal now. Now you just know that you have to go that way and balance for quality" (Urania). The need for speed appeared to be as constant in our third study as it was in the second study. The customers had gotten accustomed to high speed development and were expecting it in every project. Quality, however, was viewed as having greater importance than previously seen. Quality was associated with number of defects, customer satisfaction, and overall success. Our interviewees explained that "If you don't follow your processes, or do your documentation, that is not quality" (Urania) and that "They'll forget that you're late but they won't forget if it's bad" (Polyhymnia). Thus, at this point in time all three types of (product, process, and expectation-based) quality had become important.

5.6 Study Four Results: Boundary Spanning with Scrum

In our two studies conducted before the Dotcom bust, software development for the Internet was characterized by time pressure. In the third study changes at the market level led to a more balanced view on speed and quality; business value and costs.

In the forth study, we examined three companies that were using an agile method (Scrum) for some parts of their software development process and a more traditional approach for other parts of their development efforts. The case companies were motivated to use Scrum by an internal drive to achieve the benefits of an agile approach. The following benefits were highlighted as particularly important:

1. A closer contact with and immediate feedback from the customer.
2. Increased developer commitment and feelings of ownership.
3. The energy released from being able to focus on quick results.

At the same time, and due to the size and distributed nature of the team work as well as the criticality of the software, the interviewees stressed the need for alignment. Alignment is described as necessary to ensure that the work carried out by the Scrum teams is in line with the overall scope document, budget, and project plan. The work should also align with the major milestones of the project and broader company-prescribed methods and standards (e.g., CMMi). The wish for energy and agility and the need for overview and alignment has led all three case companies to employ 'a mixed strategy' (Abrahamsson et al. 2009) where they combine the relatively recently adopted agile approach with more well-established plan-driven ways of working (see Figure 5.4).

The three companies are very clear about how they organize to achieve the benefits of both the agile and the plan-driven approach. They explain that "We carry out project planning and management at several levels." (SuperSystem). Thus, in all three cases, the Scrum team(s) and master(s) are allowed to have a narrow focus on 'today, tomorrow, this sprint, and the next', while a project manager has the responsibility for the project and the overall alignment of plans and people, i.e. for the big, and long-term picture. This division of work is necessary because "Scrum does not help with the overall, long-term planning of the project...you need to have an additional layer of project management. Otherwise it is not possible to coordinate and oversee a project with a deadline 1½ to 2 years into the future" (SuperSystem).

As the companies have chosen to organize for both agility and alignment certain Scrum elements and key people come to play a boundary spanning role that

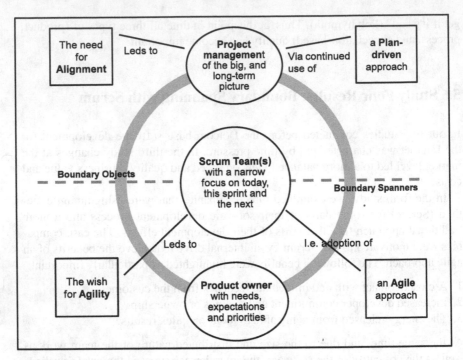

Fig.5.4 Results from the forth study

facilitates the sharing and negotiation of knowledge between several intersecting, but distinct social worlds (Levina and Vaast 2005; Star and Griesemer 1989).

5.6.1 Agility

The companies explain that they are "...true to Scrum at the team level" (SuperSystem) and that they "...use Scrum more or less 'by the book'" (GlobeRiver). Thus, Scrum helps the Scrum team conduct the work that is a part of their social world, namely the coordination and performance of tasks (related to analysis, design, development, test, integration, and release) as well as the monitoring of progress, risk, and quality for the current sprint. Moreover, Scrum plays an important role in providing a number of boundary objects that mediate the interaction that takes place between the Scrum team and the customer organization. For the product owner the prioritized user stories constitute functionality that will be a part of the next deliverable, and for the developers the user stories are (also) tasks that have to be carried out during the particular sprint. At the same time, the stories and the software allow the team members and the product owner to communicate, share knowledge, and create new meaning across the boundaries of their different worlds.

5.6.2 Alignment

In all three case companies software development was previously conducted in accordance with a sequential, document-oriented development model, and a plan-driven approach continues to be used after the introduction of Scrum. However, the plan-driven approach is now separated from the development teams and activities, and used by an appointed project manager for overseeing the project as a whole. It is explained that "...surrounding the team's work and the burn-down chart is the overall project plan, including milestones, broad-level estimates, a mapping from milestones to sprints, and a plan over external releases, as well as a risk analysis. The board-level estimates and the mapping from milestones to sprints help validate if the project and its scope can be achieved within the time frame and the budget, but the details of the sprints are not specified in these plans. That is the responsibility of the team" (SuperSystem).

DareYou also reported that, even though they are the customer organization, they consider themselves responsible for the project and its success. Consequently, they also operate with an appointed 'traditional' project manager, as well as project management tools and documents such as a written project vision, budget, overall project plan and some up-front specification of requirements. In this case, the customer's project manager is the boundary spanner who keeps the project and its plans and participants aligned, and together with the product owner she is heavily involved in and well-informed about the actual quality and progress of the suppliers' development efforts.

In GlobeRiver the overall management and responsibility for the development of new engineering products resides with the R&D department. Thus, the Indian Scrum teams carry out the software development within the frame of large, business critical projects that involve many internal departments and external suppliers and which are managed in accordance with a traditional plan driven approach. It is very important that the software meets the deadlines in the road map for the product development project as a whole and that it is in line with the requirements and quality in the specification. In this setting, the R&D project manager is also the product owner and responsible for prioritizing the already specified functionality, which the Scrum teams then develops during a number of sprints. Moreover, a third role, a Facilitator, has been introduced. The Facilitator, located in Denmark, "...is the main point-of-contact between the Danish product owner and the Indian teams and follows-up on progress and impediments on a weekly basis, or more if needed..." (GlobeRiver). The Facilitators serve as boundary spanners who use certain information objects (such as, e.g., the road map, product backlog, burn-down chart, and impediments list) to keep the Indian Scrum team informed about requirements, priorities, and deadlines and the Danish R&D manager up to date about progress, quality, and risks. In this way, the Facilitator plays an important role for the translation of information between the agile and the plan driven worlds. This in turn allows the Indian software developers and the Danish R&D

personnel to operate almost completely according to their own goals and work practices.

In sum, in all three case companies, the combined use of Scrum and a plan-driven approach has been organized so that the involved agile and plan-driven communities-of-practice (Cox 2005) can work largely in keeping with their own goals, information needs, and methods. Consequently, the translation of information and negotiation of new meaning across the different intersecting worlds is necessary. To this end, certain information elements (i.e. the overall project plans and burn-down charts) function as boundary objects, while the Scrum masters in SuperSystem, the Project manager in DareYou, and the Facilitator in GlobeRiver have boundary spanning roles, which they are fully aware of.

5.7 Discussion and Conclusion

Over the ten year time span, learning has been generated from each of the four studies. Much of this learning might be characterized as detailed and "keen insight" that is created within each of the studies and which does not bear well in brief summaries. However, it is possible to consider the learning that arises from the accumulation of insights across the four studies. A limitation of this approach lies in its assumption that the four studies provide serial episodes. Because the studies involve differing subject organizations and individuals, we cannot rule out the alternative explanation that the consistencies in the data sets are accidental.

With this caveat in mind, we can summarize and interpret the collection of four studies as follows. The central story line in the first study brought the changing landscape of software development into sharp focus. In this study, it appeared that the two main sources driving software development were incredible time pressures coupled with unknown and changing requirements. These two primary causal factors arose as the context for software development changed due to the emergence of the E-economy.

The central story line in the second study embraced a new software process that was common across the respondents. This process included customer involvement, parallel development, a release orientation, etc. The components of the new process were present in the first study, but had become more or less established practice in the second study (Baskerville and Pries-Heje 2004).

In the third study, the story shifted again, but this time away from software development in a local sense. This story line focuses instead on changing economics and the role of software in formulating business solutions and generating revenue. A balancing game arises in which business and technical factors are brought together by high speed software projects.

Finally, in the fourth study, the central story line shifts once more, but the focus falls back on software process. In this study, we find organizations which are not exactly integrating agile and planned software processes; rather they are operating these two different ways of working consistently within separate boundaries. Work is flowing across the boundaries to enable the organizations to harvest the benefits they require from each of the deployed software processes (agile and planned).Thus, boundary objects and spanners play a key role in this story.

An interesting aspect of these study settings is the historically repeating two-stage pattern where the story line first centers on a changing context and then on the software process, almost as a maturation in response to early adaptation to changes in the context (see Figure 5.5).

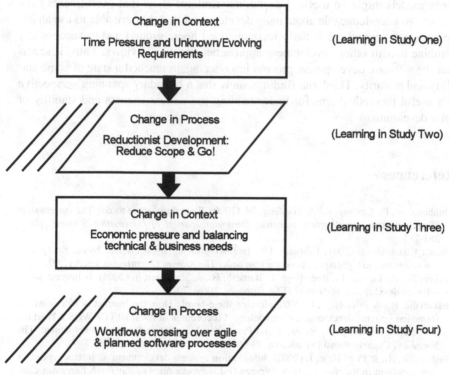

Fig. 5.5. Learning across the four studies

From one perspective, this two-stage pattern is hardly surprising. A changing context undoubtedly drives changes in software processes. However, the solid evidence of an historical stage of fairly stable maturation of software process following a stage of more chaotic, context-driven process adaptation is surprising from a different perspective. It suggests that maturation in software processes may occur in historical cycles, rather than an endless progression of maturity-model driven advance. In other words, our evidence indicates that reoccurring periods of radically changing context will interrupt software process maturation.

Software process maturation does not necessarily restart from ground zero in each episode. Our evidence clearly indicates that our settings have learned from previous experience with new software processes. However, the evidence does suggest that overall global progress in software process maturity is episodic, with the possibility that each episode begins with a reversal, and then advances. It seems likely that each episodic advance brings the software discipline to an overall position of advancement. Thus software process progress is not steady, but characterized by episodes of decline and advance.

Our findings have a number of implications for theory and practice. First, the learning that we draw from across the four studies indicates that a broadening of the primarily local way we research and view software process maturity and maturity models might be useful. Second, our findings show that practitioners have become so knowledgeable about agile development that they are able to use an agile approach beyond the initially recommended home ground and to successfully combine it with other development approaches and world views. Thus, it seems that the software development process has once again reached a state of some stability and maturity. Third, our findings show that a boundary spanning perspective is a useful theoretical lens for understanding the current success and stability of agile development.

References

Abrahamsson, P., Conboy, K., & Xiaofeng, W. (2009). 'Lots done, more to do': The current state of agile systems development research. *European Journal of Information Systems,* 18(4), 281-284.

Atlanta_Constitution. (2001, February 19). Internet growing by leaps and bytes: Study says americans trek to Cyberspace Is now a stampede. *The Atlanta Constitution,* pp. A1, A9.

Baskerville, R., Levine, L., Pries-Heje, J., Ramesh, B., & Slaughter, S. (2003). Is Internet-speed software development different? *IEEE Software,* 20(6), 70-77.

Baskerville, R., & Pries-Heje, J. (2001). Racing the e-bomb: How the Internet is redefining information systems development methodology. Proceedings of the IFIP TC8/WG8.2 Working Conference on Realigning Research and Practice in Information Systems Development: The Social and Organizational Perspective, 49-68.

Baskerville, R., & Pries-Heje, J. (2002). Information systems development @ Internet speed: A new paradigm in the making. In S. Wrycza (Ed.), *Proceedings of the Tenth European Conference on Information Systems* (pp. 282-291). Gdansk: University of Gdansk.

Baskerville, R., & Pries-Heje, J. (2004). Short cycle time systems development. *Information Systems Journal,* 14(2), 237-264.

Beck, K. (2000). *Extreme programming explained: Embrace change.* Addison-Wesley.

Beck, K., & Fowler, M. (2001). *Planning extreme programming.* Boston: Addison-Wesley.

Boehm, B. (2002). Get ready for agile methods, with care. *IEEE Computer,* 35(1), 64-69.

Boehm, B., & Turner, R. (2004). *Balancing agility and discipline: A guide for the perplexed.* Boston: Addison-Wesley.

Cockburn, A. (2002). Learning from agile software development - Part one and two. *Crosstalk - The journal of Defence Software Engineering* (September and October).

Cox, A. (2005). What are communities of practice? A comparative review of four seminal works. *Journal of Information Science,* 31(6), 527-540.

Crosby, P. B. (1980). *Quality is free: The art of making quality certain*. New York: New American Library.

Cusumano, M., & Selby, R. (1995). *Microsoft secrets: How the world's most powerful company creates technology, shapes markets and manages people*. New York: Free Press.

Cusumano, M., & Yoffie, D. (2000). *Competing on Internet time: Lessons from Netscape and its battle with Microsoft*. New York: Touchstone.

Dybå, T., & Dingsøyr, T. (2008). Empirical studies of agile software development: A systematic review. *Information & Software Technology*, 50(9-10), 833-859.

Iansiti, M., & McCormack, A. (1997). Developing products on Internet time. *Harvard Business Review*, 75(5), 108-117.

Jeffries, R., Anderson, A., & Hendrickson, C. (2001). *Extreme programming installed*. Boston: Addison-Wesley.

Levina, N., & Vaast, E. (2005). The Emergence of boundary spanning competence in practice: Implications for implementation and use of information systems. *MIS Quarterly*, 29(2), 335-363.

Orlikowski, W. (1993). CASE tools as organizational change: Investigating incremental and radical changes in systems development. *MIS Quarterly*, 17(3), 309-340.

Pries-Heje, J., Baskerville, R., Levine, L., & Ramesh, B. (2005). The High Speed balancing game: How software companies cope with Internet speed. *Scandinavian Journal of Information Systems*, 16, 11-54.

Rising, L., & Janoff, N. S. (2000). The Scrum software development process for small teams. *IEEE Software*(July/Aug), 26-32.

Smith, P. G., & Reinertsen, D. G. (1995). *Developing products in half the time* (2nd Ed.). New York: Van Nostrand Reinhold.

Star, S. L., & Griesemer, J. R. (1989). Institutional ecology, `translations' and boundary objects: Amateurs and professionals in Berkeley's museum of Vertebrate Zoology, 1907-39. *Social Studies of Science*, 19, 387-420.

Strauss, A., & Corbin, J. (1998). *Basics of qualitative research: Techniques and procedures for developing grounded theory* (2nd ed.). Thousand Oaks, Ca.: Sage.

Urquhart, C. (1997). Exploring analyst-client communication: Using grounded theory techniques to investigate interaction in informal requirements gathering. In A. S. Lee, J. Liebenau & J. I. DeGross (Eds.), *Information Systems and Qualitative Research* (pp. 149-181). London: Chapman and Hall.

Urquhart, C. (2000). Strategies for conversation and systems analysis in requirements gathering: A qualitative view of analyst-client communication. *The Qualitative Report (On-line serial)*, 4(1).

Author Biographies

Richard L. Baskerville is a Board of Advisors Professor of Information Systems and past chairman in the Department of Computer Information Systems, Robinson College of Business, Georgia State University. His research specializes in security of information systems, methods of information systems design and development, and the interaction of information systems and organizations. His interest in methods extends to qualitative research methods. Baskerville is the author of *Designing Information Systems Security* (J. Wiley) and more than 100 articles in scholarly journals, professional magazines, and edited books. He is Editor-in-Chief for *The European Journal of Information Systems* (EJIS) and serves on the editorial boards of *Business & Information Systems Engineering* (*Wirtschaftsinformatik*), and the *Information Systems Journal* (ISJ). A Chartered Engineer, Baskerville holds degrees from the University of Maryland (B.S. *summa cum laude*, Management), and the London School of Economics, University of London (M.Sc., Analysis, Design and Management of Information Systems, Ph.D., Systems Analysis).

Jan Pries Heje is Professor in Information Systems, Department of Communication, Business and IT, Roskilde University. Head of the User Driven IT-innovation Research Group. His research focuses on designing and building innovative solutions to managerial and organizational IT problems. Previous and current projects explore quality software development @ Internet speed, innovative capability in projects, the ability for an organization to improve, and how one can design a process for making better sourcing decisions. Jan Pries-Heje is Past President of the Association of Information Systems in Scandinavia (IRIS). Jan Pries-Heje serves as the Danish National Representative to IFIP Technical Committee 8 on Information Systems where he is also Chair. Jan Pries-Heje has been Associate Editor for MIS Quarterly, ISJ, and EJIS. Jan Pries-Heje's research interests include project management, information systems development, and process improvement. He focuses on organisational and managerial issues.

Sabine Madsen (PhD) is Associate professor at the Department of Communication, Business, and IT at Roskilde University, Denmark. She has been employed as a project manager in the Danish IT-industry before pursuing an academic career. She completed her Ph.D. about process and method emergence in information system development practice in 2004. Her general research interests concern IS development processes, methods, and the relationship between research and practice and she has published on these topics in journals (such as EJIS, and ISJ), book chapters, and conference proceedings. She is a regular reviewer for IS journals and conferences. Recent research and teaching are in the areas of project management, outsourcing, and agile IS development. For these themes she is particularly interested in understanding and theorizing about the practices, challenges, and changes that IS developers and managers experience as a part of their day-to-day affairs.

6 An Ideal Customer: A Grounded Theory of Requirements Elicitation, Communication and Acceptance on Agile Projects

Angela Martin, Robert Biddle and James Noble

Abstract: This chapter explores the reality of the customer role – a critical, complex, and demanding role on agile teams. Despite initial difficulties, customers love agile development and would not do it any other way, but they also encountered many difficulties in their day-to-day work. In this chapter we describe the practices that have emerged to ensure the role works effectively and sustainably, and how the role has evolved from an individual to a team. We hope customers will find this chapter helpful in performing their role, and programmers will find it useful to understand the complexities of customer's role on the project.

6.1 Introduction

"All the best talent and technology and process in the world will fail when the customer isn't up to scratch" (Beck and Fowler 2001, p17)

Most of us, based on our experience, agree with this statement, irrespective of whether the statement concerns an agile project or not. But how do we know when a customer is 'up to scratch' for an agile project? The initial agile literature (Beck 2000; Beck and Fowler 2001) provided little guidance on the practicalities of succeeding in this role.

In this chapter we summarize the results of our research into the reality of the customer role within agile projects. Firstly, we will describe our research method, grounded theory. Next we will describe the results of our research, including: the experience of customers, the emergence of an informal customer team (Martin, Biddle et al. 2009) and the practices that make the role effective (Martin, Biddle et al. 2009). We will conclude the chapter with a section that brings together and integrates the earlier three result sections as well as discussing the implications these results have to practice and theory.

T. Dingsøyr et al. (eds.), *Agile Software Development*,
DOI 10.1007/978-3-642-12575-1_6, © Springer-Verlag Berlin Heidelberg 2010

6.2 Research Method

Information Systems Development (ISD) methodology researchers (Nandhakumar and Avison 1999; Fitzgerald 2000) have expressed a growing concern that existing ISD methods do not meet the needs of today's business and software development environments. Studies (Nandhakumar and Avison 1999) in this area have begun to explore practices in natural settings in order to begin to address these issues. Given this trend, we have used grounded theory (Glaser and Strauss 1967) to explore our research questions within their natural setting, software projects. Our research questions were:

- What is the experience of the customer? While interaction between business people and developers is not new, agile does change this interaction significantly. We wanted to understand how that was really working in practice, including the positive and negative aspects of the change.
- Is the customer a single person or a team? Practitioners implementing this change were unclear who the customer should be, and if it is just one person or if it is a team of people.
- What practices enhance the effectiveness of the customer? Was it simply a matter of customers and developers interacting together daily, or was there more guidance to be offered.

The eleven case studies we present in this chapter were selected to collect data from a range of project types; see Table 6.1 for an overview of the projects:

Table 6.1 Overview of the projects studied

Company	Location	Domain	Size[1]	Team	Interviews[2]
KiwiCorp	Australasia	Telecoms	M	11	5
RavenCorp	USA	Research	S	20	6
EagleCorp	USA	Software Tools	S	16	9
FalconCorp	USA	Retail Products	S	60	7
SwiftCorp	USA	Retail	XL	20	6
HawkCorp	USA	Knowledge	S	5	6
TernCorp	Europe	Telecoms	M	20	7
SparrowCorp	UK	Energy	L	15	4
KiteCorp	Europe	Transport	M	12	5
RobinCorp	UK	Mobile software	XS	6	3
OwlCorp	UK	Health	L	20	9

---

[1] Companies were classified by the number of employees: XS <15; S <1,000; M <10,000; L <100,000 and XL >100,000.

We utilized our networks within the agile community, working with respected speakers from agile conferences to help us select the projects for the case studies. One advantage of this selection approach is that it helped to ensure that we targeted projects that were practicing XP well.

We used semi-structured in-depth one-on-one interviews as well as observations to collect the data for this chapter. The first author undertook all of the interviews and observations. She interviewed a total of 66 people across eleven projects. On all of the projects the core XP roles of "customer", "programmer", "coach" and "tester" were interviewed. The remaining core role of "big boss" was interviewed on three of the eleven projects. All interviews were taped and later transcribed in detail. The interviewees were asked to validate both the transcriptions of the interview and the interpreted findings. The project observations[3] were used to support both the interview process and the resulting findings.

This data analysis process was iterative and incremental. We created short summary labels for each significant line of the transcripts. This process is called *open coding*. We used comparative data analysis to compare and contrast the open codes, to develop the substantive codes (an abstracted category that fits multiple open codes). We also wrote *theoretical memos* that relate the codes, drawing out the potential ideas or concepts held within the data. This memoing process assisted us to focus on the core categories and the inter-relationships between the categories. We initially coded the transcripts within the margins and used index cards for the memos, as recommended by Glaser (1978). However, as the research progressed this method became unmanageable given the number of transcripts and memos, so we used the software package HyperResearch (version 2.7) (ResearchWare 2006) to assist with the coding and sorting process. The term *theoretical saturation* is used to denote when to stop this process, that is, when no or very few new codes are discovered within the data. Thus, the data collection and analysis phase stopped as theoretical saturation was reached, which occurred upon the completion of the eleventh case study.

In the sections that follow, we identify the theory as it emerged from our analysis of the data. We use a number of quotes from the interviews to illustrate our findings; names have been avoided or invented to preserve anonymity.

This study was part of a doctoral programme. The resulting PhD thesis (Martin 2009) provides a full description of our application of Grounded Theory.

---

[2] The number of people interviewed concerning each project. Sixty-six individuals were interviewed; one person was interviewed for two projects, he is only counted once in the total count of 66.

[3] We focused our observations on whole team interaction: the physical working area, artefacts produced (e.g. user stories) and activities such as the planning game, story-writing workshops, and conversational interactions involving the customer (e.g. between a programmer pair and a customer).

6.3 What is the Experience of the Customer?

The customer is the primary organisational facing role on agile projects. Their explicit responsibilities are to drive the project, providing requirements (user stories) and quality control (acceptance testing). The customer must also shoulder a number of implicit responsibilities including liaison with external project stakeholders, especially project funders, clients, and end users, while maintaining the trust of both the programmers and the wider business. One of the fundamental changes agile brings into this space is the reliance on regular (typically daily) interaction between customers and programmers during development instead of relying on large requirements documents "thrown over the wall" to the programmers.

In the projects we studied, we found that all of them had an "on-site customer" who undertook the role described above as best as they could. The on-site customers in our studies spent significant amounts of time directly interacting with the developers as well as staying engaged with their organisational work. We found that both customers and programmers love the change that agile brings, however it is not all "picture perfect":

"I think it's worked very well, but ... I don't know how long [I can] keep this pace up"
— Customer, EagleCorp

"Overall – I love this approach ... and I'd certainly like to use it again ... We probably needed about 3 of me ... it's been my life ... look at these grey hairs"
— Customer, KiwiCorp

"I think this way of working so closely with the technical team is good. I think there are an awful lot of benefits with this process ... it was a completely joint effort ... we would compromise, discuss things, share ideas, and it was really like one big team."
—Customer, OwlCorp

"I've always worked at least 70 - 80 [hrs a week] I don't even mind it, it's like what I do"
— Customer, RavenCorp

Although the existing customer practices appear to be achieving excellent results it is also clear that the customer is not able to practice the agile principle of sustainable pace in their working lives. Sadly, in a number of the projects we studied, most of the programmers were unaware of the long hours the customers were working. This situation appears to be unsustainable, and so constitutes a great risk to agile projects, especially in long duration or high-pressure projects. The remaining sections in this chapter will describe in detail the strategies we observed that helped to address the issue of customer overwork.

6.4 Is the Customer a Single Person or a Team?

The initial books about XP describe the on-site customer as a single person. In the cases we studied, we discovered that an informal team of people form to perform the on-site customer practice initially outlined by Beck (2000). While today there is a greater acknowledgement within the community that the customer is more than one person, this section provides a deeper insight into the roles required on that informal customer team. We identified the following de-facto roles in the informal customer team:

- Collaboration Guides: Geek Interpreter, Political Advisor, & Technical Liaison
- Direction Setting: Negotiator, Diplomat, Super-Secretary, & Customer Coach
- Skill Specialists: Acceptance Tester, UI Designer, & Technical Writer

In this section we will describe each of the roles and how they emerged, focusing on the first two categories, as the third is better understood[4]. We present the roles in the order that they emerged during the analysis. We first understood the detailed supporting roles and later the direction setting roles.

6.4.1 Collaboration Guides

Collaboration is an essential value of agile software development (Beck, Beedle et al. 2001), and as such significant investment is made to facilitate collaboration in agile projects (Beck 2004). During our data analysis three roles emerged that focused on enhancing the business-technical collaboration on a project: Geek Interpreter, Political Advisor and Technical Liaison.

Geek Interpreter
Quick Definition: A person who supports the business to improve their communication and collaboration with programmers.

The agile principle that business and technical people are required to work together daily changes the dynamic of the business-technical relationship in many organisations:

> "[Previously] you write a document, you get feedback on the document ... and it's not until the product comes out at the end that you realise, well somebody screwed something up ... but you get the pleasure through XP of having that close, close, close relationship in defining the product right at the time ... one of the great powers of XP ... was that ... I could leverage ... the collective intelligence of the whole developer group that I work with."
> — Customer, EagleCorp

---

[4] Skills specialists assist the customer to undertake activities such as writing stories, accepting stories, and writing end-user documentation.

The emphasis on business and technical people collaborating was perceived as fundamental in order for the "right thing to be built", but sometimes programmers and customers can talk past each other:

> "If I'm kind of thinking, how can you [Developer "A"] give me a four day [estimate] ...
> for a field on the screen, that's bonkers, I'll wander up and say [Developer "B"], I've got
> a story, what do you think? ... obviously I couldn't then quote it back to the first
> developer but it gives me an idea of what's going on ..."
> — Customer, OwlCorp

We have named this role the Geek Interpreter. The Geek Interpreter acts as a sounding board for the customer, not a bridge, simply someone to discuss a matter over with before re-engaging with the initial programmer concerned. Our interviews with the programmers revealed that most programmers value their communication skills with business people, and it might bother them that at times the customer needs to use a Geek Interpreter when communicating with them. As such, it is particularly interesting to note that the customers were aware of this and were very careful when using a Geek Interpreter. For example, one customer mentioned that they never used the advice provided by the Geek Interpreter in potentially antagonistic ways like "but [Geek Interpreter] said ...".

Words customers used to describe the person(s) playing this role included "guidance", "trust", and "on my side". Geek Interpreters were also seen as individuals who were particularly interested in the domain and able to listen to the business representatives and show respect. Finally, it is important to note that the Geek Interpreter role was never observed to be an "official" team role. We observed that their official roles were varied and included business analyst, tester, project manager or programmer (on either the same or on a different project).

Political Advisor
Quick Definition: A person who is adept at navigating the political dimensions within an organisation to assist the project to succeed.

Every organisation has a rich life. During our interviews a number of stories that illustrated the richness and diversity of organisational life were shared that help illustrate the importance of a Political Advisor[5]. One senior business executive related her ongoing frustrations with regards to working with the IT unit in her organisation, specifically the IT Manager. She was very complimentary about the specific people involved in the project and was pleased with the software that was produced. However, she was finding that continuing to "work around" the IT Unit Manager was frustrating and time-consuming. During the interview with us she noted that she intended to outsource software development in order to lessen the impact of the IT Manager. Six to twelve months after the interview the team was mostly disbanded and the software development was (mostly) outsourced. Working software was not enough for the team to keep their jobs.

---

5 In this section we wish to avoid explicitly situating the stories within cases to protect the privacy of different interviewees from the same case study, so no project pseudonyms are used.

In another project, the IT Development Manager describes a disastrous "go/no-go" meeting that occurred where the operations group vetoed the launch of the system. On reflection she realised that when assembling the key people to involve in the project steering group, she had opted for a junior member from operations as he was available, but he did not have the authority required to make the decisions necessary in this situation. She had misread the political dimensions and had no Political Advisor on the lookout for signs of unrest within the organisation.

While many of the stories from our case studies demonstrate with "negative" outcomes, the need for a Political Advisor, some demonstrate how it can work to achieve positive outcomes for the project. One customer from a large project shared a story of working closely with her executive manager (as her Political Advisor) to help her know when to break the rules. The project was seen as a success within the organisation despite breaking the rules.

Finally, although it is common for the Political Advisor to be a senior executive, we were also told stories that indicate that Political Advisors can be outside of the formal organisational hierarchy as well.

Technical Liaison
Quick Definition: A person who undertakes the liaison with related projects and technical silos within the organisation.

Most projects do not exist in isolation; projects have to interact with existing technical infrastructures and other software development projects. This role emerged very quickly in the studies, initially because it was "missing", and so caused significant overload and frustration for the KiwiCorp customer who spent about half of her time on Technical Liaison work. KiwiCorp was not alone with the need for a Technical Liaison between the project and specialized technical groups:

> "Different teams ... always comprise a project, you've got the UI, you've got deployment,
> ... you've got security, you've got infrastructure, ... the interaction between different
> systems, so you've got all these different groups that you bring together in a project."
> — Customer, SwiftCorp

The liaison undertaken at SwiftCorp seemed particularly effective. At SwiftCorp the project manager and coach invited (and encouraged) the technical specialists to attend the planning games, and daily stand-up meetings. The project manager and coach were both very aware that they needed to make it worthwhile for the technical specialists to attend, so they were careful to initially invite them only to sessions where they would get significant benefit. In their experience of using this approach, they found that over time the specialists became more involved, by choice, as they could see the benefits of being involved based on their experience. The project manager complemented this with a lot of one-on-one liaison with the technical specialists. Honious and Clark (2006) from Reed Elsevier describes a similar approach that they used to involve their operations group actively in their agile project.

A number of authors have also identified a need for cross-team coordination and communication on agile projects (Kahkonen 2004; Miller 2005; Lowery and

Evans 2007). As with our case study data, the research papers and experience reports that concentrate on these issues tend to be larger organisations: Nokia (Kahkonen 2004), BBC (Lowery and Evans 2007), Reed Elsevier (Honious and Clark 2006), and Primavera (Miller 2005).

Direction Setting

The direction setting roles comprise the core of the on-site customer role and practice outlined by Beck in the first edition of Extreme Programming Explained (Beck 2000). It is these roles that set the direction of the project, resulting in the single voice describing "what to build". The collaboration guide and skill specialist roles support the direction setting roles.

Negotiator

Quick Definition: A person who works with the end-users and other stakeholders to negotiate a single-voice of what to build.

DeMarco (1979, p. 5) suggested that negotiating "with a whole community of heterogeneous and conflicting users is a gargantuan task"; and went on to liken the Diplomatic skills required to "the skills of a Kissinger negotiating for peace in the Middle East." We use this analogy when introducing the lead role of the customer team.

On every project we studied, everyone could clearly identify the on-site customer(s), even though there was an entire customer team. One person, or in some instances a pair of people, were the identified contact point. It emerged that, like in DeMarco's analogy, the Negotiator[6] picked up the task of gaining agreement within the larger stakeholder community on the vision for the software.

For example, the EagleCorp product manager, who played the role of the Negotiator on their development project needed to bring together both internal and external stakeholders. His internal stakeholders consisted of senior executives, sales, marketing, and operational support representatives, as well as the architect from the engineering group. His external stakeholders included the Customer Advisory Group representatives from existing customers as well as representatives from potential new customers. The EagleCorp Negotiator used a number of different facilitated workshop techniques to facilitate an agreement amongst this diverse stakeholder base as to the scope of the project. Finally, it should be noted that the negotiation aspect was an ongoing activity. As new information came to hand, re-planning resulted; both small changes and dramatic changes to the initially envisioned scope needed to be negotiated and agreed on with the stakeholders. A Negotiator emerged in all of the other cases. We give them the name Negotiator to more clearly define the role, but also to more clearly allow the "onsite customer" term to refer to the customer team.

Some books (Highsmith 2000; Gottesdiener 2002) exist that would support this concept of a Negotiator or facilitator working with large or diverse groups of

---

6 Our next section elaborates on the practices the Negotiator uses when working with the stakeholder community and the programmers.

stakeholders to achieve a vision of "what to build". These texts recommend the use of facilitated workshops to achieve a shared understanding amongst the stakeholders.

We saw great variety in the background of the Negotiator, the stakeholders they would represent, and the techniques they used to obtain the agreement amongst the stakeholders. The Negotiators' backgrounds ranged from those with an IT background (e.g. business analysts, developers or project managers) to those that had no IT background at all (e.g. the KiwiCorp end-user). We have found, however, that there were also a number of similarities amongst those undertaking the role of the Negotiator. Firstly, all Negotiators knew the domain well:

> "They need to have domain knowledge, huge domain knowledge to be a customer, a strong customer. If they don't have that it's hard for them to gain the confidence of the developers to say I'm going to tell you what we're going to build and you're going to build what I tell you and that's the way its going to be. That's a great customer."
> — Programmer, SwiftCorp

Notice that this domain knowledge does not necessarily mean they are end-users or business stakeholders. For example, the programmer quoted above is referring to a business analyst, not an end-user. Other attributes the Negotiators had in common were that they:

- Understood the business drivers on the project, which may or may not have always aligned directly with their (own) needs
- Knew who to approach for information or decisions, thus were well connected within the organisation and able to use their connections effectively.
- Were aware that multiple perspectives existed, and helped people with different perspectives understand one another.
- Were comfortable working at both the "big picture" level and the detailed level.
- Were confident, decisive, and stable under intense pressure.
- Enjoyed project work and liked working with technical people.

Perhaps unsurprisingly this list of attributes aligns reasonably well with Beck's initial list of attributes of a good customer (Beck and Fowler 2001, p.18). The attributes that Beck brings up in addition to our list include:

> Is determined to deliver value regularly and is not afraid to deliver too little rather than nothing and can make decisions about what's needed now and what's needed later (Beck and Fowler 2001, p.18)

Interviewees did discuss the importance of regular delivery, which occurred through the XP process, but they did not add the aspect of not being afraid to deliver too little instead of nothing. We did, however, notice that the Negotiator was acutely aware of almost the exact opposite, which is that in some situations releasing nothing (rather than too little) may indeed be the right business decision. So it is perhaps reasonable to assume that they were very aware of delivering regularly but their emphasis was more business orientated.

We observed that Negotiators do not necessarily carry the full decision-making responsibility, that is, they will not necessarily lose their jobs if the system or project ends up being perceived as a failure. It is rare for that responsibility to be fully on their shoulders, it seems more likely that it will be on the sponsor's or Big Boss's shoulders. What was interesting, however, is the Negotiators we observed did choose to own the responsibility to obtain an agreement amongst stakeholders. These individuals chose to pick up that responsibility. This fits with Beck and Fowler's (2001) initial words, which were "willing to accept ultimate responsibility for the success or failure of the project".

Diplomat
Quick Definition: An end-user or stakeholder who brings the perspective of their group to the project.

We continue to use the treaty negotiation analogy for this next role, Diplomat. Diplomats were business representatives or technical specialist (e.g. architect) representatives. Their job is to represent the interests of their area, whether that area was a country, a business unit, or a subject area. Notice that Diplomats were members of that area, not "proxies". It is important that, as Diplomats, they articulated the view of their area well and worked with others around the table to hammer out the "treaty" or single-voice of the customer:

> "...we were representing [the business unit] and you can't please everyone ... we do research to get to the answer and ... you have to ... put your own kind of preferences aside as well and see what the best is..."
> — End-user Representative, OwlCorp

To represent the views and needs of a group of people, the Diplomat must be in touch or connected with this group of people; keeping them in the loop on trade-offs that will have to be made during the process and obtaining their buy-in to the agreement as it takes shape. Typically the projects second someone from the area to work with them on the project, so they have a deep insight into what will make a difference, please the people they represent, and get the system accepted.

So the Diplomat has a very outward facing role into the organisation. Their involvement with the programmers can vary significantly. Some Diplomats worked full-time on the project, and developed strong relationships with the programmers (e.g. OwlCorp). Other Diplomats were part-time and while they developed a strong relationship with the Negotiator, they had no relationship with the programmers (e.g. most of the programmers on the EagleCorp project we studied had not met any of the EagleCorp Customer Advisory Council members[7]).

From the examples we have presented above, it is easy to focus on the Diplomat being the end-user. While the end-user and business representatives are crucial to agile projects (Beck, Beedle et al. 2001) and real customer involvement is strongly encouraged (Beck 2000; Beck 2004), other perspectives must also be pre-

---

[7] Our next section describes the practices used by the customer team to help prevent this type of disconnect.

present to fulfil the customer role. Technical specialists have other perspectives that feed into the single-voice the customer must provide. The involvement of technical specialists in the customer team on technically focused projects might typically be expected. For example, there was a technical advisory group on HawkCorp's project and on the ChannelAdvisor project outlined by Isham (2008). Technical Specialists may, however, be crucial representatives on business-focused projects too. For example, at EagleCorp the architect was a key influence on the technology decisions made, and non-functional requirements (e.g. performance and scalability). It is important that these types of requirements are not forgotten (Hussman 2003).

Super-Secretary
Quick Definition: A person who undertakes the administrative support workload of the customer team. They also become the person that programmers approach for guidance when the Negotiator is unavailable.

There are many administration and organisational tasks that need to occur in order for the customer to be effective in their interactions with both the business and the programmers. Overloaded customer team members find it easy to either let these tasks "slip" or become a burden that results in them either not being as effective (e.g. losing stories) or working even more hours in a day. We have found that typically one person on the customer team will surface to pick up the "adminis-trivia" load from the rest of the team; we have called that role the Super-Secretary. We have found that the Super-Secretary always has another formal role[8] on the customer team, so this role is always "part-time", despite the occasionally very large amounts of work involved. The Super-Secretary will typically record and organize the stories, as well as track them through their lifecycle. The Super-Secretary also has a detailed understanding of all of the stories:

> "In fact she could have probably done my job. You know, she had a very good knowledge of the business ... She also [has] this amazing encyclopaedic knowledge of everything, so you'd say what story was this and she'd trip out the story number and the letter and everything to do with it"
> — Customer, OwlCorp

Beavers (2007) described the role "Requirements Architect" that BMC needed to introduce to improve their management, elaboration and prioritization of the projects requirements. This role appears to undertake a similar function to the Super-Secretary. Beck (2000) outlined the role of Tracker, and the Tracker role does seems to align with many aspects of this administrative role. There is, however, a focus on the requirements or customer responsibilities. From our perspective, this role is richer than that described by Beck. The richness of this role is illustrated by the remaining task that falls to the Super-Secretary, which is that of Negotiator or Diplomat stand-in. When these people are not available the programmers begin to

---

[8] The formal role that the person holds on the team can vary (e.g. BA, Tester, or Project Manager).

use the Super-Secretary as a "stand-in", obtaining his or her impressions of a story:

> "[Super-secretary], who is our tester/admin/general kicker-up-the-arse person. She is
> brilliant ... she works very closely with [the Customer] ... when we think we have
> finished a card, if [the Negotiator is not] around ... we will talk to [Super-Secretary] ...
> and she kind of gives a non-developmental look over what we have done."
> — Programmer, SparrowCorp

Perhaps it is this aspect that helps draw out why this role, despite its apparent administrative nature, is only undertaken by very experienced individuals. The Super-Secretary can often become one of the most helpful (although often underappreciated and overloaded) people on the customer team.

Customer Coach

Quick Definition: A person who supports the other customer team members to undertake their roles.

XP introduces the concept of a coach: someone who helps the team transition to XP (Beck 2000). At SwiftCorp there were two coaches: a development-focused coach and a customer-focused coach. The SwiftCorp Customer Coach worked with the customer team, supporting them to drive out and communicate the direction of the project. He was 100% customer focused, leaving another coach to focus on the development practices. The Customer Coach, however, was only part-time on the project, approximately three days a week. During that time he was the customer's personal "cheerleader" when it all seemed too much, and would help them determine how to break the task down into achievable steps. He had a lot of experience at writing stories and acceptance tests and perhaps even more importantly the soft collaborative and community building skills needed in the customer team.

The Customer Coach may also play the role of a Geek Interpreter, as they do have that interest in technical-business collaboration and typically have a technical background. However, they have a wider focus. They give the Customer someone to talk to, to help them resolve their issues, ensure they realise they are not alone and to mitigate the risk of customer burnout. We found that an effective coach is someone the customer can *trust* and they tend to have:

- A deep IT and business experience that enables them to provide effective and pragmatic support to the customer.
- An intimate understanding of how the on-site customer practice works.
- An ability to work with customers to help the customer solve their own problems, rather than solving the problem for the customer.

This practice aims to provide professional support to customers. It combines the patterns *Mentor* and *Shoulder to Cry On* outlined by Manns and Rising (2004). We have found that the Customer Coach role makes a difference to the well-being and effectiveness of the customer. While Beck (2000) introduces the role of Coach, we have discovered it to be beneficial to have a customer-focused Coach.

Hussman (2003) writes of his experiences as a Customer Coach, and his experience also seems to support the recommendation of a dedicated Customer Coach.

6.4.3 Customer Team Summary

This section has outlined the roles we identified on the informal customer teams. The first group of roles includes *Collaboration Guides* and these include the Geek Interpreter, Political Advisor and Technical Liaison. Their focus is advising or guiding the customer team as they build trusted relationships both with the programmers and in the wider organisation. These roles tend to be undertaken by people who are not formally recognized as being part of the customer team, but they are essential none-the-less. The next set of roles includes the *Skills Specialist* roles and these are the Acceptance Tester, User Interaction Designer and Technical Writer. The core function of these roles is to assist the customer to undertake activities such as writing stories, accepting stories, and writing end-user documentation. Often these roles are formal or recognized roles on the customer team, but not always. Sometimes it is sufficient to have someone on the customer team with this skill-set. The last group of roles includes the *Direction Setting* roles and these are the Negotiator, Diplomat, Super-Secretary and Customer Coach. These roles form the heart of the on-site customer practice, with the Negotiator typically being the leader of the customer team, and also the "official" customer. It emerged that the Direction Setting process is typically negotiated amongst a large group of stakeholders rather than simply "being known", as Beck seems to suggest. The aspect of real customer involvement still remains essential and the Diplomat fulfils this aspect of the on-site customer practice. The Super-Secretary and Customer Coach are the last two elements at the heart of the customer team. The Super-Secretary removes much of the administrative burden from the Negotiator, and, also importantly, often fills in as the stand-in for the Negotiator when the Negotiator is not available. Finally, the Customer Coach, when available, provides essential guidance and advice to the entire customer team, particularly the Negotiator and Diplomat, helping them to take the steps that determine the direction of the project.

6.5 What practices enhance the effectiveness of the customer?

In the second edition of his XP book, Beck (2004) introduced three overarching practices: Real Customer Involvement, Whole Team, and Energized Work. Real Customer Involvement emphasizes the direct involvement of end-users and other business stakeholders on the project. Whole Team refers to the practice of including all of the skills and perspectives on the team necessary for it to succeed. Importantly, Whole Team emphasizes the importance of the sense of team, all team members sharing a sense of purpose and supporting each other. Energized Work emphasizes working "only as many hours as you can be productive and only as many as you can sustain". We wanted to know how these practices were implemented on projects, and we were especially interested in the customer role. We have identified eight new customer-focused practices that emerged, all contributing to the three more abstract practices suggested by Beck (see Fig. 6.1).

In this section we will discuss each of the identified practices individually. In our studies we also observed wide-spread use of the already well-known customer practices including Planning Game, Short Releases, Stories and Tests (Beck 2000; Beck 2004): we do not discuss these or any of the standard business practices such as market research, business process modelling, and so forth.

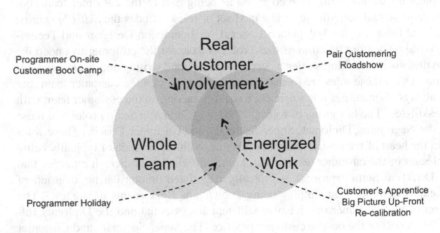

Fig. 6.1 Agile Customer Practices

6.5.1 Customer's Apprentice

Quick Definition: Programmer works on the customer team for an iteration or two so that they can understand the complexity of the customer teams' role.

We observed that people on effective Whole Teams exhibited empathy (Merholz, Wilkens et al. 2008) and respect for other team members and the roles they played on the Whole Team. It emerged that one way for developers to understand the customer was to "walk a mile in their shoes". We first encountered the dramatic nature of this experience in a story from SwiftCorp. The SwiftCorp team all described a period where the programmers were becoming increasingly frustrated with the customer as the customer was providing them with insufficiently detailed stories (and sometimes simply not enough stories for a complete iteration):

"[Programmer] said why don't I ... go and write stories with our customer and that'll help him out ... And if it turns out to be really easy then we'll continue to hit our customer and we'll track spikes through his chest. But that's not what happened. He came back and said oh wow, there's really a kind of a process to writing stories and to mine requirements and go hunt down the people in the business that want something and to get them to explain what it is that they want and so on and so forth ... It humbled them a little bit I think and that made the relationship much more productive ... And it completely turned things around for that group. In that sense the developer had a little bit of insight into the pain in the customer's world."
— Programmer Coach, SwiftCorp

In doing this, the programmer did indeed help the customer move forward, but perhaps more importantly, he gained a deeper understanding and appreciation of the extent of the customer's task, and was able to take that understanding and empathy back to the other programmers. This event was critical in helping the programmers and customers move towards becoming a Whole Team and working together more effectively.

The SparrowCorp team related a similar experience on their project. In this situation the programmer-customer bond was enhanced when the programmers attended the sessions that the customer held with external stakeholders. The programmers undertook some technical installation tasks at each visit, but more importantly they got to see the other 'face' of the customer, the positive way she projected the software and the programmers, and they got to see the pressure she faced from external stakeholders.

A number of experience reports (Hodgetts 2004; Takats and Brewer 2005) also describe situations that led to opportunities for the Customer's Apprentice practice to be used. Hodgetts (2004) describes a Government Workflow Project where the business experts were not skilled in analyzing the processes and creating a specification for the programmers, and so an "analysis backlog" developed. The issue was resolved by moving two of the programmers over to assist (and coach) the business experts for a couple of iterations. The benefits were two-fold, the business experts developed new skills, and were able to better meet the needs of the programmers, and the programmers were able to understand and help address the issues that had begun to reduce programmer morale. Takats and Brewer (2005) write of their experience at Sapient, while working with the U. S. Office of Naval Research (ONR). On this project, a few of the senior programmers were selected to assist as note-takers (or in some cases facilitators) during initial sessions that occurred on the project. This allowed them to gain a direct insight into the domain, and create relationships with the customer team prior to the development phase of the project starting.

It also emerged that programmers who have played the role of the Customer's Apprentice are more likely to see the team as a Whole Team, rather than the "us" and "them" that can often develop between the programmers and customers. This change helps to move us closer to the vision Beck had of the Whole Team practice (Beck 2004), creating a stronger and more effective business-technical collaboration. In each case the programmer assisted in reducing the burden of overload from the customer, improving their ability to experience Energized Work.

6.5.2 Programmer On-site

Quick Definition: Schedule site visits for programmers so that programmers can understand more about the end-users of the software.

Beck aspires "to reduce wasted effort by putting the people with the needs in direct contact with the people who can fill those needs" (Beck 2004). In our interviews we noticed that programmers were keen to better understand or connect with the direct end-users of the system:

> "I've always felt bad that we never talk to the [end-users] ... we just get features ... we don't see how people would use it."
> — Programmer, EagleCorp

Similar comments were discovered in other cases where we had a product manager or business analyst playing the onsite-customer. In situations like OwlCorp, where we had two end-user representatives available to the programmers full-time, we did not see comments like these. It is not as simple, however, as simply putting end-users and programmers together. At RavenCorp, for example, despite a full-time end-user representative being on-site, there was still a lack of understanding of what the end-users were trying to accomplish:

> "the software developers ... don't have as much of an interest in what ... the product we're producing is going to mean to [the domain] ... if they could ... grasp how useful ... just how cool what we're making is ..."
> — Scientist (Customer), RavenCorp

Some recent papers (Beyer, Holtzblatt et al. 2004; Broschinsky and Baker 2008) have begun to consider Real Customer Involvement, most turning in some fashion to UCD (User-Centred Design) for inspiration. Beyer, Holtzblatt and Baker (2004) provide some insight into involving real end-users in the project. Their recommendation is to use contextual inquiry, observing the end-users in their day-to-day activities, and then providing summarized models from those observations to inform the programmers. The additional, and in the context of this research important, recommendation is to include programmers as part of the cross-functional contextual inquiry team. Beyer et al. note that the inclusion of programmers on this team does not always occur in practice, but then recommended involving them as early as possible afterward and making the programmers aware of the contextual inquiry findings. Broschinsky and Baker (2008) combined the use of contextual inquiry and personas, with one of the models resulting from their use of contextual inquiry being a set of personas. They noticed that the data only resonated with the programmers once they brought actual or real end-users in to meet the programmers. It was at that point that their findings became real and believable for programmers.

Moreover, while we have tended to focus on the impact of these techniques to the programmers in the above paragraph, it is essential to remember that the benefits are always two-fold. Beyer et al. (2004) highlights that a number of misconceptions arise with Beck's concept of Real Customer Involvement including that "people cannot articulate their own work practice" and end-users and other stakeholders "are not designers". Programmer On-site is concerned with the Whole Team understanding the end user and context of use, with the programmers gaining enough information to make helpful suggestions.

6.5.3 Programmer Holiday

Quick Definition: An iteration of technical tasks so that the customer can have some time to think-ahead.

It is common practice to commence the project with a small number of programmers and to gradually increase the number of programmers assigned to the project over a period of weeks. The programmers who join early will often be working on technical tasks, not driven by stories, such as setting up the technical environment. We wondered if there was ever a need to replicate that situation once all of the programmers were onboard? We observed that the XP iteration driven approach is intense both for the customers and programmers.

> "One of the ways the [developers] deal with [the intenseness of XP] is to [have] the opportunity ... [to] choose ... to step out of the [story-driven] development process and to work ... on something that's supporting the iteration ... [called a joker card]"
> —Customer, EagleCorp

These non-story tasks included repaying technical debt, upgrading software or hardware, developing a tool to support development (e.g. a code generation tool) or conducting research into new technologies. Mackinnon (2003) describes in his experience report a similar concept, involving "gold cards". MacKinnon discovered that gold cards helped improve the programmers morale and reduced the monotony of the iterations. The SwiftCorp Coach discussed a company who took this practice to an extreme:

> "[the company had] re-factoring iterations, so they would let the team re-factor for a whole iteration ... their rule was that at the end of the iteration all the stories ... and all the unit tests ... run and ... they could do whatever they wanted under the covers. It's a little bit like giving all the developers, I mean pardon me for saying this about the developers 'cos I was one, so I can say it's like here's some lollipops and popcorn, you know, have a good time..."
> —Coach, SwiftCorp

So a mechanism to provide a "time-out" for programmers emerged, but how could a time-out of the iteration process be provided for a customer? The customer drives the iteration process, so a time-out for the customer automatically appears to have the result of programmers not having enough stories for an iteration. We faced this situation on an XP project where the project was two and a half months in, one release had been made, and the second was well on the way to completion, but the customer team was not quite sure what the functionality for release three should be. The third release was critical, but they were not sure what stories would be needed to meet its goal; they were not sure how to "break the back" of the problem. The customer team needed time to think; and the programmers were carrying a lot of technical debt and had not had a break from the story-driven iteration cycle to fix the technical debt and to research a new build and testing tool. Inspiration arose from the findings that had emerged on the research to date, and an agreement was struck. The programmers would spend an entire iteration on technical tasks of their choosing, and the customer team would step away from the iteration process and "break the back" of the third release. Typically, some of the programmers would work as a Customer's Apprentice during this period.

Programmer Holiday directly contributes to Energized Work for the Whole Team, but most importantly, from the perspective of this research, for the customer. The customer gets a break from supporting the current iteration and is able to focus almost solely on setting the direction for the next stage of the project. It is these aspects that provide the business value for a Programmer Holiday, although gold cards enable programmer-inspired work that may also have significant value.

6.5.4 Roadshow

Quick Definition: Demonstrate the software to end-users and other stakeholders to obtain their feedback on the direction of the project.

Beck (2000; 2004) would like Real Customer Involvement on XP projects, and more specifically he would like opportunities for end-users and other stakeholders to provide feedback on the software as it evolves. Software systems often have a large number of end-users and stakeholders. It emerged that the customer team typically included end-user representatives, who work as part of the customer team to represent the perspective of different sections of this community. But how did the customer team obtain the feedback on the software from the larger communities they represent? Most of the projects we studied used a practice we have called Roadshow to do this.

EagleCorp, a software product development company, described their Roadshows, and the different audiences of their Roadshows, in some detail. During our interviews it became clear that the intent of the Roadshows varied slightly based on the interests and needs of that audience, as well as what the customer team needed from that audience.

EagleCorp used a Roadshow to reach an internal audience. The internal audience consisted of the sales, marketing, operational support departments and the executive management team. The customer team used the Roadshows primarily to report progress and gain feedback on the functionality in-development. An additional side effect of these internal Roadshows was that the executive management was assured that the project was progressing towards a shippable product.

EagleCorp also used a Roadshow to reach their many external audiences. The product manager described their interaction with the Customer Advisory Group (CAG). This group met on average once a quarter, with two of those meetings typically being multi-day face-to-face meetings, and the other two meetings typically being a much shorter two hour webinar. The customer describes the importance of allowing the customers to speak during these sessions:

> "The customers [will] present to us how they're using the application at their organisation.
> ... they show us what business problems it solves for them, how they use it, how their
> groups use it, and then they'll tell us some of the challenges that they have ... it's very
> valuable because it helps me understand what some key customers are doing, some of the
> key issues that they have ... and how I should, spend my engineering ... dollars ..."
> — Customer, EagleCorp

The key focus of the Roadshow, however, is demonstrating the product and getting feedback on what has been developed since the last meeting, as well as what is on the radar for the next development period. One of the advantages that XP gave EagleCorp as a software product development company was the ability to demonstrate working software rather than discussing ideas or selling promises:

> "I think it makes a lot of difference ... until it's something that they can really look and
> feel, that they can actually touch ... this industry is still, you know, selling on a promise a
> _lot of the time. You know, [clients] over a course of time have just become very
> disillusioned with selling them promises. So, just being able to show them the application
> and show them the fact that it is functionally working, it makes a lot of difference ..."
> — Customer, EagleCorp

Scrum has a process that initially appears to be the same as the Roadshow practice we describe; the Scrum practice is called a *Sprint Review* (Schwaber and Beedle 2001). Both practices involve a regular meeting with interested project stakeholders to review the functionality developed. One of the biggest differences between these two practices is that Roadshows are tied into the pulse of the organisation rather than solely to the pulse of the development team.

6.5.5 Customer Pairing

Quick Definition: Two members of the customer team working collaboratively to provide a single-voice to the programmers.

We observed the practice of customer pairing in varying degrees in many of the cases; it particularly stood out in OwlCorp, where two end-users paired almost 100% of the time:

> "The work was quite evenly distributed. We would share a lot of ideas in conversations that we had, and we would discuss practically everything. We wouldn't make decisions on our own very often. We would always ask the other person and discuss it to make sure everything was covered. I think that helped as well, to make sure what we were asking for was right ... to not to have had a second opinion would have been very difficult... I think it would be just too hard to be the only business-person surrounded by 10 or 15 technical people. It is nothing against them, because I really like them all, but you know sometimes, you just need someone [customer pair] to see it from your point of view."
> — End-user, OwlCorp

In most of the other cases where we observed customer pairing, the pair utilized a divide-and-conquer strategy that allowed them to both work independently as well as collaborate as a pair. An illustrative example of this strategy comes from SparrowCorp. At SparrowCorp one of the business analysts was responsible for the requirements and needs of six of the regions affected by the system and the other business analyst was responsible for a similar number. This division of labour resulted in the business analysts being able to work independently, and develop the strength of relationships required with each region. However, they brought that information back into the pair in order to forge a single-voice for the programmers. The additional sounding board effect (or two heads are better than one) that the OwlCorp customer refers to also helps to create less stress for the customer that again helps to facilitate Energized Work.

6.5.6 Customer Boot Camp

Quick Definition: A customer-focused training event.

How do the customer team, be they from a traditional business analyst or from a business background (e.g. an end-user representative), learn how to interact with the programmers effectively? The OwlCorp coach, aware of this type of issue, suggested the customer team have a special customer boot camp that trained the customer team in the agile process and their role. The training would include programmers but would be focused on the customer's perspective. The key aims were to help people buy in to the process, and to gain a practical understanding of their role and what they need to do on the project. It emerged that the boot camp did not answer all of their questions, and neither did the customer retain everything, as they often needed to try to do some things in real-life before all of the concepts embedded:

> "It wasn't until I started to do it that I started to realise what everything was ..."
> — Customer, OwlCorp

However, the customer boot camp provided the customer with a "kick-start", an initial understanding of their role, the process, and some initial ideas of techniques, like story writing, that they would be expected to put into practice during the project.

A number of recent experience reports (Ganis, Leip et al. 2005; Rasmusson 2006) have also reported the importance of including customer-focused training sessions as part of an agile adoption effort. Ganis et al. (2005) write of their use of the *Extreme Construction* game when introducing XP into their environment at IBM. This non-software simulation involves specifying and building a physical model of a product using arts and crafts materials. The programmers invited their customers to attend their agile training, and as such the customers were quickly exposed to the ideas, principles and practices of XP. The non-software simulation allowed both programmers and customers to gain an appreciation for all of the XP practices. Rasmusson (2006) writes of his experiences on a number of Thoughtworks agile adoption consulting engagements. He writes of two practices that he uses, one being a four-day boot camp that occurs near the start of an engagement. The first two days of the four-day boot camp focus on aspects relevant to the Whole Team, including an introduction to agile, roles and responsibilities, release planning and team practices.

The Customer Boot Camp practice supports the customer to become an effective member of the Whole Team, as it helps them understand more about their role and responsibilities. Therefore, we believe that this practice helps us to obtain Real Customer Involvement as well as help us move towards a true Whole Team that includes the customer.

6.5.7 Big Picture Up-Front

Quick Definition: A short period of envisioning amongst the business stakeholders and programmers to set the direction of the project.

In our studies it emerged that typically the customer engaged in some activities prior to the first iteration with the programmers. The intent of these activities was to help answer the question "what to build", and to set the direction of the project.

At TernCorp the initial project concept or goal was first seriously considered by the business organisation over a year before the programmers started work. The software project began with a 14-day period where the end-user representatives worked with some of the programmers to create an initial *big picture* for the project. For this project the big picture consisted of a set of use cases and a release plan. During the project the release plan was on the wall of the project room and was a series of post-it notes on brown paper. This story is similar to the stories told to us concerning other projects in our study.

A number of published papers (Fuqua and Hammer 2003; Takats and Brewer 2005) highlight Big Picture Up-Front activities on agile projects. Fuqua and

Hammer (2003) explain that one of the key lessons from their project was: "don't try to find all of the stories up-front, and expect to throw many away". Fuqua and Hammer don't suggest the removal of that initial conception phase, but do suggest shortening its duration. Takats and Brewer (2005) describe their experiences of developing a big picture for a naval logistics command and control system, using visual models and a series of workshops to bring all of the stakeholders together to "own" the big picture.

Big Picture Up-Front also supports Whole Team, as developers are included in the workshops to help build their domain understanding and improve the estimating process. Finally, Big Picture Up-Front also supports Energized Work for the customer team.

6.5.8 Re-Calibration

Quick Definition: Plan to adjust commitments and resources regularly based on what both customers and programmers learn during the iterations.

After a few iterations, many teams realise that they are not going to deliver everything that they initially hoped they could during release planning. The velocity data from the first iteration will typically indicate that the release plan is unrealistic, but both customers and programmers typically attribute this to the effects of a new process or technology. Their expectation is that they will improve and catch up. After a few iterations, however, the Whole Team begins to gradually realise that the plan was overly optimistic. Our interviews revealed that the reaction at this point begins to differ slightly between the customer and programmer sides of the Whole Team. The programmers perceive that it was "good" that they had uncovered this situation as early as they had. Their perspective: it allows the customer team to make the scope reductions required in order to meet the deadline. The customers, however, perceived the situation as more problematic:

> "I think we agreed what would be a realistic range and what would be a stretch range.
> Not really kind of knowing what that would mean in terms of an outcome ... we had been
> told ... that we could have all the musts, all the shoulds, and some of the coulds ... And
> then it got to a point where we found out that we couldn't have any of the coulds, and
> there was some coulds that really should have been shoulds ... If we were really truthful,
> it was a bit of a quick and dirty prioritization and then we were kind of held to it. I guess
> we were a bit naïve."
> — Big Boss, OwlCorp

The primary consideration for the customer team during this period is whether any reduced set of functionality will be sufficient to deliver the necessary business value. Some stakeholders remember this process with a great deal of negative emotion. Interestingly enough, in some cases the customer's sense of "betrayal" appeared to be greater than if the situation occurred on traditional projects. One explanation perhaps is that the customer believed XP was a silver bullet.

Beck (2000) discusses the planning strategy of XP, and specifically outlines a *steering phase*. The intent of the steering phase is to update the plan based on what the team learns, including new stories, a better understanding of velocity, and estimates. Weyrauch (2006) describes the agile adoption at Medtronic. One of the barriers Medtronic faced in their agile adoption was the perception that agile projects do not need to plan. Weyrauch worked to correct that mistaken impression and the result was the new perception that agile projects are all about planning and re-planning constantly, "the exact opposite of the original worry" (Weyrauch 2006). Honious and Clark (2006) describes the path of a product Reed Elsevier was developing. The initial release plan had the product being demonstrated at a tradeshow. Reality, however, intruded on that initial plan, and it soon became clear that the deadline could not be met with the current scope and constraints. Honious emphasizes that it was unacceptable to just "drop functionality" as there was a minimal feature set required for the tradeshow, so the Whole Team developed solutions with this constraint in mind. The feature set was already the minimal acceptable for the business case, so the re-planned solution deferred features that were not required for the tradeshow users (but would be required for the full release), and they also added another programmer pair to the project.

Experience shows that initial plans are often optimistic and customers will need to regularly re-plan. Re-Calibration allows stakeholders to make changes to the plan regularly as they learn more about the project, thus supporting Real Customer Involvement. Re-Calibration contributes to creating a Whole Team as they move away from a "blame" culture towards a proactive and regular re-planning event. Finally, Re-Calibration also contributes to Energized Work as it ensures they re-plan the work for the Whole Team, including the customer.

6.5.9 Customer Practices Summary

This chapter has outlined the customer-focused practices that emerge from our qualitative study of XP projects, also identifying the inherent interwoven relationships between the practices, and how they strongly contribute to Real Customer Involvement, Whole Team and Energized Work.

The emergent practices primarily support Real Customer Involvement by preparing the business representatives for their role (Customer Boot Camp), and providing opportunities for the business representatives to contribute towards the creation and refinement of what to build (Big Picture Up-Front, Roadshow and Re-calibration). The emergent practices primarily support Whole Team by providing opportunities for the programmers to develop empathy for the customer team (Customer's Apprentice) and the end-user (Programmer On-Site). Finally, the emergent practices primarily contribute to Energized Work by reducing the intensity of the process (Pair Customering and Programmer Holiday). As with all of the XP practices, the emergent customer practices are not specific solutions, but rather focus on describing how to support Whole Teams to work together more effectively and how to ensure they "build the right thing".

6.6 Discussion and Conclusion

In this chapter we set out to explore how the role of the agile customer can be implemented effectively. To do that, we interviewed 66 people on eleven different XP projects and observed the interactions between the customer and other project roles. Our findings strongly indicated that, in the majority of cases, the customer was passionate about their role on the project and using agile. For instance, they indicated that they "wouldn't do it any other way". In the interviews both the customers and the programmers conveyed how much they had enjoyed the direct conversations and connections they had with each other, and felt that this approach contributed to creating a better quality system. Conversely, our findings also indicated that the customers were working more intensely and for longer hours than on traditional projects; the customer was not working at a sustainable pace. For instance, one customer commented upon the project "needing three of me" as she had been over-stretched concerning her working hours, and also commented on the difficulties and stress caused by the role ("look at all these grey hairs").

Our next research question sought to clarify the types of people who undertook the role, and to also understand if it was a single person or a team undertaking the role. Our findings concluded that it was always a team of people, what is more, the team of people tended to consist of up to ten distinct roles. The roles emerged as follows:

- *Collaboration Guides:* Geek Interpreter, Political Advisor and Technical Liaison. The Geek Interpreter contributes to enhancing the collaboration between the customers and programmers. The Political Advisor contributes to enhancing the collaboration between the customer and the larger organisational life of the business, ensuring the customer is better able to navigate the political dimensions necessary for the project to succeed. The Technical Liaison contributes to enhancing the collaboration between this project and other related projects, as well as any technical specialist silos that might exist within the organisational structure.
- *Skills Specialists:* Acceptance Tester, UI Designer and Technical Writer. All of these roles support the customer to undertake their on-site customer responsibilities. The Acceptance Tester supports the customer by assisting with the acceptance testing of the software. The UI Designer supports the customer by lending their UCD (User-Centred Design) skills to assist the customer in deciding and designing what to build. The Technical Writer supports the customer by lending their specialist writing skills to create user documentation to accom-

pany the software when released. Each specialist skill-set helps to reduce the workload of the customer and improves the resulting software released. The skills specialist roles that emerged support Beck's identification of the potential roles that he outlined in XP second edition(Beck 2004).

- *Direction Setting:* Negotiator, Diplomat, Super-Secretary and Coach. Each of these roles contributes significantly to deciding what to build. The Negotiator is the lead role; responsible for working with a large group of end-users and other stakeholders to create a single-voice describing what to build to the programmers. The Diplomats are the end-users and other stakeholders that are around that negotiating table. They provide their experiences and perceptions of what is needed, and work with the Negotiator and other Diplomats to create a single-voice. The Super-Secretary supports the Negotiator by providing administrative support and also by filling in for them with the programmers when the Negotiator and Diplomats are not available. All of these roles work towards ensuring there is a strong and coordinated focus on understanding and communicating what to build, which appears to be what Beck initially hoped to achieve with the onsite-customer practice (Beck 2000). We used the analogy from DeMarco (1979) where he likened the role of an analyst to Kissinger negotiating for peace in the Middle East to help form the emerging roles that allow Beck's initial vision to be fulfilled.

Our finding that a team of people implements the on-site customer practice is useful, but we then wanted to know if this finding had any bearing on the passion and overwork issues found in our early findings. Figure 6.2 depicts our interpretation of the relationship. The three corners of the figure show the sets of roles and our interpretation of their impact on both passion and overwork, which are depicted at the centre. Not all customer teams studied implemented all of these roles, but the customer teams we saw with the majority of the roles implemented (for example, OwlCorp) tended to report significantly less overwork, and hence the impact of their passion was more pronounced. Therefore, our conclusion is that the customer team roles help to increase the passion, and decrease the overwork experienced by the customer.

Notice that each of the role groups helps in a particular way to support this change. The Collaboration Guides tend to further enhance the collaboration and sense of Whole Team, which so many customers were passionate about retaining, and had enjoyed experiencing to a much greater degree on an XP project. The Skill Specialists tend to increase the customer's certainty (or abilities) concerning a task such as writing a story, or testing the software, therefore improving their perception and passion for the task at hand. The Direction Setting roles primarily help to provide a clear focus for the core function of the customer: deciding what to build. The roles also assist to reduce the workload experienced by the customer, particularly the Skill Specialists, Technical Liaison and Super-Secretary. These roles should address the problem of overwork and reduce comments from the customer such as "we needed three of me".

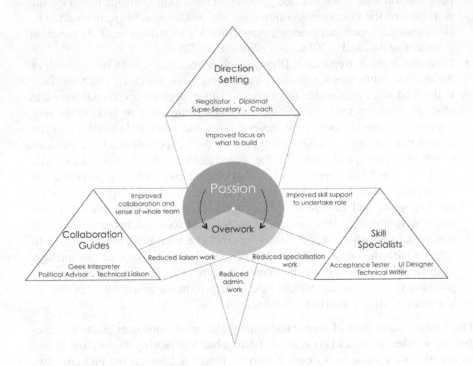

Fig. 6.2 Impact of Customer Team Roles on Being a Customer

Our final question for this research sought to uncover the practices the customers and developers were using to enhance the effectiveness of the on-site customer. Eight new practices emerged:

- Customer's Apprentice: A programmer joins the customer team for a few iterations so that they can understand the complexity of the customer teams' role as well as assisting to reduce the overload experienced by the customer.
- Programmer On-Site: The customer schedules site visits for the programmers so that they have the opportunity to understand more about the end-users.
- Programmer Holiday: The customer schedules a technically focused iteration so that the customer can step outside the iterations to reset the project direction.
- Roadshow: The customer demonstrates the software and planned stories to end-users and other stakeholders to obtain feedback on the direction of the software.
- Customer Pairing: Two customers collaborate to provide a single-voice to the programmers. The customers could be performing the same roles (e.g. two Diplomats) or different roles (e.g. a Negotiator and a UI Designer).
- Customer Boot Camp: A customer-focused training event for both customers and programmers. The training should cover the role of the customer as well as

the techniques (e.g. story writing) and practices (e.g. Programmer On-site) with opportunities for the whole team to put what they have learnt into practice in a safe and fun environment (e.g. a simulation).

- Big Picture Up-Front: A relatively short period of design amongst the business stakeholders and the customer team to set the direction of the project and create an initial release plan. The most common technique used to develop the big picture were facilitated workshops involving the stakeholders, customer team and programmer representatives.
- Re-Calibration: The customer schedules regular sessions (every few iterations) with the end-users and stakeholders to adjust commitments and resources. The adjustments will be made to take into account what both customers and programmers learn during the iterations.

Our studies were all practicing XP as described by Beck (2000), commonly referred to as XP first edition. During our data analysis it became clear that the eight new practices helped to enhance or support the three second edition (Beck 2004) practices: Real Customer Involvement, Whole Team and Energized Work. As with the roles, it also emerged that the practices changed the experience of the customer. Our interpretation of the impact of the practices to the variables of passion and overwork is depicted in Figure 6.3. The practices associated with Whole Team and Real Customer Involvement are shown as promoting the increase in passion, with the practices associated with Energized Work are shown as decreasing overwork. The practices are depicted in bold with two asterisks where they are a primary contributor and in faded text where they are a secondary contributor.

Our conclusion is that the practices help to increase the Real Customer Involvement and the feeling of an effective Whole Team. It is these points that customers and programmers identify as those that increase their passion or preference to not "do it any other way". Additionally, and just as importantly, there are a significant number of practices that directly address overwork, providing a break from the intensity of agile projects, and reducing the amount of overwork experienced by the customer.

Figure 6.4 depicts the significant change to the passion to overwork ratio when the team roles and customer practices are combined. At the centre of the figure we depict the expected increase of passion and decrease of overwork that accompanies the experience of being an on-site customer when all of the team roles and practices are utilized. The figure categorizes the roles and practices by Real Customer Involvement, Whole Team and Energized Work. For readability purposes only the primary contributors to each second edition practice are depicted, but it is important to remember that the team roles and practices create a much more interwoven set than that depicted in Figure 6.4.

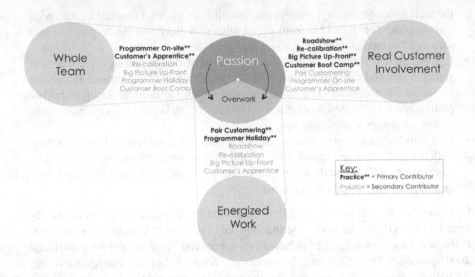

Fig. 6.3. Customer Practices Impact on Customer Passion and Overwork

During the last three years of our six-year study we have presented our research to well over 300 practitioners and academics in the form of a conference tutorial at a number of conferences, including: OOPSLA 2005, XP2006, Agile 2006, OOPSLA 2006, Agile 2007, and XP Day 2007. The feedback from this tutorial has given us an insight into the "grab" of the theory, particularly from industry practitioners wishing to improve the effectiveness of the customer and programmer interaction on their agile project. Feedback from attendees was positive, with many of them finding it helped provide them with a much deeper insight into the experience of the customer, and how to improve their own approach to implementing the agile customer role. Additionally, the first author has worked with a number of teams, both Scrum and XP teams, as an agile coach, and has used this research to help guide these teams in their (successful) agile adoption efforts.

Finally, the emphasis on workload in our interviews and observations suggests that even the roles and practices that we identify do not completely eliminate overwork, but they do reduce its impact. The roles and practices reduce overwork to a more manageable level, but perhaps customers will also need to take a break between projects.

We hope this qualitative work has raised a number of interesting questions and framed opportunities for both qualitative and quantitative future research.

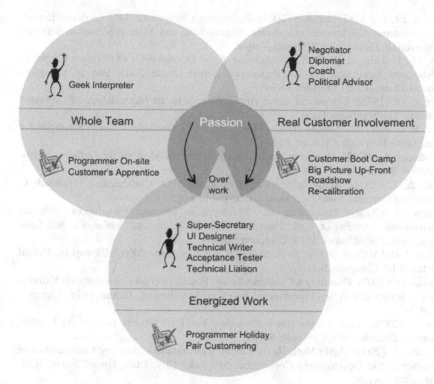

Fig. 6.4. The roles and practices impact on passion and overwork

References

Beavers, P. A. (2007). Managing a Large "Agile" Software Engineering Organization. Agile 2007, Washington D.C, United States, IEEE Computer Society.

Beck, K. (2000). eXtreme Programming Explained: Embrace Change, Addison-Wesley.

Beck, K. (2004). eXtreme Programming Explained: Embrace Change. Second Edition., Addison-Wesley.

Beck, K., M. Beedle, et al. (2001). "Manifesto for Agile Software Development." from http://agilemanifesto.org/.

Beck, K. and M. Fowler (2001). Planning Extreme Programming, Addison-Wesley.

Beyer, H., K. Holtzblatt, et al. (2004). An Agile Customer-Centered Method: Rapid Contextual Design. XP Agile Universe, Calgary, Alberta, Canada.

Broschinsky, D. and L. Baker (2008). Using Persona with XP at LANDesk Software, an Avocent Company. Agile 2008, Toronto, Canada, IEEE Computer Society.

DeMarco, T. (1979). Structured Analysis and System Specification, Prentice-Hall.

Fitzgerald, B. (2000). "Systems Development Methodologies: The Problem of Tenses." Information Technology and People 13(3): 174 - 185.

Fuqua, A. M. and J. M. Hammer (2003). Embracing Change: An XP Experience Report. Fourth Internal Conference on Extreme Programming and Agile Processes in Software Engineering, Genoa, Italy, Springer-Verlag.

Ganis, M., D. Leip, et al. (2005). Introducing Agile Development (XP) into a Corporate Webmaster Environment - An Experience Report. Agile 2005, Denver, Colorado, United States, IEEE Computer Society.

Glaser, B. G. (1978). Theoretical Sensitivity: Advances in the Methodology of Grounded Theory., The Sociology Press.

Glaser, B. G. and A. L. Strauss (1967). The Discovery of Grounded Theory: Strategies for Qualitative Research. Chicago: Aldine.

Gottesdiener, E. (2002). Requirements by Collaboration: Workshops for Defining Needs, Addison-Wesley.

Highsmith, J. (2000). Adaptive Software Development: A Collaborative Approach to Managing Complex Systems., Dorset House Publishing.

Hodgetts, P. (2004). Refactoring the Development Process: Experiences with the Incremental Adoption of Agile Processes. Agile Development Conference, Salt Lake City, Utah, United States, IEEE Computer Society.

Honious, J. and J. Clark (2006). Something to Believe In. Agile 2006, Minneapolis, United States, IEEE Computer Society.

Hussman, D. (2003). Coaching a Customer Team. Fourth Internal Conference on Extreme Programming and Agile Processes in Software Engineering, Genoa, Italy, Springer-Verlag.

Isham, M. (2008). Agile Architecture is Possible - You First Have to Believe. Agile 2008, Toronto, Canada, IEEE Computer Society.

Kahkonen, T. (2004). Agile Methods for Large Organisations - Building Communities of Practice. Agile Development Conference, Salt Lake City, Utah, United States, IEEE Computer Society.

Lowery, M. and M. Evans (2007). Scaling Product Ownership. Agile 2007, Washington D.C, United States, IEEE Computer Society.

Mackinnon, T. (2003). XP - Call in the Social Workers. Fourth International Conference on eXtreme Programming and Agile Processes in Software Engineering., Genoa, Italy, Springer-Verlag.

Manns, M. L. and L. Rising (2004). Fearless Change: Patterns for Introducing New Ideas, Addison-Wesley.

Martin, A. (2009). Exploring the Role of Customers in Extreme Programming Projects. PhD Thesis. New Zealand. http://researcharchive.vuw.ac.nz/handle/10063/877, Victoria University of Wellington. PhD: 150.

Martin, A., R. Biddle, et al. (2009). The XP Customer Team: A Grounded Theory. Agile 2009, Chicago, IEEE Computer Society.

Martin, A., R. Biddle, et al. (2009). XP Customer Practices: A Grounded Theory. Agile 2009, Chicago, IEEE Computer Society.

Merholz, P., T. Wilkens, et al. (2008). Subject To Change: Creating Great Products and Services for an Uncertain World, O'Reilly.

Miller, L. (2005). Case Study of Customer Input for a Sucessful Product. Agile 2005, Denver, Colorado, United States, IEEE Computer Society.

Nandhakumar, J. and D. E. Avison (1999). "The Fiction of Methodological Development: A Field Study of Information Systems Development." Information Technology and People 12(2): 1 - 28.

Rasmusson, J. (2006). Agile Project Initiation Techniques - The Inception Deck and Boot Camp. Agile 2006, Minneapolis, United States, IEEE Computer Society.

ResearchWare (2006). HyperResearch Qualitative Analysis Tool.

Schwaber, K. and M. Beedle (2001). Agile Software Development with Scrum, Prentice-Hall.

Takats, A. and N. Brewer (2005). Improving Communication between Customers and Developers. Agile 2005, Denver, Colorado, United States, IEEE Computer Society.

Weyrauch, K. (2006). What Are We Arguing About? A Framework for Defining Agile in our Organization. Agile 2006, Minneapolis, United States, IEEE Computer Society.

Author Biographies

Angela Martin wrote her doctoral thesis on "The Role of Customers in Extreme Programming Projects" at Victoria University of Wellington, New Zealand. This chapter is based on her thesis. She is currently a lecturer at Waikato University in Hamilton, New Zealand. She also teaches the Agile Methods course within the Software Engineering Programme at Oxford University in the United Kingdom. She has over fourteen years of industry experience, including as an agile coach, and has served a two-year term on the Agile Alliance Board of Directors.

Robert Biddle is Professor of Human-Computer Interaction at the Institute of Cognitive Science at Carleton University in Ottawa, Canada, and is also an Adjunct Professor in the School of Engineering and Computer Science at Victoria University of Wellington, New Zealand. His interests are in "the secret life of software": how software can work in rich and subtle ways with human expression and human behaviour. His active research is in computer security, agile software development, and computer games.

James Noble is Professor of Computer Science and Software Engineering at Victoria University of Wellington, New Zealand. His research centres around software design, ranging from object-orientation, aliasing, design patterns, and agile methodology, via usability and visualization, to postmodernism and the semiotics of programming.

7 Pair Programming: Issues and Challenges

Kim Man Lui, Kyle Atikus Barnes, and Keith C.C. Chan

Abstract: Pair programming, two programmers collaborating on design, coding and testing, has been a controversial focus of interest as Agile Software Development continues to grow in popularity both among academics and practitioners. As a result of the many investigations into the effectiveness of pair programming in the last decade, many have come to realize that there are many hard-to-control factors in pair programming in particular and in empirical software engineering in general. Because of these factors, the results of many pair programming experiments are not easy to replicate and the relative productivity of pair and solo programming are still not fully understood. So far, it has been concluded by previous studies that pair programming productivity can vary, but few have shown how and why this is the case. In this chapter, we discuss a number of challenging factors in the adoption of pair programming and present an approach to deal with them. We discuss how different factors may affect our experimental outcomes and improve experiment design to reveal how and why pair programming can be made productive, at least, in controlled situations.

7.1 Introduction

Pair programming involves two programmers collaborating side-by-side while working on any type of programming task. These tasks include problem solving, system design, coding, and testing. Whether set of pair programmers or an individual is better for a specific programming task depends on several factors such as the capabilities of each programmer and the unique demand of each task. As the popularity of eXtreme Programming (XP) has increased (Kent 2000), the practice of pair programming has continued to draw much attention in the software community (Williams 2000).

Over the years, empirical studies in software engineering have consistently focused on how to determine which programmers are faster or more capable through assessment methods such as Program Aptitude Tests (PAT). Contrary to past programming studies, we use pair programming to better understand how the collaboration of programmers can build higher quality software in less elapsed time while also being adaptable to unpredictable changes in requirements and the challenges of personnel turnover. Therefore, we can expect the number of programmers with

T. Dingsøyr et al. (eds.), *Agile Software Development*,
DOI 10.1007/978-3-642-12575-1_7, © Springer-Verlag Berlin Heidelberg 2010

pair programming skills to increase and the popularity of pair programming to continue its upward trend.

Many different variations of pair programming experiments have been reported but the results of these studies vary substantially (Williams 2000; Flor 1991; Nosek 1998; Nawrocki 2001; Hulkko 2005; Arisholm 2007; Ciolkowski 2002; Bellini 2005; Lui 2006; Lui 2008). This is mainly due to several consistent variables, which are difficult to control. The difficulties these variables imply extremely limit the ability of researchers to replicate previous experiments. Replication gives us the opportunity to justify pair programming and the chance to examine under what settings it could be adopted in the real world of software development. A recent meta-analysis by Hanney et al has recently been conducted, which reveals renewed perspective on many of these prior empirical studies (Hanney 2009).

Almost all empirical experiments consist of two core elements, subjects and the tasks they complete. The relationship between the elements is clear; the subjects perform the task so that we may observe the results. When we are interested in particular variables, we set up a control group and a treatment group. During the experiment one group is affected by the variables, which we are interested in, while the other group is unaffected in order to establish a baseline for comparison. After the experiment is conducted, statistics can be drawn from the collected data and used as a tool to understand our topic of interest.

When conducting a pair programming experiment, we must have two groups of subjects where one of the groups is composed of pairs. Each group is then presented with a number of tasks to complete. Human subjects can be assigned to groups using either random assignment (Nosek 1998; Nawrocki 2001; Bellini 2005) or a type of pre-test evaluation (Williams 2000; Arisholm 2007). Assigning subjects using either of these methods allows the results to be less affected by this variable. Most importantly, it establishes an initial basis for the results while maintaining consistency. After pairs have been formed, the experiment engages each set of subjects with a programming assignment. The tasks involved with these assignments may have different degrees of difficulty. When subjects are given tasks with varying degrees of difficulty; for example from simple to difficult or from difficult to simple, it must be noted that such factors may cause inconsistent results. The process of grouping people and task handling can become complicated; therefore replication becomes even more difficult.

The layout of this chapter is as follows: Section 7.2 discusses a classic Horse-Trading Problem. This exercise can be easily replicated to prove that collaborative problem solving makes a difference when comparing pairs and individuals. Section 7.3 reviews several initial studies that have impacted empirical research in pair programming. We go on to introduce other studies, which have resolved the problems of these initial studies, while introducing the new areas of research they have revealed. The section ends with a discussion on what outstanding issues should be explored in future pair programming experiments. Section 7.4 describes the process of Repeat Programming and how its experimental results can be used to better understand what challenges lie ahead in the future of pair programming studies. Section 7.5 concludes our discussion.

7.2 Horse Trading Problem: Understanding Pair vs. Solo

Before introducing these empirical studies, we will begin with a simpler experiment that provides insight and understanding while justifying the legitimacy of the collaborative problem solving processes.

7.2.1 Human Subjects and a Simple Task

A well-known problem called the Horse-Trading Problem by Maier can help us explore collaborative problem solving. We have replicated this experiment; the following summarizes the preparation and results.

The Horse-Trading Problem is a simple question as seen in Figure 7.1.

A man buys a horse for $60 and then sells it for $70. Later he buys the horse back for $80 and sells it again for $90. So, how much did the man earn?

Fig. 7.1. Classic Horse-Trading Problem

In 2006, we taught a course on eXtreme programming. One of the lectures focused on pair programming; as an exercise, the students were asked to solve a Horse-Trading Problem. The problem was part of a class activity intended to show the students the validity of collaborative problem solving. This experiment was carried out on students for learning purposes; therefore the experiment was not strictly monitored. Students were asked to solve the problem either alone or in pairs, they were also allowed to form their own groups with as many members as they preferred (see Table 7.1).

Table 7.1. Group Distribution

	Group Number					
	1	2	3	4	5	6
Members per Group	10	10	4	1	3	1

Afterward, each group was handed a piece of paper with the problem printed on it. Groups were allowed to refer back to the question as needed throughout the problem solving process, and were able to use as much time as necessary to solve the problem. Finally, each group wrote down their respective answers and submitted it to us. We immediately checked the answers and revealed the results of the exercise to the class for discussion.

Most of the groups were able to work out a solution in around three minutes. The time needed to determine a solution is not considered, as the difference in solution times may be large in terms of percentage, but overall the time is not significant as these differences are too short. More importantly, though, not all groups were able to correctly solve the problem by calculating the amount the man actually earns.

7.2.2 Results

Our observations revealed significant improvements in the average percentage of accuracy when comparing a group with only one member to a group with more than three members. Groups 1 and 2 offer a strong statistical basis as evidence and such results are consistent with sociological research findings (Maier 1969) (see Figure 7.2). However, when the group size consists of five or more, the correction percentage dropped slightly. This result could be related to ergonomics as the classroom seats arranged in fixed rows. A group of two may be able to communicate side-by-side effectively, but for groups larger than three a round table is needed to facilitate communication and collaboration.

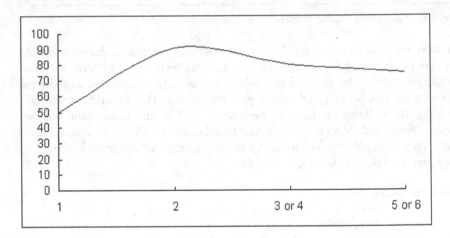

Fig. 7.2. Collaborative Problem Solving Results

7.2.3 Discussion

Although the Horse-Trading Problem is simple, it brings to light several benefits. First, the Horse-Trading Problem experiment is easily replicated. This allows other researchers, like us, to quickly verify the results by repeating the experiment. Using such methods can steadily advance our knowledge, thus demonstrating that the previous works of others provides a strong foundation for the exploration of potential improvements. Finally, any such experiment should quickly resolve any debate concerning the validity of previous findings.

Second, the experiment stimulates us to consider an interesting quandary. Why is the Horse-Trading Problem easy to replicate, but a specific pair programming experiment not? Pair programming is simple in principle, but to create such an experiment is challenging. In order to complete the Horse-Trading Problem, one only needs an elementary education in basic reading and arithmetic; however, programming requires a unique skill set and experience which must be developed over time. A pair programming experiments requires that human subjects be classified according to their level of ability. A subject's skills and experience in pair programming is a significant factor when considering the results of any such experiment. Additionally, the task to be completed in the Horse-Trading Problem is solid and limited to one possible answer. We know from programming that any programming assignment has unlimited solutions. If programming tasks in pair programming experiments could be limited to one specific activity, for example writing a program to compute the average of a set of numbers, then pair programming experiments by others could more easily be replicated. Therefore, when we consider the Horse-Trading Problem, we realize the task is specific. Solving the task requires no particular skill set and hence we need not be concerned with how the subjects pair. This is the reason why the Horse-Trading Problem is easy to replicate. However, how the subjects pair up and the methodologies used are significant considerations in any pair programming experiment.

The Horse-Trading Problem is not related to programming, but this experiment gives us insight and goals for empirical studies in pair programming. We should bear in mind that pair programming experiments should be designed so that they can be easily replicated and validated, even though such objectives may not be easily achieved in reality.

The Horse-Trading Problem is beneficial to people who are learning pair programming or pair programming coaches that are looking for a significant result, which clearly demonstrates the value of collaborative problem solving.

7.3 Pair Programming Studies

This section investigates five major pair programming experiments. Although three of these experiments were executed over a decade ago, it does not undermine their value. Our key interest is to understand the handling of variables in each experiment, so that by the end of our discussion we can develop a list of variables, which will have the strongest affect on the results of future studies.

Before discussing these empirical experiments, we must point out that limited sample sizes may seem to be a critical factor. However, despite the sample size, we still may find that the statistics obtained are significant. Nevertheless, some may argue that the sample size may cause the results to be misleading. According to Miller (Miller 1986), the results of an experiment can be more informative with a small number of subjects rather than having a large set of statistical data from a larger group of subjects.

The key focus of our discussion is to determine the effect of pair programming combinations and the difficulty of the tasks to be completed.

7.3.1 Relative Effort Afforded By Pairs: REAP

There are two important methods that can be used to measure productivity achieved over a period of time when undergoing a pair programming experiment. We can consider the elapsed time to complete a task or the total effort divided by the time required for the programmers to complete the task. Lui and Chan (Lui 2006) developed a single measurement to include both of these methods. This measurement is known as Relative Effort Afforded by Pairs (REAP). In order to better understand the results of previous pair programming studies, each of their results have been converted into REAP equivalents.

$$REAP = \frac{(finish\_time\_of\_pair) \times 2 - (finish\_time\_of\_individual)}{finish\_time\_of\_individual} \times 100\%$$

All together there are five possible results when computing REAP. Each result gives us a quantitative value to measure both productivity and time in a pair programming session.

(i) REAP *less than* 0: The total time / effort needed for pair programmers is less than the time needed for an individual programmer. Using pair programmers is less costly than individual programmers; therefore pair programming is actually more efficient than a single programmer.

(ii) REAP *approximately* 0: Pair programming halves the total time / effort required for an individual programmer. Opportunities and product life cycles have become much shorter over the past few years. In order to take advantage of premium pricing and the advantages of early movement in a market, such situations make it worthwhile for companies to focus more on short-term development costs (Kalantone 2000).

(iii) REAP *greater than* 0 but *less than* 100: Pair programmers require more total man-hours / effort, but the pair is still faster than an individual programmer. As the elapsed time for pairs is less than individual programmers, such situations can be useful when time-to-market is a critical issue (Williams 2000; Nosek 1998). Division and reallocation of programming tasks involves planning and a significant amount of time. Pair programming allows for individual programmers to group their tasks and work in parallel. Overall, it provides an alternative method to speed up the development process.

(iv) REAP *approximately* 100: Programmers engaged in pair programming need about the same amount of time as an individual programmer. Pair programming, therefore, doubles the total-man hours / effort in comparison to individual programming.

(v) REAP *greater than* 100: Pair programmers need more time / effort than an individual programmer.

7.3.2 Nosek

In 1998, Nosek reported the first quantitative findings involving pair programming. His empirical experiment involved fifteen full-time system programmers. Five sets of pair programmers and five individual programmers were asked to write a UNIX script that performed a database consistency check (DBCC) on a Sybase database.

Throughout the course of the experiment, the subjects wrote a program that would start the consistency check, review the database log for errors, and finally send a warning e-mail if any errors were detected. After executing the DBCC command, the status of the database would be returned in a log file.

Nosek's results in terms of REAP are shown in Table 7.2. In order to determine the quality of the software, two independent graders evaluated the readability and functionality of each pair's or individual's code. Readability was assigned a score between 0 and 2: 0 for an unreadable solution, 2 for a readable solution, and 1 for those cases in between. Functionality was assigned a score between 0 and 6. Those solutions with a score of 0 did not achieve the goal at all, while those receiving a score of 6 achieved the goal in its entirety. Although the two graders examined the code of all the subjects with an inter-grader reliability of 90%, it must be noted that human judgment was involved in verifying the quality of each piece of software.

Nosek's experiment forms five sets of pair programmers, but how these pairs were made was not taken into consideration. As for the task, the process itself should be straightforward, especially for professional system programmers. In this case, we can suspect that the only area where the system programmers lacked experience was the use of DBCC commands. Nevertheless, it is impossible for us to understand how difficult this task was for the subjects. In short, the initial study reveals positive results, which should lead us to explore further issues in pair programming. Specifically, two variables need further consideration – the formation of pairs and the level of task difficulty.

7.3.3 Williams

In 2000, Williams reported on a pair programming experiment involving forty-one junior and senior university students. Each of the students was randomly assigned to work either as a pair programmer (total 14 pairs) or a single programmer (total 13 singles). The student subjects were taught how to use Active Server Page (ASP), and then asked to write web scripts with dynamic content. The project involved querying and updating a Microsoft Access Database. Williams' students had little to no experience with ASP, however, they all had approximately three years of programming experience with C++. The application developed was similar to typical e-commerce web site solutions (Williams 2000).

Although students were assigned to be pair programmers randomly, Williams argued that the distribution of many different spreads is better than randomization when working with pairs in a pair programming experiment. Therefore, pairs were arranged according to their GPAs. The spread of distribution included high-high, high-average, high-low, average-average, average-low, and low-low pair groupings. The REAP was approximately 15% on average.

All the students, both pairs and singles, completed four assignments over a six-week period. The students recorded their time spent on the project using a web-based tool. It should be noted that the experiment was not monitored by any on site research assistant, nor were the pairs monitored to confirm how closely they practiced pair programming. In order to test each assignment, a teaching assistant executed automated testing to analyze the program's quality. In general, pair programmers passed more automated post-development test cases compared to single programmers.

After the first assignment, REAP was 60%. However, after the initial adjustment period, the total hours the pairs needed to complete the second and third assignments decreased substantially. REAP was then 15% on average (Williams 2000). Due to data entry problems, the completion times for the fourth assignment were not accurate. Thus, the results and time performance of the fourth assignment were not reported.

In terms of quality, pairs passed the test cases within the following range: 86.4-94.4%, whereas singles only passed the test cases 70.4-78.1% of the time (see Table 7.2).

Williams' experiment is extensive and has taken into consideration several variables that were not considered in Nosek's experiment. The pairing situation has been done randomly to determine singles and pairs, and further pretesting (GPA) was used to arrange pair formations.

Strictly speaking, one may argue that the experiment took place in too loosely of a controlled environment. As the students were not monitored, we cannot be sure that some of the students did not work on the project while at home. Another factor is the four assignments and their order of completion. We can assume that each task was given in order (1, 2, 3, 4), but we must consider the order of the tasks and their relative level of difficulty. Williams' past work has also observed the effects of pair learning and its significance. Therefore, one should not ignore the effects concerning the order of tasks and their difficulties.

Another issue is re-submission, up until all test cases have passed. Williams' experiment does not allow for the student to re-submit their work. Therefore, how each test case was written to measure software quality would be a significant factor. We will come back to re-submission to facilitate quality measurement in pair programming experiments in Section 7.3.4.

Finally, the combination of novice-novice programmers vs. expert-expert programmers has not been considered as all the students represented only novice programmers.

In summary, Williams resolved many of the problems introduced by Nosek's experiment. Furthermore, her work opened us up to explore the above mentioned problems in pair programming experiments. Such factors must be given clear consideration in future experiments. Topics such as the combination of tasks, the effects of novice-novice pairs vs. expert-expert pairs, and re-submission to insure basic level of software quality are good areas for further exploration.

7.3.4 Nawrocki and Wojciechowski

In 2001, Nawrocki and Wojciechowski conducted an experiment on twenty-one fourth-year university students. The students were divided into three groups and asked to complete an assignment using one of three different methodologies. Methodology 1: five pairs using XP (referred to as pair XP); Methodology 2: five singles using XP but without pair programming (referred to as single XP); and Methodology 3: six singles using Personal Software Process (PSP). Nawrocki was primarily interested in two specific comparisons involving the three methodologies: single XP vs. PSP and single XP vs. pair XP. However, in this chapter, we are only interested in the comparison of pairs and singles using the same methodology. Therefore, we have selected single XP vs. pair XP for our review.

All of the subjects had more than two years of formal study in C and C++ programming. They were asked to write four programs, which would find the mean and standard deviation of numerical data samples. Additionally, the program would determine the linear regression parameters, count the number of lines output in the program, and count the total lines of code (LOC) used to create the program.

The results of the experiment revealed that singles and pairs needed around the same amount of time to complete the first three assignments. Each assignment needed 2.4, 1.3, and 2.4 hours respectively (Nawrocki 2001). Therefore, REAP is equal to 100%. During the fourth assignment, pairs needed 3.5 hours and singles needed 4.3 hours, which results in REAP equal to 63%. Although the improvement seems to support pair programming, Nawrocki remarked that such improvement was due only to the fact that the single programmers misunderstood the program requirements. Additionally, the number of re-submissions was also counted, as groups were required to re-submit their work until their program had no errors and passed acceptance testing.

The experiments of Nawrocki and Williams have similarities but several design factors differ. Group pairs have been formed using different methods and the degree of difficulty has been altered. The most interesting point is that Nawrocki's results do not support pair programming, whereas Williams' results do. It should be noted, however, that the subjects are monitored throughout the entire process in Nawrocki's experiment, thus giving the data a higher probability of accuracy.

Another key factor is required re-submission. The need for re-submission greatly depends on how the test cases are written. We cannot say that all test cases are fairly used to measure the quality of a program, as a test cannot measure the absence of faults. For example, Program A is more robust but unfortunately neglects a few points addressed by the test cases, while Program B is less robust but just happens to better cover the test cases. Therefore, any successful program in an experiment depends on test cases for both functionality and exception handling. However, it should be noted that we should not regard this as a major factor as we believe the experimenter should design quality test cases while planning the experiment.

As long as a pair may re-submit, even if the program fails the first test case, the program can still be fully reviewed in order to determine its true quality.

7.3.5 Arisholm et al

In 2007, Arisholm et al conducted a pair programming experiment involving 295 subjects who were hired from 29 software companies in Norway, Sweden, and the UK. The subjects were grouped by their organization as well as their performance based upon a pre-test. The pre-test involved a maintenance task, which was simpler, but similar to the actual experimental task (Arisholm 2007). The experimental task was a change task focusing on seven class and 354 lines of code. Pairs were grouped according to their level of expertise (junior-junior, intermediate-intermediate, and senior-senior). Arisholm's experiment was large scaled, well planned, and successfully implemented. The results in terms of REAP are show in Table 7.2.

Arisholm et al showed that pairs did not increase correctness or significantly reduce the total elapsed time. An important factor in this experiment was that the subjects were limited to one type of task: a change task. This is substantially different from experiments where subjects are asked to write programs from scratch (Williams 2000; Nosek 1998; Nawrocki 2001; Hulkko 2005; Lui 2006). Maintenance tasks, however, are advantageous as they can easily be measured in a more objective way. For example, subjects can attempt to make a minimum number of changes to complete the task, and then the number of lines modified and added can be counted. When the experimental task is a development task, each group of subjects has the opportunity to create a different design or implementation of the solution. Evaluation of design and implementation in comparison with other subjects is difficult and the process can be quite subjective. Therefore, the task is usually restricted to specific requirements to cover these issues and/or the final product must pass several pre-defined test cases.

The major difference between Arisholm and previous experiments (Williams 2000; Nosek 1998; Nawrocki 2001) is that the task involves a maintenance task rather than a development task. Nevertheless, we still cannot easily conclude that pair programming, as it has been originally addressed, is not only concerned with writing code but also with the program's greater design. In Arisholm's experiment, programmers need to understand the design before they can begin the maintenance task; therefore they may run the original program several times to determine what should be changed as it is impossible to test unwritten software. More importantly, Arisholm's experiment is more realistic for the software industry as many programmers are responsible for maintaining code rather than writing original code (Lui 2008).

Over the duration of Arisholm's experiment, many different Java development tools were used (i.e. JBuilder, Eclipse, IntelliJ, NetBeans, Emacs, and Javac). The decision to use certain tools was left up to the discretion of the subjects. The subjects' familiarity with the tool and the tool's ability to affect productivity or facilitate Java program maintenance was not measured. For example, Eclipse is a popular Integrated Development Environment (IDE) for Java while Emacs is multi-OS text editor. This factor increases the complexity of the pair programming experiment, as the use of a development tool or tools is an uncontrolled variable.

7.3.6 Lui, Chan, and Nosek

An individual's performance on a programming aptitude test (PATs) has proven to be a strong indicator of their future programming performance (Bateman 1973; Denelsky 1974; Tukiainen 2002) therefore many organizations have adopted such tests to pre-screen potential programming candidates before their interviews.

Lui, Chan, and Nosek conducted two controlled experiments with full-time professional programmers. The subjects worked on increasingly complex programming aptitude tasks related to problem solving and algorithmic design. Each experiment revealed that pairs significantly outperformed individuals, thus providing solid evidence for the value of pairs in program design-related tasks.

These experiments brought up a number of questions: Is pair programming better for design tasks rather than implementation tasks, or vice-versa? Or is pair programming better for both? Design and implementation are two separate processes when considering traditional software development, but the nature of pair programming combines both design and implementation. Therefore, if pair programming is good for design, then implementing that design is not only easy, it is also a natural process. This is an important idea for the future exploration of pair programming.

Table 7.2. Summary of Pair Programming Experiments

	Nosek	Williams	Nawrocki and Wjciechowski	Arisholm, et al.	Lui, Chan, and Nosek
Subjects	Full-time pro-grammers	University stu-dents	University stu-dents	Full-time pro-grammers	Full-time pro-grammers
Sample Size	15	41	21	295	15
Same Organization	Yes	Yes	Yes	No	No
Day Split	No	Yes	No	No	No
Pre-Test	No	Yes	Yes	Yes	No
Subjects already know algo-rithms needed to solve prob-lems before the experiment	No	No	Yes	Not Examined	No
Tasks	Simple Development Task	Moderate Development Task	Simple Development Task	Moderate Maintenance Task	Programming Aptitude Test (PAT)
Quality assessment	Rated by two independent graders	Post-development test cases	Pass all pre-defined test cases	Correctness analysis by two independent senior consult-ants	Pass all PAT questions
REAP (%)	41.7	15	100	84	-1.8 ~ 21
General Conclusions	PP is productive	PP is productive	PP is not productive	PP is not productive	PP is productive

Lui and Chan have proposed an approach to better understand pair programming known as Repeat Programming. This information is not shown in Table 7.2 as this experiment will be discussed in Section 7.4.

7.3.7 Outstanding Issues

There are many other studies that consider grouping and tasks in several different contexts. No matter the context, we must focus on subjects and tasks. Therefore, the fundamental question to answer is: *How should we group the subjects and set their respective tasks?* Once we have clearly answered this question, we will have a solid foundation on which to move forward. Let us consider the following four major factors:

Pairing of Programmers: The grouping of subjects into pairs and individuals is a non-trivial matter; however, how this is handled can greatly affect the outcome of the experiment. As discussed above, researchers have already recognized this fact. Therefore, they have grouped subjects according to their organization or class, and then allowed them to freely select their partners (Ciolkowski 2002). Yet other researchers have used randomization to ensure a thorough distribution of programmer characteristics between groups of pair programmers and individuals (Nosek 1998; Nawrocki 2001; Bellini 2005). It should be noted that we are looking for general all purpose cases in empirical studies on pair programming. The determined general cases will be the best alternative in many, but clearly not all, situations. We are not seeking universal applicability; as to do so only undermines human nature and the essence of the software engineering industry.

Programming Tasks: Designing appropriate programming tasks can be more challenging than the pairing of programmers. For example, in experiments that evaluate the performance of pairs against individuals in non-programming related tasks, it is easier to control variables and reproduce the original experimental results (Forsyth 1999). In pair programming experiments, tasks are more complicated and entail the programmers to understand requirements, software design, coding, testing, and debugging. Still such tasks must focus either on Design Difficulty or Implementation Difficulty, and the results of any task must be measurable. Pair programming makes this difficult to achieve, as programming tasks can never be as specific as the horse-trading problem. The complexity of programming tasks is not the issue, rather there is not one single task that can be used in pair programming, which can objectively measure pair performance as well as the task's relative complexity. Such factors are representative of the industry and its constant challenges.

Combination of Programming Tasks: Measuring the degree of difficulty for one programmer is already difficult. However, measuring the degree of difficulty for a group of subjects with varied skills and experience is even more challenging. Therefore, we must consider how to develop different programming assignments that can be distributed amongst a group of subjects that will lead to consistent results. Consider three tasks that are completed in succession (A -> B -> C), which steadily become more difficult. Now consider the same three tasks completed in reverse (C -> B -> A) where the tasks only become much easier. The combination of these tasks will inevitably have a large effect on the overall factor of pair learning.

Programming Hidden Variables between Programming Tasks: When discussing pair programming tasks we must determine a fair basis for comparison. Simply using the control group (i.e. individual programmers) as the baseline for comparison could be problematic and should be dealt with carefully. A more appropriate baseline includes the combination of both subjects and their tasks. In this case, all of the above-mentioned factors (i.e. 1 – 3) should be used to create the baseline of the experiment; otherwise pair programming experiments cannot be accurately measured.

If a set of pair programmers is late in completing task A, then we can assume that they will be late for task B. This of course does not makes much sense, the same as a set of pair programmers that are fast in completing task A must then be fast for task B. In order to justify such assumptions, we must clarify the correlation, if any, between tasks A and B. The key factor is the similarity of the tasks. Once the relationship between tasks A and B is established, this relationship then becomes the baseline.

In most cases there are distinct differences that exist or take place between tasks. These differences could involve a change of programming languages, the introduction of specialized domain information, or simply the fact that the set of pair programmers had a cup of coffee before taking on the next task. Each difference is a type of hidden variable, which must be clearly considered and in all possible cases controlled throughout the pair programming study. If such hidden variables are ignored, then the baseline can never be fixed.

Pair programming with partner rotation: Recent innovations in pair programming methodology consider many programmers pairing together and then rotating partners based upon a fixed constraint (i.e. time interval or completion of a number of classes). In such situations, the effect of pair jelling (Williams 2000) and the time needed to jell must not be discounted. Nevertheless, this issue creates yet another unique situation needing further study and investigation. However, before the effects of partner rotation can be fully considered, the four issues above must be understood. Thus, those issues are the focus of this chapter.

7.4 Repeat Programming

In 2005, we conducted an experiment known as "repeat programming." In this experiment subjects were asked to write the same program several times. The experiment was not meant to simulate a real world situation; therefore it was a controlled lab experiment. In reality, a programmer will never rewrite a program exactly the same way. Actually, programmers actively solve problems of similar nature using design patterns they have developed from their own experiences. As repeat programming does not simulate an industrial environment, its purpose is to create a controlled environment to assess the productivity of pair programming versus solo programming.

Repeat programming can be considered as a method for measuring programmer experience and how this experience is affected throughout the process of repeat programming. It should be noted, however, that the experience of solving a particular problem many times should not be misconstrued with "experienced programmers" (i.e. years of experience, skills, etc.).

7.4.1 Experiment

The above experiment was conducted in 2004 and used part-time masters students with full-time programming jobs as subjects. All together there were thirty-nine subjects who were taking the course, "Agile Software Development and eXtreme Programming", as a requirement for their double Masters Degree jointly organized by the Hong Kong Polytechnic University (Hong Kong) and The Graduate School of Chinese Academy of Science (Beijing).

The students were divided into groups of threes. Subjects were placed with other programmers with "nearly-identical" abilities. This way any disparities in programming ability would be minimized. In order to determine each programmer's ability, a pre-assessment test was taken by each programmer. The test consisted of fifty multiple-choice questions, which were taken from Munzert's (1994) computer aptitude test.

The experiment incorporated three major phases:

1) Select capable and "nearly-identical" subjects to group (pre-assessment).
2) Familiarize subjects with the practice of Pair Programming.
3) Have subjects repeatedly write the same program.

As none of the subjects had any formal experience with pair programming, it was mandatory for groups to practice pair programming for at least four hours before being able to work separately. As a warm-up exercise, each group was asked to write *Tower of Hanoi*, a simple puzzle game. This pre-experiment was not recorded; its only intention was to ease the subjects into a pair-programming environment. Each group determined their own organization of pair and single programming amongst the three members. Thus, this minimized the impact on those group members who may have simply preferred solo programming or had any bias against pair programming. Furthermore, to minimize the possibility of conflict amongst group members, we suggested that in situations of disagreement, the final decision was to be made by the group member currently controlling the keyboard/mouse. All of the subjects fully understood that internal conflict and self-assertion would only reduce productivity and run counter to the objective of the experiment.

The task asked the subjects to write a FIFO warehouse application with the following requirements: in/out operations, reserved stock, bin management, and good return using SQL Server and ASP (or JSP if subjects were not as familiar with ASP). As the subjects were already full-time programmers, they were all familiar with popular programming languages and scripts like SQL and ASP (or JSP). The requirements of the tasks were determined during our initial study; however, we simplified the requirements so that the program could be completed in a shorter amount of time. More specifically, the program was to be completed over a weekend (approx. two days) as all the subjects had full-time jobs. The duration of the experiment was eight weeks, thus groups selectively chose four weekends over the eight-week period to complete the program repeatedly during four separate sessions. During each session the subjects were responsible for keeping their own total elapsed time.

Fifty test cases were written and used to assess the quality of each group's software. Many test cases were used in order to assess each program's quality objectively, rather than subjectively using human judgment. Each group's software had to pass all fifty test cases before the program was considered to be satisfactory. The test cases involved specific application requirements as well as exception handling. Such measurements were appropriate for two major reasons. First, quality could be objectively measured rather than by relying on human subjectivity. Secondly, from a client's perspective, users would be more satisfied with software products that have undergone extensive testing and would regard them as higher quality. Traditionally, developers and customers tend to see software quality differently.

7.4.2 Result

After the first round of programming, the individuals completed the program in 635 minutes on average. Predictably, after the second round they accomplished the task much faster. Clearly, they were able to shorten their learning curves, especially in the areas of design and algorithm formation. Upon inspection of each version of their work, we found that design for the most part remained the same; however, syntax, naming standards, and ordering of statements were different in each version.

7.4.3 Discussion

The implementation of repeat programming provides substantial feedback to the design of the software as there is no up-front design phase. Therefore, in our experiment, the steepness of the slope reveals a stronger influence on design throughout the coding process, rather than coding solely for implementation. These results have a direct implication on the impact of pair design due to the difference in steepness between the two slopes. Therefore, we can conclude that pair programming is better for design; otherwise if there was no effect on design, then the steepness of slopes for pair and solo should be more similar. During the first and second iterations the focus for both pairs and solos is the design, whereas during the third and fourth iterations the focus is coding. Now, let us once again consider the four major factors and how they relate to repeat programming:

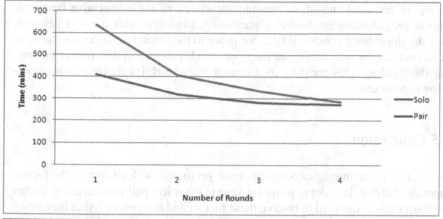

	1st Round	2nd Round	3rd Round	4th Round
Solo (mins)	635	407	334	285
Pairs (mins)	410	320	281	272
REAP	29%	57%	69%	91%

Fig. 7.3. Summary of Repeat Programming Results

Pairing of Programmers: As described earlier, our goal in a pair programming experiment is to ensure at least one of two issues. Programmer ability amongst subjects must be either well distributed between all groups or each subject's ability must be matched to their respective group members. Repeat programming groups programmers with similar abilities as determined by the pre-assessment test. Thus we avoid any issues that may arise due to ambiguous pairing and no extremes will be found in any pair combination.

Programming Tasks: In repeat programming we can focus less on the task and more on the interaction of pairs as the task never changes throughout the experiment. Programmers may be considered as novices with the program during the first iteration, but by the end of the fourth iteration, they all become experts.

Combination of Programming Tasks: In repeat programming, the level of task difficulty steadily becomes easier as the subjects continually repeat their design. Therefore in the experiment the affects of pair programming are minimized as the order of tasks does not matter.

Programming Hidden Variables between Programming Tasks: In repeat programming, a programmer's capability is not as important as the fact that the program is repeated numerous times, which enables the programmer to inactively learn the program while focusing on collaboration. Thus, as we are able to control the hidden variables we can easily see the differences between pairs and solos without depending on the expertise of the programmers. Most importantly, we must establish a fair baseline. Initially we use pair vs. solo as a baseline; this is good, but not solid enough to measure the effects of the consecutive iterations. Repeat programming establishes a standardized baseline after the first iteration, thus the slope drops considerably as we move to the second iteration. As the iterations continue we can clearly see the slope steadily decrease, thus further enhancing the baseline. This provides us a clearer framework for future pair programming experiments.

7.5 Conclusion

So far, pair programming experiments have yet to deal with all four of the factors mentioned above. In order to move forward in empirical pair programming studies we must make it our goal to resolve these factors and the greater issues they introduce. The Horse-Trading Problem we first introduced can be used as a contrast with collaborative programming situations, but the Horse-Trading Problem does not deal with all the factors that emerge during pair programming experiments. Repeat programming, on the other hand, considers the four main factors and gives us better insight on how we can adjust our baseline for future contributions in empirical pair programming experiments.

Repeat programming gives us insight to explore these four factors; unfortunately though, it will be better to design an experiment that mimics a real world situation while taking all four factors into consideration. Pair programmers, coaches, and researchers alike will be confident of our understanding in order to explore more issues, including extensions of pair programming experiments such as Side-by-Side Programming and Software Process Fusion.

Finally, we are not saying that pair programming and its applicability should limit its focus only to these four factors. However, we should pay close attention to these four factors because of their potential to affect our experimental results. Empirical studies such as Arisholm et al, which consider new approaches such as maintenance tasks in pair programming, and meta-analytical studies like those of Hanney et al are key to understanding the effects of these four major factors (Arisholm 2007; Hanney 2009).

References

Adair, G. (1984). "The Hawthorne effect: A reconsideration of the methodological artifact" *Journal of Appl. Psychology* vol 69, no 2, 334-345.

Arisholm, E., Gallis, H., Dybå, T. and Sjøberg, D.I.K. (2007). "Evaluating pair programming with respect to system complexity and programmer expertise," *IEEE, Transactions on Software Engineering*, vol. 33, no. 2, pp. 65-86.

Bateman, C.R. (1973). "Predicting performance in a basic computer course," *Proceedings of the Fifth Annual Meeting of the Amer. Inst. for Decision Sciences*, Boston, Mass.

Bellini, E., G. Canfora, F. Garcia, M. Piattini, C.A. Visaggio (2005). "Pair designing as a practice for enforcing and diffusing design knowledge",Journal of Software Maintenance and Evolution: Research and Practice, Volume 17,Issue 6, pp 401 - 423.

Calantone, R.J. and Di Benedetto, C.A. (2000). "Performance and time to market: accelerating cycle time with overlapping stages," *IEEE Transactions on Engineering Management*, vol 47, no 2, pp 232-244.

Ciolkowski, M. and Schlemmer M. (2002). "Experiences with a case study on pair programming," *Proceedings of the Workshop on Empirical Studies in Software Engineering*, Rovaniemi, Finland.

Curtis, B. (1986). "By the way, did anyone study any real programmers?" In E. Soloway and S. Iyengar (eds), *Empirical Studies of Programmers*, First Workshop, Ablex Publishing Corporation, Norwood, NJ, pp 256-262.

Denelsky, G.Y., and McKee, M.G. (1974). "Prediction of computer programmer training and job performance using the AABP test," *Personal Psychology*, vol 27, no 1, pp. 129-137.

Flor, N. and Hutchins, E. (1991). "Analyzing distributed cognition in software teams: a case study of team programming during perfective software maintenance," *Proceedings of Empirical Studies of Programmers: Fourth Workshop*, Norwood, NJ: Ablex.

Forsyth, D. R. (1999). *Group dynamics (3rd ed)*, Belmont, Calif.: Brooks/Cole,.

Garbus, J.R. Solomon D.S. and Tretter, B. (1995). *SYBASE DBA survival guide*, Indianapolis, Ind.: Sams Pub.

Hanney, Jo E., Dybå, Tore, Arisholm, Erik, Sjøberg, Dag I.K.. (2009). "The effectiveness of pair programming: A meta-analysis." *Information and Software Technology*, vol 51, pp 1110-1122.

Hulkko and Abrahamsson, P. (2005). "A multiple case study on the impact of pair programming on product quality," *Proceedings of the 27th International Conference on Software Engineering*, St. Louis, MO, USA, pp 495-504.

Hunt, Andrew and Thomas, David. (1999). "The Pragmatic Programmer: From Journeyman to Master." October. The Pragmatic Bookshelf.

Kent, B. (2000). *Extreme Programming Explained: Embrace Change*, Reading, Mass: Addison-Wesley.

Lorenzen, T. and Chang, H.L. (2006). "MasterMind: a predictor of computer programming aptitude," *ACM SIGCSE Bulletin*, vol 38, no 2, pp 69 – 71.

Lui, K.M. and Chan, K.C.C. (2006). "Pair programming productivity: novice-novice vs. expert-expert," *International Journal of Human Computer Studies*, vol 64, pp. 915-925.

Lui, K.M., Chan, K.C.C. (2008). "Software process fusion by combining pair and solo programming," *IET Software*, vol 2, no 4, pp 379-390.

Lui, K.M., Chan, K.C.C., Nosek, J. (2008). "The effect of pairs in program design tasks," *IEEE Transactions on Software Engineering*, vol 34, no 2, pp 197-211

Maier, Norman R.; Burke, Ronald J. (1967). "Response Availability as a Factor in the Problem-Solving Performance of Males and Females." Journal of Personality and Social Psychology. Vol. 5(3), Mar, 304-310.

Microsoft (2003). *MCAD/MCSE/MCDBA Self-Paced Training Kit: Microsoft SQL Server 2000 Database Design and Implementation, Exam 70-229*, (2nd Edition), Microsoft Corporation.

Miller, R.G. (1986). *Beyond ANOVA, Basics of Applied Statistics*, New York: John Wiley & Sons.

Müller, M.M. (2006). "A preliminary study on the impact of a pair design phase on pair programming and individual programming," *Information and Software Technology*, vol 48, no. 5, pp 335-344.

Munzert, A. (1994). "Part IV: Computer I.Q.– Program Procedure," *Test Your IQ, third Edition*, Random House, pp.112-117.

Nawrocki, J. and Wojciechowski, A. (2001). "Experimental evaluation of pair programming," *Proceedings of the 12th European Software Control and Metrics Conference*, London, April, pp 269–276.

Nosek, J. (1998). "The case for collaborative programming," *Communication of ACM*, vol 41, no 3, pp 105-108.

Tukiainen, M. and Mönkkönen, E. (2002). "Programming aptitude testing as a prediction of learning to program," *Proceedings 14th Workshop of the Psychology of Programming Interest Group*, Brunel University, pp 45-57.

Williams, L. and Kessler, R.R. (2003). *Pair programming illuminated*, Boston, Mass.: Addison-Wesley.

Williams, L., Kessler, R.R., Cunningham, W. and Jeffries, R. (2000). "Strengthening the case for pair-programming," *IEEE Software*, vol 17, no 4, pp 19-25.

Wohlin, C., Runeson, P., Höst, M., Ohlsson, M.C., Regnell, B., Wesslén, A. (2000)."Experimentation in software engineering - An Introduction," Springer.

Author Biographies

Kim Man Lui has worked in a number of IT positions in the commercial sector from system engineer, analyst programmer, system analyst, project leader and IT manager. Dr. Lui was a certified Sybase Database Administrator in 1996, a certified Oracle Database Administrator in 1999 and a SUN certified Java Programmer in 2002. Dr. Lui is an author of three books: two books written in Chinese on CMM and Agile Software Development in Beijing SPI and *Software Development Rhythms*, Wiley, 2008. The book is being translated in Chinese and is scheduled to be published by Publishing House of Electronics Industry.

Kyle Atikus Barnes is a professional software engineer working in both the United States and Asia. Mr. Barnes completed his Bachelor of Arts Degree in Business Administration and International Studies from Queens University of Charlotte, North Carolina (2005), and recently graduated with distinction from Hong Kong Polytechnic University (2010) with a Master of Science Degree in Information Technology focusing on Agile Software Development. Mr. Barnes has worked in numerous industries including Travel, Logistics, and Education. Currently, Mr. Barnes works in implementing agile practices and methodology as Owner / Manager of Seattle Software Solutions, LLP.

Prof. Keith Chan received a B.Math. (Hons.) degree in Computer Science and Statistics in 1984 and a M.A.Sc. and Ph.D. degree in Systems Design Engineering from the University of Waterloo, Ontario, Canada in 1985 and 1989 respectively. He had worked as a senior analyst at the IBM Canada Laboratory, Toronto, Canada and as an Associate Professor at the Department of Electrical and Computer Engineering at Ryerson University, Toronto, Ontario, Canada. He joined the Hong Kong Polytechnic University (PolyU) in 1994 and is currently a Professor and Head of the Department of Computing. He is a Guest Professor of the Graduate School, the Chinese Academy of Sciences (CAS), Beijing and is also the Co-Director of the CAS-PolyU Joint Software Engineering Laboratory. Prof. Chan's research interests are in software engineering and data mining. Prof. Chan is active in consultancy and has served as consultant to government agencies as well as large and small to medium enterprises in Hong Kong, China, Singapore, Malaysia and Canada.

8 Architected Agile Solutions for Software-Reliant Systems

Barry Boehm, Jo Ann Lane, Supannika Koolmanojwong, Richard Turner

Abstract: Systems are becoming increasingly reliant on software due to needs for rapid fielding of "70% capabilities," interoperability, net-centricity, and rapid adaptation to change. The latter need has led to increased interest in agile methods of software development, in which teams rely on shared tacit interpersonal knowledge rather than explicit documented knowledge. However, such systems often need to be scaled up to higher level of performance and assurance, requiring stronger architectural support. Several organizations have recently transformed themselves by developing successful combinations of agility and architecture that can scale to projects of up to 100 personnel. This chapter identifies a set of key principles for such architected agile solutions for software-reliant systems, provides guidance for how much architecting is enough, and illustrates the key principles with several case studies.

8.1 Introduction

Systems are becoming increasingly reliant on software due to needs for rapid fielding of "70% capabilities," interoperability, net-centricity, and rapid adaptation to change. This trend is shown in Figure 8.1, illustrating the percentage of aircraft functionality that relies on software versus time, and the resulting system challenges as software was used to adapt to change (Van Tilborg, 2006).

In (Boehm and Turner 2004), we identified two fundamental approaches to developing software systems: agile and plan-driven. Given that there is a broad spectrum between these two extremes, we characterized "home grounds" that describe the sets of conditions under which each is most likely to succeed. The more a particular project's conditions differ from the home ground conditions, the more risk there is in using one approach in its pure form, and the more valuable it is to blend in some of the complementary practices from the opposite method. Table 8.1 summarizes these home grounds.

Overall, small, less mission-critical projects with high rates of change are best accomplished by highly skilled agile teams able to operate on shared, tacit knowledge and little documentation. Large, more mission-critical projects with less change and mixed developer skill levels are more successful using explicit documented knowledge, such as architectural views and project plans, to succeed. If the requirements of these large projects are relatively stable, architectures and

T. Dingsøyr et al. (eds.), *Agile Software Development*,
DOI 10.1007/978-3-642-12575-1_8, © Springer-Verlag Berlin Heidelberg 2010

plans will change infrequently, so a pure documented-architecture approach will succeed. However, as seen in Figure 8.1, large projects increasingly need product and process architectures that enable them to use agility to support more volatile requirements in areas like user interfaces, competition-critical features, or interfaces with independent, rapidly evolving external systems.

Also, our experiences in the commercial and public-service sectors indicate that a growing number of systems must integrate into larger enterprise software frameworks and systems of systems. This leads to complex interactions with evolving COTS products, legacy systems, and external systems, with the tacit expectation that these systems "never fail." Emergent requirements, rapid changes, reused components, high levels of assurance, and dynamic market factors further complicate integration or incorporation.

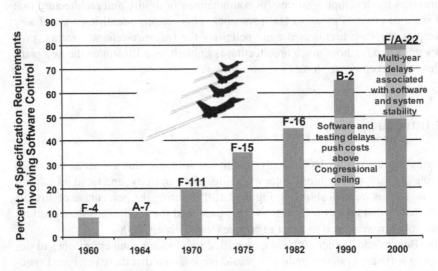

Fig. 8.1. Trends in Software-Reliant Systems: Aircraft

The relative importance of these different application sectors depends on what is counted. Organizations dealing mainly with large numbers of small, dynamic, less-critical projects will count the number of such projects. Organizations dealing with a mix of large and small projects will more likely count the investment costs and skilled effort that are consumed by their projects.

Figure 8.2 shows how the relative importance of agility and architecture varies when counting numbers of projects or percentage of costs. Drawn from Appendix E of (Boehm and Turner 2004), the information is based on data provided in (Highsmith 2002) of the relative number of projects in three size ranges across various business sectors. The particular data shown in Figure 8.2 is from the financial sector, with 65% of the projects having less than 10 people, 25% between 11 and 50 people, and 10% over 50 people.

Table 8.1. Agile and Plan-Driven Method Home Grounds

Characteristics	Agile	Plan-Driven
Application		
Primary Goals	Rapid value, responding to change	Predictability, stability, high assurance
Size	Smaller teams and projects	Larger teams and projects
Environment	Turbulent, high change, project-focused	Stable, low-change,, project/organization focused
Management		
Customer Relations	Dedicated on-site customers, focused on prioritized increments	As-needed customer interactions, focused on contract provisions
Planning and Control	Internalized plans, qualitative control	Documented plans, quantitative control
Communications	Tacit interpersonal knowledge	Explicit documented knowledge
Technical		
Requirements	Prioritized informal stories and test cases, undergoing unforeseeable change	Formalized project, capability, interface, quality, foreseeable evolution requirements
Development	Simple design, short increment, refactoring assumed inexpensive	Extensive design, longer increments, refactoring assumed expensive
Test	Executable test cases define requirements, testing	Documented test plans and procedures
Personnel		
Customers	Dedicated, collocated CRACK* performers	CRACK* performers, not always collocated
Developers	Continuing critical mass of high-capability personnel	Early critical mass of high-capability personnel, lower level OK later
Culture	Comfort and empowerment via many degrees of freedom (thriving on chaos)	Comfort and empowerment via framework of policies and procedures (thriving on order)

* Collaborative, Representative, Authorized, Committed, Knowledgable

The boundary between Low and High Size projects is taken as 25 people. In 1999, eXtreme Programming (XP) innovator Kent Beck said, "Size clearly matters. You probably couldn't run an XP project with a hundred programmers. Not fifty. Not twenty, probably. Ten is definitely doable." (Beck 1999). Since then, 20-25 person pure-agile projects have succeeded; for larger projects, investments in architecture are needed (Elssamadisy and Schalliol 2002). The relative stability data come from cost model Requirements Volatility parameter trends, in which High stability means less than 5% change in requirements per year.

By % of Projects			By % of Costs		
Criticality, Size / Stability	Low (78%)	High (22%)	Criticality, Size / Stability	Low (28%)	High (72%)
High (20%)	Either	Arch	High (20%)	Either	Architecture
Low (80%)	Agile	Both	Low (80%)	Agile	Both

Fig. 8.2. Relative Importance of Agility and Architecture

In this chapter, we identify key principles for balancing agility and architecture in the largest-cost sector where both agility and architecture are needed. In this sector, the software development activities must be lean and agile but also need a strong flexible architecture undergirding software functionality. If either is not adequately addressed, the software will not be viable over the long term. It will be late to market (or late to the crisis), too difficult to evolve, quickly reach a dead-end, and suffer a relatively short life. We define this hybrid approach as "architected-agile."

We also introduce a risk-driven process framework, the Incremental Commitment Model (ICM). Using the ICM, projects can determine the best mix of agile and architected approaches for their system situation. We will also provide quantitative results showing that the best mix is usually determined by the system's size, criticality, and requirements volatility. We then analyze case studies of one of the most successful mixed approaches, the Architected Agile approach, and present critical success factors for applying the approach.

8.2 Key Principles

Several analyses of successful programs have determined the kind of processes that satisfactorily address current trends and challenges (OUSD AT&L 2008; Pew and Mavor 2007). The strengths and difficulties of current process models have also been analyzed (Pew and Mavor 2007), finding that, while each had strengths, each needed further refinements to address all of the identified challenges. The most important conclusion, though, was that there were key process principles that address the challenges, and that the form of the process models was less important than the ability to adopt the principles. These key principles are:

1. Commitment and accountability of success-critical stakeholders

2. Stakeholder satisficing based on success-based negotiations and tradeoffs
3. Incremental and evolutionary growth of system definition and stakeholder commitment
4. Iterative system development and definition
5. Concurrent system definition and development allowing early fielding of core capabilities, continual adaptation to change, and timely growth of complex systems without waiting for every requirement and subsystem to be defined
6. Risk management – risk-driven anchor point milestones that are key to synchronizing and stabilizing all of this concurrent activity

A new process model framework, the Incremental Commitment Model (ICM) (Boehm and Lane 2008), was developed to build on the strengths of current process models: early verification and validation concepts in the V-model, concurrency concepts in the Concurrent Engineering model, lighter-weight concepts in the Agile and Lean models, risk-driven concepts in the spiral model, the phases and anchor points in the Rational Unified Process (RUP), and recent extensions of the spiral model to address SoS acquisition. The model framework, illustrated in Figure 8.3, explicitly:

• Emphasizes concurrent engineering of requirements and solutions
• Establishes Feasibility Rationales as pass/fail milestone criteria
• Enables risk-driven avoidance of unnecessary documents, phases, and reviews
• Provides support for two concurrent activities: a stabilized current-increment development activity and a separate change processing and rebaselining activity that prepares for appropriate and stabilized development of the next increment.

Figure 8.3 shows the relationship between the concurrently engineered life cycle phases, the stakeholder commitment review points with their use of feasibility rationales to assess compatibility, and the resulting risk assessment to decide how to proceed at each commitment review point. There are a number of alternatives at each commitment point, leading to many risk-driven paths through the life cycle. These are:

1. the risk is negligible and no further analysis and evaluation activities are needed to complete the next phase;
2. the risk is acceptable and work can proceed to the next life cycle phase:
3. the risk is addressable but requires backtracking; or
4. the risk is too great and the development process should be rescoped or halted.

Risk is assessed by the system's success-critical stakeholders, whose commitment will be based on whether the current level of system definition gives sufficient evidence that the system will satisfy their value propositions.

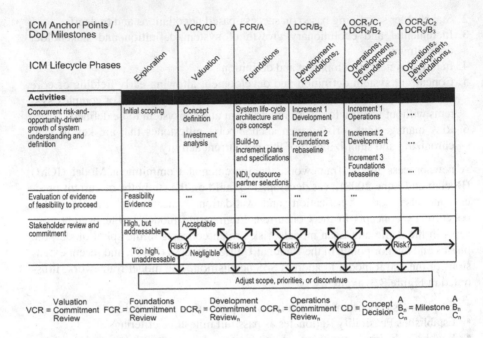

Fig. 8.3. ICM Overview

The ICM integrates

1. agile processes assessing the system environment and user needs and planning the implementation of new and modified system capabilities;
2. plan-driven (often time-boxed) processes to develop and field new capabilities; and,
3. continuous verification and validation (V&V) to provide high assurance of the requisite system qualities.

Figure 8.4 shows one of the risk-driven process patterns of the ICM that best fits the need for simultaneously accommodating rapid change and the need for high assurance on larger projects. High assurance is achieved by

- Stabilizing a build-to-specification development team
- Anticipating foreseeable change and architecting for its easy accommodation
- Providing continuous V&V to ensure rapid and efficient defect fixes
- Diverting unforeseeable changes to the concurrently-operating agile team assessing the changes and rebaselining the plans and specifications for development of the next increment

The ICM framework acknowledges there can be no "one size fits all" process model and that a key feature of any successful framework is the ability to tailor processes based on key project characteristics and risks. The ICM uses project characteristics and risks to determine how much process agility or rigor is enough to satisfy the system's objectives subject to its constraints. As a result, several common types of software-intensive systems have been identified, along with guidance for tailoring the ICM framework for each case (Boehm and Lane 2008). These common types range from small agile types of projects, through the larger-project pattern in Figure 8.4, to more complex, adaptive processes for systems of systems. The goal of the ICM tailoring process is to establish the right amount of rigor, assurance, and predictability, while remaining agile and timely.

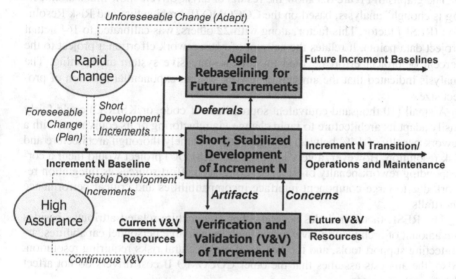

Fig. 8.4. Hybrid Agile/Plan-Driven Process Pattern (Boehm and Lane 2008)

Successfully satisficing with respect to a diverse set of stakeholders in a multi-team development environment is critical to larger software projects. Studies (Carlile 2002) focused on knowledge management and transfer between different groups, such as stakeholders and product developers and distributed development teams, have identified key "boundary objects" used to guide the development and integration of new products such as software. These include key models, such as architecture and data models, that allow the different developers to quickly communicate with non-technical stakeholders and other developers and to synchronize work so that pieces come together quickly in the integration environment (OUSD (AT&L), 2008). As shown in the next section, cost estimation models can support mutual understanding of cost implications of project decisions—including how little or how much to invest in up-front architecting.

8.3 How Much Architecting is Enough?

Size, criticality, and volatility are key decision drivers for focusing on agile or architected approaches. But critical questions remain about how much architecting is enough for a particular project. Here we provide a quantitative approach that has helped projects address this question. It extends the Return on Investment (ROI) of SE analysis described in (Boehm 2008).

The graphs in Figure 8.5 show the results of a risk-driven "how much architecting is enough" analysis, based on the COCOMO II Architecture and Risk Resolution (RESL) factor. This factor, along with 22 others, was calibrated to 161 actual project data points. It relates the amount of extra rework effort on a project to the percent of project effort devoted to software-intensive system architecting. The analysis indicated that the amount of rework was an exponential function of project size.

A small (10 thousand equivalent source lines of code, or KSLOC) could fairly easily adapt its architecture to rapid change via refactoring or its equivalent, with a rework penalty of 14% between minimal and extremely thorough architecture and risk resolution. However, a very large (10,000 KSLOC) project would incur a corresponding rework penalty of 91%, covering such effort sources as integration rework due to large-component interface incompatibilities and critical performance shortfalls.

The RESL factor includes several other architecture-related attributes besides the amount of architecting investment, such as available personnel capabilities, architecting support tools, and the degree of architectural risks requiring resolution. Also, the analysis assumes that the other COCOMO II cost drivers do not affect the project outcomes.

The effects of rapid change (volatility) and high assurance (criticality) on the sweet spots are shown in the right-hand graph. Here, the solid lines represent the average-case cost of rework, architecting, and total cost for a 100-KSLOC project as shown at the left. The dotted lines show the effect on the cost of architecting and total cost if rapid change adds 50% to the cost of architecture and risk resolution. Quantitatively, this moves the sweet spot from roughly 20% to 10% of effective architecture investment (actually 15% due to the 50% cost penalty). Thus, high investments in architecture and other documentation do not have a positive return on investment due to the high costs of documentation rework for rapid-change adaptation.

The dashed lines at the right represent a conservative analysis of the effects on the project's effective business cost of correcting architecting shortfalls and illustrate the architecting sweet spot. It assumes that the costs of architecture shortfalls are not only added rework, but also losses to the organization's operational effectiveness and productivity. These are conservatively assumed to add 50% to the project-rework cost of architecture shortfalls to the organization. In most cases for high-assurance systems, the added cost would be considerably higher.

Quantitatively, this moves the sweet spot from roughly 20% to over 30% as the most cost-effective investment in architecting for a 100-KSLOC project. It is good to note that the sweet spots are actually relatively flat "sweet regions" extending 5-10% to the left and right of the sweet spots. However, moving to the edges of a sweet region increases the risk of significant losses if some project assumptions turn out to be optimistic.

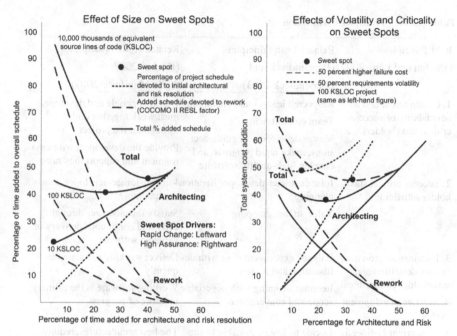

Fig. 8.5. How Much Architecting is Enough?

8.4 Early Architected-Agile Success Cases

Most successful large-scale projects have learned to balance architecting and agility. When these projects find a good balance, they can set up a battle-rhythm using a process somewhat akin to the hybrid agile/plan-driven process described in Figure 8.4. A product backlog allows the projects to welcome and manage change, using stakeholder priorities to plan capabilities for multiple future increments. They stabilize development for the current increment by defining the changes to be incorporated into the update cycle. Development is supported by continuous V&V, often with mature integration and test environments that support experimentation as well as quality assessments.

A comparison of the six key ICM principles (Boehm and Lane 2008; Poppendieck and Poppendieck 2003; Agile Manifesto 2009) with characteristics of lean and agile principles was conducted and a summary of the results are shown in

Table 8.2. Although there are differences in the level of detail in the way each set of principles is specified, there are no substantial differences with respect to architecting. All focus on efficiently performing value-adding activities at the appropriate point in the development life cycle and eliminating activities that don't add value.

Table 8.2. Key Principles Comparison

ICM Principles (Boehm and Lane 2007)	Related Lean Principles (Poppendieck and Poppendieck 2003)	Related Agile Principles (Boehm 2007; Agile Manifesto 2007)
1. Commitment and accountability of success-critical stakeholders	Respected leaders and champions Team commitment Master developers to guide decisions, make rapid progress, and develop high-quality software	Business people and developers must work together daily throughout the project Provide the developers with environment and support they need
2. Success-critical stakeholder satisficing	Joint customer-developer iteration planning Value stream mapping	Joint customer-developer iteration planning Satisfy the customer through early and continuous delivery of valuable software
3. Incremental growth of system definition and stakeholder commitment 4. Iterative development cycles	Balance experimentation with deliberation and review Iteration planning with negotiable scope and convergence	Deliver working software frequently Working software is the primary measure of progress
5. Concurrent engineering	Decide as late as possible to support concurrent development while keeping options open Ensure emergence of a good architecture through reuse, integrated problem solving, and experienced developers	The best architectures, requirements, and designs emerge from self-organizing teams.
6. Risk-based activity levels and milestones	Eliminate waste Value stream mapping	Team reflects periodically on how to become more effective, then tunes and adjusts its behavior accordingly Simplicity--the art of maximizing the amount of work not done--is essential.

This section provides five examples. First, we summarize three architected-agile case studies involving multinational US and European corporate transformations. In each, top management commissioned an internal technical and management expert to lead a corporate-wide effort to transform the company's software development practices into a more agile Scrum of Scrums approach. All used a transformed corporate information architecture and framework that enabled compatible agile development while satisfying various corporate assurance and governance needs, such as medical safety, physical platform safety, always-on availability, and US Sarbanes-Oxley corporate information management accountability (Highsmith 2002).

Next, we summarize a Scrum of Scrums approach evolved by a large US aerospace company to enable more rapid and cost-effective logistics support for an evolving product line of aerospace vehicles. Finally, we describe the Composite Health Care System (CHCS) (Lane and Zubrow 1996, E-Health Designs 2009). As part of a major process improvement effort, this large government health care system evolved a more lean and architected-agile approach, while providing continuity of service across more than 700 Department of Defense (DoD) hospitals and clinics worldwide. Each of these case studies has risk-driven approaches similar to the Supply Chain Management example in Boehm-Turner (Boehm and Turner 2004), but with additional considerations of transforming their enterprises across multiple user sites and applications.

8.4.1 Architected Agile Corporate Transformations

The first of these corporate transformations involved a US medical services company with over 1000 software developers in the US, two European countries, and India. The corporation was on the brink of failure, due largely to its slow, error-prone, and incompatible software applications and processes. A senior internal technical manager, expert in both safety-critical medical applications and agile development, was commissioned by top management to organize a corporate-wide team to transform the company's software development approach. In particular, the team was to address agility, safety, and Sarbanes-Oxley governance and accountability problems.

Software technology and project management leaders from all of its major sites were brought together to architect a corporate information framework and develop a corporate architected-agile process approach. The resulting Scrum of Scrums approach was successfully used in a collocated pilot project to create the new information framework while maintaining continuity of service in their existing operations.

Based on the success of this pilot project, the team members returned to their sites and led similar transformational efforts. Within three years, they had almost 100 Scrum teams and 1000 software developers using compatible and coordinated architected-agile approaches. The effort involved their customers and marketers in the effort. Expectations were managed via the pilot project. The release management approach included a 2-12 week architecting Sprint Zero, a series of 3-10 one-month development Sprints, a Release Sprint, and 1-6 months of beta testing; the next release Sprint Zero overlapped the Release Sprint and beta testing. Their agile Scrum approach involved a tailored mix of eXtreme Programming (XP) and corporate practices, 6-12 person teams with dedicated team rooms, and global teams with wiki and daily virtual meeting support—working as if located next-door. Figure 8.6 shows this example of the Architected Agile approach.

The second and third corporate transformations were similar. The second involved a World-100 European products company with major software sites in Europe, the US, India, and China. The third involved a large European IT company with major development centers in Europe, India, and Israel. Each applied the six key principles above of (1) stakeholder commitment (top management, developers, external stakeholders); (2) stakeholder satisficing (e.g., via Scrum prioritized backlogs); (3,4,5) incremental, evolutionary, iterative, concurrent development starting with a talented early-success core team from all major sites; and (6) risk-driven commitment milestones for expanding the number and distribution of the Scrum teams (over 30 in three years for company-2, including development of a new corporate architecture; over 40 in one year for company-3, which already had a strong corporate architecture).

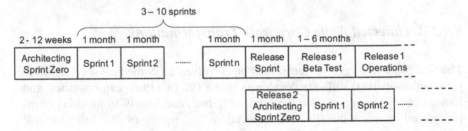

Fig. 8.6. Example of Arcitected Agile Process

In each of the three cases, the teams needed to deal with a continuing stream of asynchronous change requests to accommodate new technology or COTS opportunities; changing requirements and priorities; changing external interfaces; low-priority current increment features being deferred to a later increment; and user requests based on experience with currently-fielded increments (including defect fixes).

Figure 8.7 shows how the Scrum team leaders interact with the change proposers, current-increment scrum teams, and the manager of future-increment to evaluate proposed changes and their interactions with each other and to update the prioritized backlog for the next release.

8.4.2 Automated Maintenance Support System

This project, performed by a major aerospace company on a government contract, involved an advanced, highly automated vehicle maintenance application. The system implemented extensive on-board trend and anomaly analysis on each vehicle that used net-centric capabilities to communicate impending service needs to the nearest relevant vehicle maintenance center. The multi-mission vehicle versions and components can encounter many unanticipated interaction effects, leading to a high rate of change in the maintenance and diagnostic software.

Originally, the project used a Scrum of Scrums organization similar to those involved in the three corporate-internal case studies above. But the project encountered numerous coordination challenges across the multi-mission, multi-owner vehicle versions. These included decision priorities for common components and product backlog, multi-team requirement implementations, and needs for teams to interrupt their progress to help other teams. The number and magnitude of these challenges caused the classic single-owner Scrum of Scrums architected-agile approach to lose momentum.

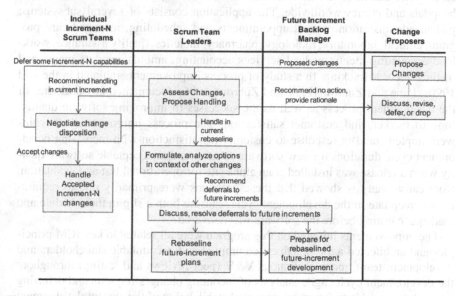

Fig. 8.7. Agile Change Processing and Rebaselining

The project recognized this and evolved to a more decentralized Scrum-based approach, with centrifugal tendencies monitored and resolved by an empowered Product Framework Group (PFG) consisting of the product owners and technical leads from each development team, and the project systems engineering, architecting, construction, and test leads. The PFG meets near the end of an iteration to assess progress and problems, and to steer the priorities of the upcoming iteration by writing new backlog items and reprioritizing the product backlog. A few days after the start of the next iteration, the PFG meets again to assess what was planned vs. what was needed, and to make necessary adjustments.

This approach has been successful in keeping the project's momentum at a high level and pointed in the right direction. This example and similar multi-mission, multi-stakeholder net-centric systems of systems have led to somewhat different combinations of agility and architecture. But overall, each has found ways to succeed by applying the six critical success factor principles discussed above. It is also important to remember that it takes qualified people to understand when and how to apply these principles to determine, tailor, and apply processes or architectures to complex system situations.

8.4.3 Composite Health Care System (CHCS)

CHCS (Lane and Zubrow 1996, E-Health Designs 2009) is an automated health care system that in 1996 was installed in about 500 Department of Defense (DoD) hospitals and clinics worldwide. The application consists of several subsystems: patient administration, patient appointments and scheduling, managed care program, clinical, laboratory, radiology, pharmacy, dietetics, quality assurance, workload accounting menu, medical services accounting, ambulatory data menu, and medical records tracking. In a study of process improvements initiated in the mid 1990s, Lane and Zubrow (Lane and Zubrow, 1996) documented key attributes of the development process as well as the successes in improving software quality, time to market, and customer satisfaction. The process improvement activities were implemented in response to customer dissatisfaction with increasing development cycle durations for new software releases and unacceptable software quality when a release was installed at an alpha site for operational test and evaluation. Root cause analysis showed that these problems were primarily due to requirements creep late in the development cycle, causing both a slip in the schedule and inadequate testing before the software was delivered.

The improvements initiated on this program were all related to key ICM principles and architected agile practices: committed and accountable stakeholders and development team, more continuous V&V (peer reviews and testing) throughout the development cycle, agile analysis of incoming changes requests and deferring as much as possible to future releases, and stabilization of the current development cycle. This stabilization of the development cycle resulted in development teams working in parallel on the current major release and two maintenance updates while planning the next major release instead of the previous approach of continuing to slip new features into the current release right up until delivery.

To quantify the impact of these planned changes, the organization collected a set of measurements with respect to the previous software release and established this as their baseline (V4.11). These sets of measures were customer satisfaction, developer productivity (average number of logical source statements (LSS) output per month during the development cycle), cost per LSS (average number of dollars expended to develop each LSS), cycle time (number of months from software release start to delivery at an alpha site), and error rates (number of defects detected during the first 30 days of operation and the number detected during the first year of operation). The measures where then captured for the next release (V4.2) in which the process improvements had been implemented and compared to the baseline. Figure 8.8 shows the results of this initial comparison as well as subsequent trend analysis for several additional software development cycles.

Figure 8.8 shows that in the first increment after the process changes were implemented, the cost per LSS dropped 29%, cycle time dropped 46%, and error rates at the alpha site dropped 90% in the first release after the initial set of improvements were implemented. Figure 8.8 also shows that additional improvements were achieve with further development environment tool upgrades and the application of more advanced processes, but none of the subsequent results were as dramatic as the first set.

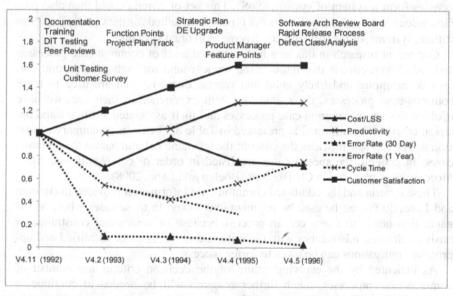

Fig. 8.8. Results of Incorporating Process Changes Related to Architected Agile ICM Principles. (Lane and Zubrow 1996)

Key to continuing to deliver new, high quality capabilities every year were a stable but flexible software architecture and a core database managed by a single database team, continual stakeholder involvement, managing the contents of each upgrade, frequent status checks with committed and accountable stakeholders to manage obstacles and make timely decisions, minimal documentation, and continuous V&V. High priority features were assigned to each major increment and lower priority features in the product backlog were incorporated when the associated code was undergoing change for a high priority feature. As would be expected for a health care system, patient safety was a top priority and continuous testing was necessary to meet this goal.

8.5 Implications for Practice and Future Research

The above cases illustrate successes in the use of architected agile and show different approaches for using an architected agile process as well as the business drivers that led to the migration of an architected agile process. One would like to have a set of criteria for determining when to use an architected agile process versus a pure agile process versus a pure architected process. In addition, one would also like a set of criteria for determining which of a number of common-case system and software engineering processes to use, including cases where multiple systems form a system of systems (SoS). This set of criteria could then also provide guidance for selecting the process type(s) best suited for the various SoS constituent systems, or for parts of very diverse individual systems.

Our recent research in this area has identified a set of common-case processes and risk-driven criteria that indicate the homeground for each process, and also provide examples and likely build and release durations that are used in these common-case processes. Over time and with experience in their use, we have evolved this set of common-case processes and their associated attributes and decision criteria. The information presented in Table 8.3 below is a summary of version 4. The top row provides the criteria; the left-hand column names the common cases. In general, the special cases are listed in order of complexity and rigor. More detail is provided in Chapter 5 of (Boehm and Lane, 2008).

These criteria and the additional common-case information provided in (Boehm and Lane, 2008) can be used by organizations today. In those cases where an organization needs to use a certain process because of contractual constraints or business drivers, mismatches with the criteria and risks can be identified and appropriate mitigations can be taken to foster success.

As indicated by the evolving nature of the decision criteria and number of common-case processes, much further research will be needed to continue to evolve these and add detail about their characteristics and implementation subprocesses. We are continuing to address these, but welcome further improvements based on others' experience and research.

8.6 Conclusion

There are no single one-size-fits-all process or product models that can be applied to the wide variety of systems needing to be addressed, now and in the future. However, there are key principles (stakeholder commitment and accountability;

stakeholder satisficing; incremental and evolutionary growth of system definition and stakeholder commitment; iterative system development and definition; and risk management) for determining appropriate process and product models for different system situations.

Table 8.2 showed how these principles are addressed by three approaches: lean development, agile development, and the Incremental Commitment Model (ICM). Each of these has strengths. The ICM provides the most explicit risk-based decision criteria for determining which overall process category fits each particular situation, and for tailoring variations within and among the process categories, as illustrated in the Corporate Transformations, AMSS, and CHCS examples. An expanded set of common-case processes and decision criteria for determining which to use in various situations is provided in Table 8.3.

Another key set of decisions involves how much of agility and architecting is enough. A multivariate analysis of 161 projects, represented in Figure 8.5, provides additional guidance for such decisions, depending primarily on project size, criticality, and volatility. Finally, it is important to remember that these are aids to thought and not substitutes for thought, and that it takes good, qualified people to understand when and how to select and apply these principles and processes to complex system situations.

Table 8.3. Homegrounds for Common Software-Intensive System Processes

Common Case	Size, Complexity	Change Rate (%/Month)	Application Criticality	Available NDI Products	Organizational and Personnel Capability
Use NDI				Complete	
Agile	Low	1-30	Low-Med	Good; in place	Agile-ready Med-high
Architected Agile	Med	1-10	Med-High	Good; most in place	Agile-ready Med-high
Formal Methods	Low	0.3	Extra High	None	Strong formal methods experience
HW with embedded SW component	Low	0.3-1	Med-Very High	Good; in place	Experienced; med-high
Indivisible IOC	Med-High	0.3-1	High-Very High	Some in place	Experienced; med-high
NDI- intensive	Med-High	0.3-3	Med-Very	NDI-driven architecture	NDI- experienced;

Common Case	Size, Complexity	Change Rate (%/Month)	Application Criticality	Available NDI Products	Organizational and Personnel Capability
			High		med-high
Hybrid agile/ plan-driven	Med- Very High	Mixed parts; 1-10	Mixed parts; Med-Very High	Mixed parts	Mixed parts
Multi-owner system of systems	Very High	Mixed parts; 1-10	Very High	Many NDIs; some in place	Related experience, med-high
Family of systems	Med- Very High	1-3	Med-Very High	Some in place	Related experience, med-high
Brownfield	High- Very High	0.3-3	Med-High	NDI as legacy replacement	Legacy re-engineering
Net- Centric Services— Community Support	Low-Med	0.3-3	Low-Med	Tailorable service elements	NDI- experienced
Net-Centric Services—Quick Response Decision Suppport	Med-High	3-30	Med-High	Tailorable service elements	NDI- experienced

Legend : HW: Hardware; IOC: Initial Operational Capability; NDI: Non-Development Item; SW: Software.

References

Beck, K. (1999); Extreme Programming Explained. Reading, MA: Addison-Wesley.

Boehm, B. (2007); "Agility and quality." IBM Agile Conference, May 15, 2007; ICSE Workshop on Software Quality, May 21, 2007.

Boehm, B. and Turner, R. (2004); Balancing agility and discipline: a guide for the perplexed. Addison-Wesley, Boston.

Boehm, B. and Lane, J. (2008); Incremental Commitment Model Guide, version 0.5, Center for Systems and Software Engineering Technical Report, December 31, 2008, http://csse.usc.edu/csse/TECHRPTS/2009/usc-csse-2009-500/usc-csse-2009-500.pdf.

Boehm, B., Valerdi, R., and Honour, E. (2008); "The ROI of Systems Engineering: Some Quantitative Results for Software-Intensive Systems," Systems Engineering, Vol. 11, No.3, Fall 2008, pp. 221-234.

Carlile, P. (2002); "A pragmatic view of knowledge and boundaries: boundary objects in new product development." Organization Science Vol. 13: 442-455.

Elssamadisy, A. and Schalliol, G. (2002); "Recognizing and Responding to 'Bad Smells' in Extreme Programming," Proceedings, ICSE 2002, pp. 617-622.

Highsmith, J. (2002); Agile Software Development Ecosystems. Boston: Addison-Wesley.

Lane, J. and Zubrow, D. (1996); "Metrics focus brings about improvement in health care software development. Proceedings, SEI Software Engineering Process Group Conference, March 1996.

E-Health Designs, LLC, Legacy System Saviors, http://www.ehealthdesigns.com/?page_id=246, accessed on 12/8/2009. Office of the Under Secretary of Defense for Acquisition, Technology and Logistics (OUSD AT&L), (2008); Systems engineering for systems of systems, Version 1.0. Washington, DC: Pentagon.

Pew, R. and Mavor, A. (2007); Human-system integration in the system development process: a new look. National Academy Press, 2007.

Poppendieck, M and Poppendieck, T. (2003); Lean software development, an agile toolkit. Addison Wesley.

Van Tilborg, A., Acting DUSD(S&T), (2006); "Advancing Software-Intensive Systems Producibility: Charge to NRC Committee," September 27, 2006 (citing Defense Acquisition University as source).

Principles behind the agile manifesto, http://agilemanifesto.org/principles.html. accessed on 8/4/2009.

Author Biographies

Dr. Barry Boehm is the TRW professor of software engineering at the University of Southern California; and the Director of Research of the DoD-Stevens-USC Systems Engineering Research Center (SERC). He was previously in software engineering, systems engineering, and management positions at General Dynamics, Rand, TRW, and DARPA, where he managed the acquisition of more than $1 billion worth of advanced information technology systems. Dr. Boehm originated the spiral model, the Constructive Cost Model, and the stakeholder win-win approach to software management and requirements negotiation. He is a Fellow of INCOSE, ACM, AIAA, and IEEE, and a member of the US NAE. Contact him at boehm@usc.edu.

Dr. Jo Ann Lane is a Research Assistant Professor at the University of Southern California conducting research in the areas of system of systems (SoS) cost models, tailorable evolutionary acquisition systems and SoS engineering processes, and the application of lean principles in the SoS engineering environment. She is a member of the INCOSE and IEEE and in 2007 received the INCOSE Foundation/Stevens Doctoral Award for promising research in Systems Engineering and Integration. She was previously a key technical member of Science Applications International Corporation's Software and Systems Integration Group, responsible for the development and integration of software-intensive systems and SoS. Contact her at jolane@usc.edu.

Supannika Koolmanojwong is currently a PhD student at the University of Southern California Center for Systems and Software Engineering. Her primary research area focuses on software process modeling and software process improvement especially in rapid-fielding software development, Architected Agile, NDI-Intensive, and Net-Centric Services areas. Prior to this, she was a lecturer at Faculty of Science and Technology, Assumption University, Thailand and a RUP/OpenUp Content Developer at IBM Software Group. Contact her at koolmano@usc.edu.

Dr. Richard Turner is a Distinguished Service Professor at Stevens Institute, a Visiting Scientist at the Software Engineering Institute of Carnegie Mellon University and a respected researcher and consultant with thirty years of international experience in systems, software and acquisition engineering. Dr. Turner is co-author of three books: Balancing Agility and Discipline: A Guide for the Perplexed, CMMI Distilled, and CMMI Survival Guide: Just Enough Process Improvement. Contact him at rturner@stevens.edu.

9 Agile Interaction Design and Test-Driven Development of User Interfaces – A Literature Review

Theodore D. Hellmann, Ali Hosseini-Khayat, Frank Maurer

Abstract: This chapter describes the development of GUI-based applications, from usability engineering and prototyping to acceptance test-driven development, in an agile context. An overview of current agile interaction design practices will be presented, including a thorough analysis of the current role of prototyping and current attempts to facilitate test-driven development of GUI systems, as presented in academic and industrial literature. Traditional usability engineering approaches shows that if user input is taken into consideration early in the development process by repeatedly conducting usability tests on low-fidelity prototypes of the GUI system, the final version of the GUI will be both more usable and less likely to require revision. The major risk associated with test-driven development of GUIs is the high likelihood of change in the target GUI, which can make test development unnecessarily expensive and time consuming. A unification of these styles of development will be presented, along with a prediction of how this process can be used to simplify creating testable GUI-based applications by agile teams.

9.1 Introduction

Currently, agile quality assurance practices like test-driven development, continuous integration, and acceptance testing have been widely adopted into mainstream agile development teams. The purpose of this chapter is to introduce two additional types of testing that have yet to be widely integrated into agile software development: usability evaluation and testing of graphical user interfaces.

Traditional usability engineering approaches show that if user expectations are taken into consideration early in the development process by repeatedly conducting usability tests on low-fidelity prototypes of the graphical user interface (GUI) of a system, the final version of the GUI will be both more usable and less likely to require revision. Usability testing focuses on improving the ease of use of a GUI. On top of this, automated testing of GUIs can improve their stability and reliability. In an agile context, test-driven GUI development seems to be an obvious approach and has been discussed by the community (Poole 2005). However, a major risk associated with test-driven development of GUIs is the high likelihood of change in the target GUI and the resulting fragility of tests, which can make test-driven development unnecessarily expensive and time consuming. In this chapter, we will give an overview on the related work on agile interaction design, automated GUI testing and test-driven development of user interfaces. We will then

T. Dingsøyr et al. (eds.), *Agile Software Development*,
DOI 10.1007/978-3-642-12575-1_9, © Springer-Verlag Berlin Heidelberg 2010

present a unification of these two GUI-related approaches, along with a prediction of how this process can be used to simplify the creation of tested GUI-based applications.

9.2 Agile Interaction Design

Software usability has the potential to determine the success or failure of a software system. As such, usability engineering practices such as prototyping (Buxton 2007) and usability testing (Barnum 2002) have become increasingly common in software development projects, particularly for commercial software. Adapting usability techniques for use in combination with agile methods is an ongoing process that is gaining increasing attention by usability practitioners and proponents of agile methods[1]. This section presents the motivation behind interaction design in agile methods, the basic concepts of interaction design and adaptation of these concepts for use by agile teams. While some research in this area exists, the integration efforts are currently driven by industry practitioners. As a result, we are discussing both industrial as well as academic resources in our literature review.

9.2.1 Usability and Usability Evaluation

Software with poor usability can have negative effects on productivity and acceptance. If the software is a commercial product to which users have an alternative, poor usability can cause customers to reject the product and choose a competitor's product instead. However, if usage is mandated, bad usability can result in reduced productivity for the end-user and decreased sales for the developer. Bad usability in software developed for in-house use can lead to users circumventing the system and generally reduced productivity. In some cases, bad usability can lead to the failure of a project because of end-users rejecting the system and fighting against its use. It is clear that these effects are all undesirable to varying degrees for the entities involved.

On the other hand, software with good usability can result in increased productivity, customer satisfaction and revenue (Barnum 2002; Nielsen 1994). Additionally, a user interface that has gone through multiple usability evaluations is more likely to be relatively stable in terms of changes needed because of the discovery of usability flaws in later stages. Software usability is receiving increasing attention particularly for commercial products. The first step in improving usability is typically creating prototypes of the user interface based on an analysis of user

---

[1] Retrieved from agile-usability Yahoo! Group: http://tech.groups.yahoo.com/group/agile-usability.

needs and tasks. Prototypes usually start with sketches of user interfaces (so called low-fidelity prototypes) and can then be refined into medium or high fidelity prototypes. Typically, the next step involves evaluating the design of the prototype using a variety of techniques (see below). Finally, the results of the evaluation are analyzed and the design is improved to alleviate any usability issues that may have been found. The process is then started again using the updated design, forming an iterative design process in which each iteration improves upon the design until a satisfactory design is obtained.

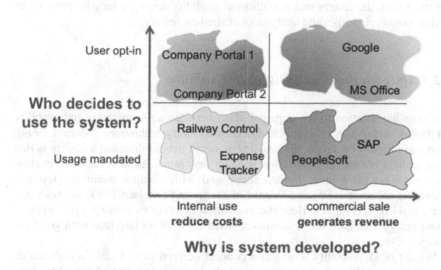

Fig. 9.1. Usability quadrant (Image Source (Maurer 2009))

9.2.2 Traditional Usability Evaluation and Conflicts with Agile Methods

Traditionally, large amounts of design work and usability evaluation are done prior to any implementation. Implementation of a release only starts once the entire iterative user experience design process is completed, including prototype design, evaluation, analysis and redesign. Once the design has been finalized, it is handed over to the developers for implementation of that phase. Before the next release, the designers gather feedback from the latest release and incorporate it in the design for the next release. In this way design flaws found in a release, either during development or post-release, are corrected in the next release of the software. This results in a large gap between when a flaw is identified in a release and when it is actually fixed, if it is not found and corrected in the initial design phase.

The traditional usability evaluation process appears to have some fundamental conflicts with the principles of agile methods, particularly the need for short iterations, the preference towards minimal up-front design work and the non-functional design artifacts. Agile methods prescribe devoting minimal time to designing and creating design documents in the start of a project. Instead, design is done during each iteration for the features involved in that particular iteration. Clearly, this poses a problem when employing traditional usability techniques, where all the design work should be finished prior to any other work on the project. Short iterations are another concept found in agile methods. This practice can be problematic if a complete traditional usability testing process is attempted at the beginning of each iteration as that process is a lengthy one. Recruiting participants and collocating them with the testers makes traditional usability testing a lengthy process, as well as prototype design and analysis of evaluation results.

9.2.3 Agile Methods and Discount Usability

One possible solution to the apparent clash between agile methods and usability evaluation techniques is to utilize discount usability techniques (Nielsen 1994), proposed initially by Jakob Nielsen. The concept behind discount usability is that some amount of usability evaluation is better than none. As such, usability evaluation is done with a more limited scope and with cheaper methods. Heuristic evaluation (Nielsen 1995) and Wizard of Oz testing (Nielsen 1993) are both discount usability techniques. Heuristic evaluation involves evaluating a prototype or actual design against a set of heuristics based on what an interface with good usability is like.

Wizard of Oz usability testing is a concept derived from Frank Baum's novel, The Wonderful Wizard of Oz (Baum 1900). In the story, one of the characters, known as the Wizard of Oz, manipulates a contraption from behind a curtain, deceiving the main characters into thinking the contraption is a working one. In usability terms, the concept of Wizard of Oz testing is showing a test subject a view of a non-working prototype, observing the user's input or reaction and manipulating the view of the prototype as appropriate, thereby giving the illusion that the prototype actually works.

When used in discount usability approaches, the prototype used for Wizard of Oz testing is typically a pen and paper, low-fidelity prototype. One of the test conductors acts as the "wizard" while another observes the users' behavior and reactions. By observing the users' actions and behavior the designers can get an idea of what the user is expecting, whether or not an element is located in the right place and many other indications of usability flaws. Often the Wizard of Oz testing approach is accompanied by a think aloud protocol (Nielsen 1994), whereby participants are asked to articulate their thoughts as they interact with the prototype. Prototypes can have multiple levels of detail, although the most commonly used level of detail for Wizard of Oz testing is a low-fidelity one. The following section will describe the different levels of detail and their benefits and disadvantages.

9.2.4 Prototype Levels of Detail

User interface prototypes can be categorized by their level of detail into one of three categories: low-fidelity, high-fidelity or mixed-fidelity. Low-fidelity prototype refers to prototypes that resemble (or are) sketches of the user interface. Wireframe designs, pen and paper sketches and whiteboard drawings are examples of low-fidelity prototypes (Nielsen 1990).

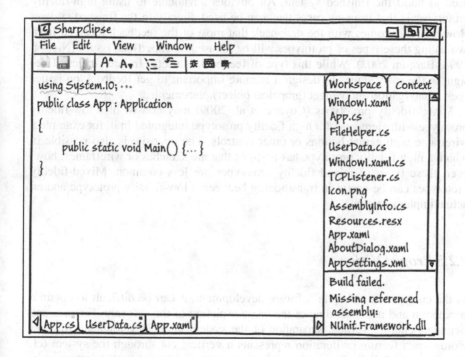

Fig.9.2. Low-fidelity prototyping

Low-fidelity prototypes are a concept adopted from similar design artifacts in other fields, such as movie production, where storyboards (Hart 1999; Bailey et al. 2001) are created prior to the bulk of the production process. Low-fidelity prototypes have the advantage of focusing the attention of test participants and reviewers on basic and essential usability questions such as the placement of buttons, navigational issues and organization of the interface. This is opposed to the feedback that is obtained based on higher level prototypes or finished systems, where users tend to focus on superficial issues such as fonts and colors. Another advantage of low-fidelity prototypes is that they are easy to create, cheap in terms of time and resources and can easily be discarded or modified. Additionally, when providing feedback on these types of prototypes users feel that input they provide that requires major modifications will have a better chance of being taken into account, since the system does not appear finalized. Due to the fact that they are cheap, easy to modify and require minimal upfront design work they are ideal for integrating usability methods with agile methods. Additionally they provide good ROI, as a relatively smaller amount of time is spent designing and testing them while still addressing and discovering the most serious issues.

High-fidelity prototypes are ones that closely resemble a finished system. These prototypes are typically built with GUI-builder tools, often the same tools that are used to build the finished system. An obvious advantage to using high-fidelity prototypes is that in many cases they can be used directly in the finished system. However, this comes with the drawback that most of the feedback received from evaluating these types of prototypes will be focused on superficial issues (Nielsen 1994; Barnum 2002). While this type of feedback is useful in later stages of design, in the early stages of design it is more important to get feedback on issues such as navigation and widget (graphical object) placement.

Mixed-fidelity prototypes (Coyette et al. 2009) may consist of a low-fidelity prototype with elements of a high-fidelity prototype integrated in it, for example a wireframe with actual buttons or other controls. The opposite is also possible in which a high-fidelity prototype has portions that are sketches or wireframes; however, these types of mixed fidelity prototypes are less common. Mixed-fidelity prototypes can be useful in transitioning between a low-fidelity prototype and an actual implementation.

9.2.5 Project Vision

In the current state of agile software development, it can be difficult to obtain a perception and understanding of the broader picture of the software. Features and iterations entail a vertical separation of the system under development. In other words, each feature or iteration represents a vertical cut through the system (cf. Fig. 9.3), which is limited to the parts of the system relevant to that feature or iteration. As a result, maintaining a consistent and unified vision throughout the many iterations of development can be difficult.

As an aid to obtaining a broad view of the system, prototypes of varying detail and fidelity can be designed and utilized (Patton 2002; Meszaros and Aston 2006). In addition to providing the broader picture, they also serve as design artifacts necessary for performing usability evaluation. Prototypes are abstracted representations of the user interface of a software system in the sense that they generally do not have any underlying business code and in some cases do not contain any form of implementation at all. The need for a broad project vision early in the project can be considered as motivation for designing prototypes.

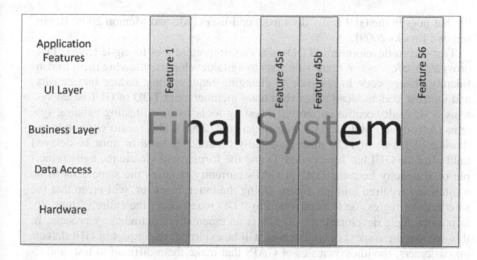

Fig. 9.3. Vertical slices through system from iterative and incremental development

9.3 User Interface Test-Driven Development

There are two ways of testing a GUI-based application (GAP): with or without automation. In manual GUI testing, a tester interacts directly with the AUT. This sort of testing is time-consuming, meaning that fewer tests can be run over the course of a project, and distinctly un-agile. In automated GUI testing, tests are written to simulate user interaction with a GAP, and can be run as part of a continuous integration setup. Automated tests can be run faster and more regularly than manual GUI tests, but at a price. First, a GUI test must mimic the way in which a real user would interact with the system, which can be difficult since widgets are often hard to interact with from test programs. Next, GUI tests tend to be fragile, and maintenance can be expensive: it has been estimated that Accenture Technology Labs spends between $50 and $120 million annually to repair broken GUI test scripts (Grechanik et al. 2009). Compounding this, GUIs are very likely to change over the course of development, virtually ensuring that test maintenance will be required. Finally, GAP tests are difficult to write in the first place due to the degree of freedom GUIs allow users. This is because GUIs can enter a large number of possible states in response to user input, and it is often difficult to determine the validity of a given state in an automated fashion. Given these difficulties, it might be tempting to declare automated GUI testing too expensive to do and to focus on testing the underlying application instead. However, any untested code should be viewed as a potential source of bugs. Even using a model-view-controller -style architecture does not obviate the need for GUI testing – especially since 45-60% of a GAP's code may lie in its GUI (Memon 2001). Despite this, automated GUI testing in practice is generally done inadequately despite the reality that bugs in the GUI really do impact end-users (Xie and Memon 2008; Robinson and Brooks 2009).

Test-driven development (TDD) is a very important tool for agile teams. TDD provides a safety net of regression tests to agile developers, allowing them to confidently change code in response to changing requirements, reduce bug density, and increase communication between team members, but TDD of GUI-based systems is difficult because current GUI testing tools focus on testing existing systems (Jeffries and Melnik 2007; Nagappan et al. 2008). This means either that authoring GUI tests in TDD must essentially be done by hand or must be delayed until after the GUI has been coded. Doing the former will violate the agile principle of simplicity because TDD of GAPs currently requires the same tests to be written and repaired multiple times. Doing the latter, however, will mean that the safety net of regression tests provided by TDD won't cover the entire system. So, at present, agile development of GAPs is an essentially contradictory process. In this section, the context of GUI testing will be explored: the impact of GUI defects on customers; the idiosyncrasies of GAPs that make them difficult to test; and finally the difficulties and advantages to attempting to apply test-driven development to GAPs. Previous attempts at test-driven development of GAPs will be explored, and conflicts between the requirements of these attempts and the tenets of agile software will be explored, followed by a discussion of possible reconciliations.

9.3.1 What Makes GUI Testing Difficult?

The difficulties encountered in GUI testing are no different from those encountered in other kinds of testing. They are simply less avoidable here than they are in other contexts. Three key encumbrances for testing in general become very difficult to address when performing GUI testing: complexity, verification, and change. Individually, each encumbrance represents a significant challenge; together, they make GUI testing nearly impossible to perform in an agile fashion.

Complexity
The more freedom is allowed a user, the larger an application's interaction space becomes. Work by Xie and Memon (Xie and Memon 2008) has shown that the number of possible event sequences increases exponentially with the length of a test case for a GAP. Compounding this, experimentation (Xie and Memon 2006) by the same group has shown that there are two important factors in determining how effective a test suite will be: the number of events from the GUI's interaction space that have been used in the test suite; and the number of different states in which these are triggered. In other words, the interaction space in which testing can be performed on GAPs is truly huge, and testing only a portion of it is very likely to have a negative impact on the test suite's ability to detect defects.

Without an effective suite of regression tests, agile developers can't be as confident when making changes to existing code, but creating tests comprehensive enough to deal with the complexity of GUIs is a daunting task – especially when attempted in a test-driven fashion.

Verification

Any test consists of two parts: a test procedure and a test oracle. A test procedure might consist of a set of actions to take on the system, whereas a test oracle contains information that will be used to check whether the system responded appropriately to these actions. Since automated testing is constrained by the way in which test oracles are defined and used (Kaner and Bach 2005), the fact that it's difficult and/or expensive to create useful GUI test oracles makes it difficult to create good GUI tests. In work by Memon, Banerjee, and Nagarajan (Memon et al. 2003), both the information contained in an oracle ("oracle information") and the way this information is compared to the GAP at test-time ("oracle procedure") are explored. In short, GUIs are usually composed of windows, each of which contains a set of widgets. Since the state of a widget can be described as the parameters it exposes and their values, the state of a window can be described as the state of its widgets. If tests are being generated automatically, this information can be compared to the application under test (AUT) either after each step of the test or after the entire test has completed. It was found that more complex oracles have stronger fault-detection ability. For example, oracles that store more information about the state of the AUT and that compare this information to the AUT after each step. Of course, these will take more time to run and space to store. This, combined with the complexity issue, implies that GUI test suites are likely to grow very large very quickly. This makes automated GUI testing of an application very difficult in an agile environment due to the overhead involved in test suite creation and the fact that rapid feedback will be less likely as the project continues. Commonly used GUI testing tools also require the GUI to be available before they can be used.

Change

Unfortunately, the fact that GUI testing is best done with complex test oracles makes these oracles exceedingly vulnerable to changes in the GUI. GUIs are also likely to be changed on a regular basis during the course of development, which means that GUI test suites will be broken again and again. Research has shown (Memon and Soffa 2003) that it is possible for over 74% of GUI test cases for a GAP to become unusable after modifications to its GUI. When this happens, test cases have to be repaired or rerecorded.

Traditionally, tool support for repairing broken GUI tests has been lacking, but several interesting tools have been proposed recently. In work by Memon and Soffa (Memon and Soffa 2003), a compiler-inspired approach is taken. GUI test suites are scanned for sequences that are illegal in the new version of the GUI, and events are deleted or inserted until the sequence is again found to be legal. Fu, Grechanik, and Xie take a different approach, one that focuses on how objects are used in test scripts rather than their specific type at runtime (Fu et al. 2009). Their system, TIGOR, is able to determine information about the types of widgets used in test scripts and make this explicit, making manual repair of broken GUI tests less difficult. The same team has also developed another system, REST (Grechanik et al. 2009), which is able to determining which objects in the GUI have been changed between revisions and then generate suggestions based on where in a test script a failure is likely to happen, and why. Similarly, Actionable Knowledge Models (Yin et al. 2005) have been used to store test data so that revisions can be propagated between many tests quickly.

However, while these tools represent a step in the right direction, the frequent breaking and subsequent repair of GUI tests remains a significant problem. The most significant danger here is that, as has been reported on agile projects in the past (Holmes and Kellogg 2006), team members may begin to dismiss failing tests as "the test's fault," in which case the credibility of an automated test suite will be significantly reduced. While repairing broken tests is a significant advance, a better solution would be to find a way to increase the robustness of GUI tests.

It's interesting to note that change remains a significant challenge to GUI testing even within agile teams. While agile teams should be able to react to and embrace change, the level of complication involved in GUI testing means that change remains a significant risk even to agile development efforts. A solution to the problem of TDD of GAPs, then, must be able to address to the triple threat of change, validation, and complexity if it is to be of use to agile teams.

9.3.2 GUI Testing – An Overview

To test a GUI, a test script must first be defined. A test script consists of a series of actions to be performed on the AUT. Scripts can be used without a test oracle, in which case a crashing AUT signifies a failed test. This sort of testing can be executed by either a manual tester or an automated test runner. More advanced tests can be created by adding a test oracle to a script, which allows for more detailed testing. It's possible to write GUI test scripts by hand, but GUI testing is generally done using a capture-replay tool (CRT). CRTs capture user interactions and store them as a script that can be replayed later as a regression test.

While CRT-based tools are popular for writing GUI tests, invariant-based and model-based methods show promise. Invariant-based testing is done by defining a set of invariants, or things that are not allowed to change, about a system, and verifying that the GUI upholds each invariant after each step in a test script. Model-based testing is done by creating an intermediate representation of an AUT and using this to automatically create a test suite that will meet certain criteria. In this section, each of these techniques will be explained.

Capture-Replay Tools

CRTs were initially very basic systems. They would simply record mouse movements, clicks, and keyboard input as scripts, which would later be replayed. Relying on screen coordinates has the distinct disadvantage of creating fragile tests, since refactoring of the GUI, such as rearranging its widgets, will cause test failures even though the AUT itself is functioning appropriately (Fu et al. 2009; Grechanik et al. 2009). For example, even cosmetic refactoring of an application's

GUI, refactoring that changed the location of widgets without changing any of the functionality of the system, would break tests. Because of this, a system called testing with object maps was developed to ease widget identification (Fu et al. 2009; Grechanik et al. 2009). In this system, detailed information about a widget is recorded so that a best-fit match can be made when the test is run. While more robust, this sort of test is difficult to write by hand, so keyword-based identification has been gaining popularity (Ruiz and Price 2008; Chen et al. 2005; Ruiz and Price 2007). In this system, developers assign a unique identifier to each widget so that it can be easily located in test fixtures.

While modern CRTs allow rapid creation of relatively stable scripts, there are two main disadvantages to their use on agile projects. First, it is often faster to simply discard and re-record a broken test than it is to attempt maintenance, leading to a gap between TDD of GUIs and maintenance of GUI tests. Since tests are likely to break frequently, the same tests are likely to be recorded multiple times in different versions of the GUI. Care must be taken to ensure that the newly-recorded tests remain identical to the now non-working tests they are replacing, lest the regression suite drift away from the functionality it was intended to test. If this were to happen, it would compromise the usefulness of the regression suite of GUI tests as a safety net for development. Second, since CRTs record a user's interactions with a working GUI, a GUI must exist in order to use a CRT, meaning that test-driven development is not currently possible from a CRT itself, which forces agile teams to choose between TDD or CRTs.

Invariant-Based Testing

In invariant-based testing, rules which define expected or prohibited system behavior are created (Mesbah and van Deursen 2009). Mesbah and Deursen have applied this technique to the testing of AJAX-based web-based applications (WBAPs) (Mesbah and van Deursen 2009). In their study, invariants were applied to characteristics like the DOM tree; for instance, the DOM should never contain error messages. As a script is executed on the AUT, invariants are checked after each step. This method ties in nicely with the issue of GUI complexity in that it is testing for a wide range of possible errors at each step of the test, and each invariant is based on some functional expectation of the AUT rather than on whether the AUT matches an ideal version of itself. The distinction is that what is being tested with invariants is closer to "is the system correct?" than it is to "does the actual system match an ideal version?" When verifying a GUI against an ideal version, that ideal version must first be created. Also, the correctness of the actual GUI will be largely dependent on the correctness of the model. On the other hand, testing for system correctness is only limited by the correctness of the customer's specifications, so agile teams are already familiar with correcting the sort of errors that these tests can incur.

Model-Based Testing

Model-based testing requires generation of an intermediate version of the GUI, either by reverse-engineering a working GUI or generating one based on specifications. This model is then used for automatic test case generation. Model-based GUI testing has recently explored the use of Hierarchical Predicate Transition

Nets (Reza et al. 2007), UML diagrams (Vieira et al. 2006), Labeled State Transition Systems (Jaaskelainen et al. 2009), and Event-Flow Models (Memon 2007; Lu et al. 2008). Advantages of these systems include ease of automation, increased code coverage, reduced coupling between the implementation of a test and the implementation of a GUI, and increased cohesion within the test suite. Disadvantages are that a model of the GUI must first be created, and this model must be maintained or regenerated when the system changes. This, again, violates the agile principle of simplicity in that additional work must be done on a regular basis in order to support testing.

9.3.3 Test-Driven Development

In test-driven development (TDD), a developer will first write tests based on the requirements for the feature s/he's about to implement, which will be capable of verifying that the new feature is working correctly. Next, s/he will write just enough code in order to make the new tests pass - without, of course, breaking any other tests. Finally, the new code should be refactored until it is not just passing the tests, but well implemented as well.

TDD is an incredibly important core process of agile software engineering. Over time, TDD forms a safety net of tests covering the entire application. This safety net means that developers can confidently change code in response to changing requirements since regression errors will be caught immediately by existing tests. TDD also encourages communication between customers and developers, which is central to the success of an agile project (Jeffries and Melnik 2007). Most importantly, there is evidence that TDD is able to and increases quality by decreasing the defect density (bugs per KLOC) of an application without significantly decreasing productivity ((Nagappan et al. 2008), for example), though that remains an open subject (Jeffries and Melnik 2007).

However, the most straightforward methods of testing GUIs require the GUI to exist before the tests can be recorded, which makes performing TDD on GUI-based applications difficult. So how has TDD of GUIs been done so far?

9.3.4 Test-Driven Development of GUI-Based Applications

Test-driven development of user interfaces has been discussed in the agile community for some time now (Poole 2005). However, no broadly used solutions have been found for agile teams. Several methods that have been proposed will be described, along with a short explanation of why these approaches aren't ideal for agile development environments.

TestNG-Abbot and FEST
Ruiz and Price (Ruiz and Price 2007) developed an integration of TestNG, a Java testing framework, and Abbot, a library for testing Swing GUIs, which facilitates TDD of GUIs. TestNG-Abbot makes writing GUI tests manually much easier in that it hides much of the complexity of coding GUI tests in two ways. First, it makes it easier to find widgets using enhanced matcher objects. Second, it makes it easier to interact with widgets by wrapping complicated Robot functionality inside more coder-friendly methods. The result is that this integration overcomes some of the dissociation between test code and widgets in that it makes it possible for tests to treat widgets in the GUI in much the same way as it would treat objects in the rest of the application. The TestNG-Abbot integration grew into FEST, which makes writing GUI tests even simpler and further enables TDD of GAPs (Ruiz and Price 2008) .

GUI Testing Tool
GTT (GUI Testing Tool) enables TDD of GAPs through specification-based testing (Chen et al. 2005). In this system, testers define sets of user interactions and the expected system response based on a list of pre-defined GUI components. Note that manual test development in GTT is done at a more abstract level than in the above, where tests are coded directly. Additionally, because a GUI is likely to change once it has been developed, breaking existing tests, GTT is integrated with a CRT to facilitate test maintenance.

Selenium and Similar Software
Testing WBAPs is similar to testing GAPs in that both can be tested through their user interfaces, and similar progress has been made in this field. TDD of WBAPs through directly coding tests is possible using Selenium (and many other mostly-analogous applications). However, a study done by Digital Focus found that using this method for TDD seldom works seamlessly (Holmes and Kellogg 2006). Tests written in a test-first fashion would rarely work after a feature is implemented. Further, this usually happened for minor reasons - for example, misidentification of a widget, or the test running faster than the WBAP could respond. Because of this, developers got into the habit of writing a test, then writing application code, and then getting the test to pass afterwards. It is interesting to note that Selenium gives multiple options for how tests can be repaired: developers can of course manually alter test code, but they also have the option of using Selenium's CRT to re-record a test on the new version of an interface.

All of these approaches suffer from basic faults that prevent them from being an ideal solution for TDD of GAPs. The most important of these faults is that no attempt is made to minimize the amount of change that GUIs will need to undergo during development. At present, GUIs are very likely to change over the course of development, which is likely to break their attendant tests, which will have to be repaired or recoded – either by hand, as in FEST, or through a CRT, as in Selenium and GTT. This is the opposite of the core agile principle of maximizing work not done in that it requires the same work to be done multiple times.

Also, these systems create a gap between TDD and test maintenance. When the GUI actually exists, a broken test can be more simply fixed by using a CRT to re-record it on the actual GUI than it is to repair the test by hand. This means that a new test, written in a different manner from the first test, is being substituted into the regression suite for the application. When tests are rewritten in this manner, extreme care needs to be taken that new tests are semantically identical to the tests they are replacing. Otherwise, there is a risk that the suite of regression tests carefully created through TDD will no longer be able to act as an adequate safety net, and developers may find themselves once again coding without a suite of tests to ward against regression errors.

9.3.5 Future Directions: Using Prototyping for TDD of GUIs

So far, we addressed both GUI testing and TDD of GUIs. Existing approaches provide frameworks that make it easier to write GUI tests by hand and for maintaining these tests once a GUI has been developed. Before these approaches can be smoothly integrated into agile development environments, several conflicts with agility must be resolved.

First, when great effort must be placed on maintenance of GUI tests, emphasis shifts towards the tool used for creating or running these tests and away from the original intent of the tests - namely, to prove to all interested parties that the software being developed meets the customer's requirements. Similarly, a large, fragile, or untrustworthy test suite makes it very difficult to welcome change, much less embrace it or use it for the customer's advantage, due to the amount of extra work that must be done to ensure the integrity of the tests.

Second, writing GUI tests according to TDD must become a simpler process. While writing GUI tests from an existing GUI is relatively simple, and while test-first development of a GUI is technically possible, it remains difficult to write tests that will actually assist in GAP development. TDD of GUIs must become an intrinsic part of the rest of the testing process, rather than representing an obstacle to it.

Third, the limitations of GUI TDD negate many of the benefits associated with TDD. Namely, TDD should increase a developer's confidence in the code base, but a fragile test suite does the opposite. In this situation, developers will be reluctant to embrace changes due to the technical limitations of GUI testing.

In order to enable GUI TDD in a straightforward, robust manner, it is necessary to integrate it into the existing agile testing framework. First, a stable basis for GUI testing must be established. We believe this can be done through an agile usability evaluation process. This would involve repeated usability evaluation, through which an application's GUI would be prototyped, tested, and analyzed. Because of this, usability issues are more likely to be discovered before the GUI is actually implemented, making the GUI more stable during the course of development.

Additionally, if a low-fidelity prototype were decorated with realistic automation information, including widget identification information and information about how widgets will cause the GUI to transition between states, these interactions could be recorded and used for TDD of the actual GUI. We are currently conducting research to support this proposed approach.

9.4 Conclusion

In this chapter, agile usability evaluation and test-driven development of GUI-based applications have been covered. We covered the conflicts between traditional usability testing and agile methods. The current solution in the agile community – the use of discount usability testing – is also addressed. Recent advances in the testing of GUI-based applications were discussed, as well as attempts at enabling test-driven development of these systems. Issues preventing the adoption of test-driven GUI development into agile development practices were presented, and an overview on a possible solution to these obstacles was given.

References

Bailey, B. P., Konstan, J. A., & Carlis, J. V. (2001). DEMAIS: designing multimedia applications with interactive storyboards. Proceedings of the Ninth ACM International Conference on Multimedia (pp. 241-250). Ottawa: ACM Press.

Barnum, C. (2002). Usability Testing and Research. New York, NY: Pearson Education.

Baum, F. (1900). The Wonderful Wizard of Oz. Chicago: George M. Hill Company.

Buxton, B. (2007). Sketching User Experiences: Getting the Design Right the Right Design. Morgan Kaufmann.

Chen, W., Tsai, T., & Chao, H. (2005 March). Integration of Specification-Based and CR-Based Approaches for GUI Testing. Proceedings of the 19th International Conference on Advanced information Networking and Applications, 1, 967-972.

Coyette, A., Kieffer, S., & Vanderdonckt, J. (2009). Multi-fidelity prototyping of user interfaces. In Human-Computer Interaction - INTERACT 2007 (pp. 150-164). Berlin / Heidelberg: Springer.

Fu, C., Grechanik, M., & Xie, Q. (2009 April). Inferring Types of References to GUI Objects in Test Scripts. Proceedings of the 2009 International Conference on Software Testing Verification and Validation, 1-10.

Grechanik, M., Xie, Q., & Chen, F. (2009 May). Maintaining and evolving GUI-directed test scripts. Proceedings of the 2009 IEEE 31st International Conference on Software Engineering, 408-418.

Hart, J. (1999). The Art of the Storyboard: Storyboarding for Film, TV, and Animation. Focal Press.

Holmes, A., & Kellogg, M. (2006 July). Automating Functional Tests Using Selenium. Proceedings of the Conference on AGILE 2006, 270-275.

Jaaskelainen, A., Katara, M., Kervinen, A., Maunumaa, M., Paakkonen, T., Takala, T., et al. (2009 May). Automatic GUI test generation for smartphone applications - an evaluation. 31st

International Conference on Software Engineering - Companion Volume, 2009. ICSE-Companion 2009, 112-122.

Jeffries, R., & Melnik, G. (2007 May/June). Guest Editors' Introduction: TDD--The Art of Fearless Programming. IEEE Software, 24(3), 24-30.

Kaner, C., & Bach, J. (2005 Fall). From Center for Software Testing Education & Research: http://www.testingeducation.org/k04/documents/BBSTOverviewPartC.pdf

Lu, Y., Yan, D., Nie, S., & Wang, C. (2008 December). Development of an Improved GUI Automation Test System Based on Event-Flow Graph. Proceedings of the 2008 International Conference on Computer Science and Software Engineering - Volume 02, 2, 712-715.

Maurer, F. (2009 July). Agile methods and interaction design: friend or foe? Proceedings of the 1st ACM SIGCHI Symposium on Engineering interactive Computing Systems, 209-210.

Memon, A. M. (2001). A Comprehensive Framework for Testing Graphical User Interfaces. Doctoral Thesis, University of Pittsburgh.

Memon, A. M. (2007 September). An event-flow model of GUI-based applications for testing. Software Testesting, Verification, and Reliability, 17(3), 137-157.

Memon, A. M., & Soffa, M. L. (2003 September). Regression testing of GUIs. Proceedings of the 9th European Software Engineering Conference Held Jointly with 11th ACM SIGSOFT International Symposium on Foundations of Software Engineering, 118-127.

Memon, A., Banerjee, I., & Nagarajan, A. (2003 October). What test oracle should I use for effective GUI testing? Proceedings. 18th IEEE International Conference on Automated Software Engineering, 164-173.

Mesbah, A., & van Deursen, A. (2009 May). Invariant-based automatic testing of AJAX user interfaces. Proceedings of the 2009 IEEE 31st International Conference on Software Engineering, 210-220.

Meszaros, G., & Aston, J. (2006). Adding Usability Testing to an Agile Project. Proceedings of the Conference on AGILE 2006, (pp. 289-294). Washington, DC.

Nagappan, N., Maximilien, E. M., Bhat, T., & Williams, L. (2008 June). Realizing quality improvement through test driven development: results and experiences of four industrial teams. Empirical Software Engineering, 13(3), 289-302.

Nielsen, J. (1990). Paper versus computer implementations as mockups scenarios for heuristic evaluation. Proceedings of the IFIP Tc13 Third Internationl Coneference on Human-Computer Interaction, (pp. 315-320). Amsterdam.

Nielsen, J. (1993). Usability Engineering. Morgan Kaufmann.

Nielsen, J. (1994). Guerilla HCI: using discount usability engineering to penetrate the intimidation barrier. In J. Nielsen, R. Bias, & D. Mayhew (Eds.), Cost-Justifying Usability (pp. 245-272). Orlando, FL: Academic Press.

Nielsen, J. (1995). Usability inspection methods. Conference Companion on Human Factors in COmputing Systems, (pp. 377-378). Denver, Colorado.

Patton, J. (2002). Hitting the Target: Adding Interaction Design to Agile Software Development. OOPSLA 2002 Practitioners Reports, (pp. 1-ff). Seattle, Washington.

Poole, C. (2005). Test-Driven User Interfaces. Proceedings of Extreme Programming and Agile Processes in Software Engineering, 6th International Conference, XP 2005, 285-286.

Reza, H., Endapally, S., & Grant, E. (2007 April). A Model-Based Approach for Testing GUI Using Hierarchical Predicate Transition Nets. Proceedings of the international Conference on information Technology, 366-370.

Robinson, B., & Brooks, P. (2009 April). An Initial Study of Customer-Reported GUI Defects. Proceedings of the IEEE international Conference on Software Testing, Verification, and Validation Workshops, 0, 267-274.

Ruiz, A., & Price, Y. W. (2007 May). Test-Driven GUI Development with TestNG and Abbot. IEEE Software, 24(3), 51-57.

Ruiz, A., & Price, Y. W. (2008 August). GUI Testing Made Easy. Proceedings of the Testing: Academic & industrial Conference - Practice and Research Techniques, 99-103.

Vieira, M., Leduc, J., Hasling, B., Subramanyan, R., & Kazmeier, J. (2006 May). Automation of GUI testing using a model-driven approach. Proceedings of the 2006 international Workshop on Automation of Software Test, 9-14.

Xie, Q., & Memon, A. M. (2006 November). Studying the Characteristics of a "Good" GUI Test Suite. Proceedings of the 17th international Symposium on Software Reliability Engineering, 159-168.

Xie, Q., & Memon, A. M. (2008 Nov.). Using a pilot study to derive a GUI model for automated testing. ACM Trans. Softw. Eng. Methodol., 18(2), 1-35.

Yin, Z., Miao, C., Shen, Z., & Miao, Y. (2005 September). Actionable Knowledge Model for GUI Regression Testing. Proceedings of the IEEE/WIC/ACM international Conference on intelligent Agent Technology, 165-168.

Author Biographies

Theodore D. Hellmann is the lead developer of LEET. He has experience with user interface automation, acceptance and unit testing, and the .NET Framework. His research interests include acceptance testing, test-driven development, and GUI testing. He joined the Agile Software Engineering lab at the University of Calgary after graduating magna cum laude from Christopher Newport University with B.Sc. in Computer Science.

Ali Hosseini-Khayat is a PhD student at the University of Calgary under the supervision of Dr. Frank Maurer. He holds a Master's degree in Computer Science from the University of Calgary. He is the lead developer of ActiveStory Enhanced and has experience with user interface design, usability evaluation and the .NET Framework.

Frank Maurer, is currently a full professor at the University of Calgary. His research has included work in artificial intelligence, agile software engineering, acceptance testing, and many other areas of software development. Over the course of his career he has formed many industrial, research, and governmental partnerships. Most recently, Frank is the principle investigator of an NSERC Strategic Network grant (the largest grant available from the Canadian National Science and Engineering Research Council).

Author Biographies

10 Organizational Culture and the Deployment of Agile Methods: The Competing Values Model View

Juhani Iivari, Netta Iivari

Abstract: A number of researchers have identified organizational culture as a factor that potentially affects the deployment of agile systems development methods. Inspired by the study of Iivari and Huisman (2007), which focused on the deployment of traditional systems development methods, the present paper proposes a number of hypotheses about the influence of organizational culture on the deployment of agile methods.

10.1 Introduction

Agile methods have received considerable attention during the last ten years (Dybå and Dingsøyr 2008). When compared with other systems development methods, they seem to be exceptionally well-received by practitioners. What is the explanation for this success? One possibility is, of course, the fashion factor, i.e. the early excitement with the idea. Although we cannot exclude this possibility, one can conceive of more fundamental changes in the systems development terrain that favor agile methods.

When arguing for agile systems development methods (SDMs), its proponents often refer to the increased turbulence and unpredictability of the world around us, that organizations and enterprises need to be more agile, more responsive to changes (Sherehiy et al. 2007). Ideally, agile methods support this organizational agility. Software development - also in the information systems (IS) context - is increasingly commodified and/or outsourced making it a relationship between an identifiable customer and a supplier. Although the requirements may be vague and volatile, the customer is assumed to be able to decide about them without potentially complex and time-consuming negotiation between different stakeholders on the customer's side. Much of software development is also evolutionary development of existing software product with a given architecture and technical design. The abundance of requirements and their prioritization is the problem in this evolutionary development rather than the identification and elicitation of requirements (Cusumano and Selby 1995). It may well be that under conditions like these agile

T. Dingsøyr et al. (eds.), *Agile Software Development*,
DOI 10.1007/978-3-642-12575-1_10, © Springer-Verlag Berlin Heidelberg 2010

methods really are better in terms of the speed and efficiency of development and the quality of developed system than alternative methods. Yet, there is not definite empirical evidence on this (Dybå and Dingsøyr 2008).

Despite the above positive trends, the adoption of the agile methods is not necessarily unproblematic. Compatibilities and incompatibilities between agile methods and organizational culture have been recognized as one explanation of the encountered difficulties (Cockburn and Highsmith 2001; Boehm and Turner 2005; Nerur et al. 2005; Chow and Cao 2008; Vijayasarathy and Turk 2008; Chan and Thong 2009). There are also more specific studies on the relationship between organizational culture and agile methods (Robinson and Sharp 2005; Siakas and Siakas 2007; Tolfo and Wazlawick 2008; Tolfo et al. 2009; Strode et al. 2009).

The purpose of the present paper is to analyze the relationship between organizational culture and the post-adoption deployment of agile methods, which is a largely neglected area in the case of agile methods (Abrahamsson et al. 2009). The analysis is inspired by Iivari and Huisman (2007), who studied the relationship in the case of traditional SDMs. They found that the hierarchical culture orientation increased the deployment of these methods as perceived by IS developers and the rational culture decreased it as perceived by IT managers. As an outcome they suggested a number of propositions and hypotheses to explain the findings. The present paper attempts to contrast agile methods with their findings.

The composition of the paper is the following. Section 10.2 introduces organizational culture and the competing values model (Denison and Spreitzer 1991) as a theoretical background of the present paper. The competing values model distinguishes four culture types: hierarchical culture, group culture, rational culture and developmental culture. Agile organization or enterprises in this framework represents developmental culture. Section 10.3 proceeds to the analysis of the relationship between organizational culture and the deployment of agile methods, contrasting agile methods with traditional ones. Section suggests a number of hypotheses to describe the relationship. Finally, Section 10.4 concludes the paper.

10.2 Organizational Culture and the Competing Values Model

10.2.1 Organizational Culture

Organizational culture forms the context in which systems development takes place. Although there is not much prior research into the relationship between organizational culture and the deployment of SDMs (Leidner and Kayworth 2006), there are good *a priori* reasons to believe in a relationship between the two. However, before going into detail in connection that, it needs to be emphasized that culture is a very complex concept with a multiplicity of definitions even in anthropology from which the concept originates (Kroeber and Kluckhohn 1952).

Also organizational culture has been approached from numerous viewpoints (Smircich 1983). One reason is that it can be construed to cover almost everything in an organization - basic assumptions and beliefs, attitudes, values, norms, morals, models of behaviour, customs, rituals, practices, habits, specific languages, ideas and symbols, heroes, art, artifacts, knowledge and technology (cf. Kluckhohn 1952; Gagliardi 1986; Hofstede et al. 1990; Keesing and Stratherns 1998). Therefore it is understandable that it has several interpretations (Smircich 1983,; Allaire and Firsirotu 1984; Czarniawska-Joerges 1992; Leidner and Kayworth 2006). Despite the differences, there seems to be an agreement that organizational culture includes several levels with a varying degree of awareness on the part of the culture-bearers (Schein 1985; Hofstede et al. 1990).

Among the variety of culture conceptions adopted in IS research Schein's (1985) model, the Competing Values Model (CVM) (Denison and Spreitzer 1991) and Hofstede's (1991) culture dimensions have been relatively popular. There are also divergent conceptions of the relationship between organizational culture and different kinds of IT efforts, such as the introduction of an information system or the deployment of SDMs.[1] Several researchers have emphasized the importance of cultural compatibility or fit (e.g. Gallivan and Srite 2005; Leidner and Kayworth 2006), postulating that the organizational culture should be compatible with the IT effort in question in order to succeed. Yet, their recommendations of how to achieve the compatibility differ (Iivari 2006).

10.2.2 Existing Research into the Relationship Between Organizational Culture and Agile Methods

There are a few studies that have investigated the relationship between organizational culture and agile methods (Robinson and Sharp 2005, Siakas & Siakas 2007, Tolfo and Wazlawick 2008, Tolfo et al. 2009, Strode et al. 2009). They clearly demonstrate that organizational culture can be conceptualized in a number of ways. Robison and Sharp (2005) apply a categorization of four culture types from Cockburn (2001) to analyze the relationship between organizational culture and XP in three empirical cases, finding that XP is culturally flexible so that it can thrive in different organizational cultures.[2] Siakas and Siakas (2007) identify an ideal organizational culture to embrace 'agile professional culture' by relying on a typology of organizational cultures influenced by the cultural dimensions identi-

---

[1]IT efforts are interpreted to include efforts related to the development, implementation, adoption, use, operation or management of IT artifacts.

[2]The four culture types are *hierarchical* (central command and control), *random* (little or no central command and control), *collaborative* (consensus-based on command and control) and *synchronous* (where work is co-ordinated with no explicit evidence of command and control).

fied by Hofstede (2001). The culture types are labeled as Clan, Democratic, Hierarchical and Disciplined, of which the Democratic culture type is brought up as the most suitable one (Siakas and Siakas 2007). Tolfo and Wazlawick (2008) discuss six dimensions of organizational culture using one case organization to illustrate each dimension.[3] They identify a number of favorable and unfavorable aspects in relation to XP adoption in the case of each dimension. Tolfo et al. (2009) applies Schein's (1985) framework to contrast organizational culture of three case companies from Tolfo and Wazlawick (2008) with an idealized agile culture. Finally, Strode and colleagues (2009) study the relationships between 24 culture indicators adopted from the competing values model (see below) and the weighted sum of agile (XP) technique usage in the case of nine projects, four of which are characterized as non-agile. The Spearman correlations coefficients show most consistently significant associations with the group culture (with five of six indicators of group culture) and more weakly with the developmental culture (with two of the six indicators of developmental culture).

All these studies rely on the assumption of cultural compatibility or fit. They identify characteristics of an ideal organizational culture for agile methods. However, there are clear differences in their recommendations related to how to achieve the compatibility. Some studies argue for changing the culture so that it is compatible with agile methods (Tolfo and Wazlawick 2008; Tolfo et al. 2009), although acknowledging that this is difficult. It is also reminded that researchers are dealing with a complex anthropological and sociological phenomenon that is quite unique in every organization (Tolfo et al. 2009).

A number of studies imply that there might be difficulties involved in separating the 'organizational culture' from the 'agile method usage' and that there might be interaction between the cultural context and the agile methods.[4] Robinson and Sharp (2005), emphasize the cultural flexibility of agile methods, based on the finding that XP has succeeded to thrive in very divergent organizational cultures as interpreted in their study. Siakas and Siakas (2007) underline that the agile approach should be considered as a culture of its own (Siakas and Siakas 2007), in a way analogous to professional cultures.[5] Sharp and Robinson (2004) identify characteristics of a 'XP culture', which is not presented as an ideal one *per se*, but is based on an ethnographic examination of a particularly mature XP team.

Following Iivari and Huisman (2007), this paper will apply the competing values model (Quinn and Rohrbaugh 1983; Quinn and Kimberly 1984; Denison and

---

[3]The dimensions are: innovation and risk, detail orientation, outcome orientation, people orientation, team orientation, aggressiveness, and stability.

[4]Taking into account the semantic broadness of the concept of "culture" the difficulty is understandable.

[5]Although Siakas and Siakas (2007) speak about "agile professional culture", we are hesitant to characterize it professional for two reasons. First, software developers or engineers or similar occupations cannot be considered "professionals" in the sense of being members of "professions" as understood in sociology of professions. Second, it may well be that many software developers or engineers do not regard agile methods particularly "professional" in the sense of representing the "best practices".

Spreitzer 1991) as a theoretical model of organizational culture, and identity a number of hypotheses connected to the relationship between organizational culture and agile method deployment. The model focuses on values as core constituents of organizational culture and therefore helps us to avoid the problem of overlap between the 'organizational culture' and the 'agile method use'.

10.2.3 Competing Values Model

Competing values model (CVM) is based on two distinctions: *change* vs. *stability* and *internal focus* vs. *external focus* (Figure 10.1). Change emphasizes flexibility and spontaneity, whereas stability focuses on control, continuity and order. Internal focus underlines integration and maintenance of the socio-technical system, whereas external focus emphasizes competition and interaction with the organizational environment (Denison and Spreitzer 1991). The opposite ends of these dimensions impose competing and conflicting demands on the organization.

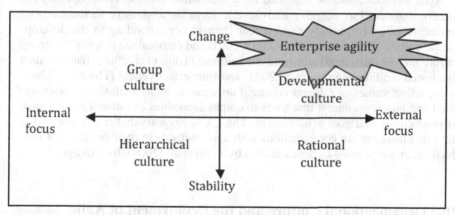

Fig. 10.1. The competing values framework for organizational culture and enterprise agility

Based on the two dimensions, one can distinguish four types of culture. *The group culture* (change and internal focus) is primarily concerned with human relations and flexibility. Belonging, trust and participation are its core values. Effectiveness criteria include the development of human potential and member commitment. The *developmental culture* (change and external focus) is future-oriented, considering what might be. The effectiveness criteria emphasize growth, resource acquisition, creativity and adaptation to the external environment. The *rational culture* (stability and external focus) is achievement-oriented, focusing on productivity, efficiency and goal achievement. The *hierarchical culture* (stability and internal focus) is oriented towards security, order and routinization. It emphasizes control, stability and efficiency through the following regulations. Each of the cultural types has its polar opposites (Denison and Spreitzer 1991). A group culture, which emphasizes flexibility and internal focus, is contrasted with a rational culture, the latter stressing control and external focus. A developmental culture, which is characterized by flexibility and external focus, is opposed by a hierarchical culture, which emphasizes control and internal focus.

Organizational or enterprise agility in this framework represents developmental culture. Sherehiy et al. (2007) provide a recent review of the concept rooting it into contingency theory and especially into the distinction between mechanistic and organic organizational forms (Burns and Stalker 1961), and Overby et al. (2006) and van Oosterhout et al. (2006) discuss it more from viewpoint of IT. Enterprise agility is usually associated with adaptivity and flexibility, i.e. an organizations' ability to adjust in response to changes in the environment (Sherehiy et al. 2007) implying external focus and change.

The four culture types are ideal types in the sense that an organization is unlikely to reflect only one type (Denison and Spreitzer 1991). CVM stresses a reasonable balance between the opposite orientations, although some cultural types may be more dominant than others. This imposes paradoxical requirements for effective organizations (Cameron 1986).

Agile methods illustrate this need for a reasonable balance. Although they are usually introduced as adaptive and flexible methods responsive to the environmental volatility (especially requirement change) corresponding to the developmental culture (Highsmith and Cockburn 2001) and emphasize values of the group culture such as trust, motivation and commitment (Tolfo et al. 2009), features such timeboxed deadlines (Aydin et al. 2005) and team effectiveness (The Agile Manifesto) reflect values of rational culture. Furthermore, agile methods are often applied in a business context that tends to emphasize values of rational culture such as productivity and goal achievement. The CVM suggests that it is naïve to believe that there are not contradictions with agile methods in their emphasis of productivity and efficiency as demonstrated by Tolfo et al. (2009), for example.

10.3 Organizational Culture and the Deployment of Agile Methods

10.3.1 The Theoretical Model

Iivari and Huisman (2007) conducted a survey on the relationship between organizational culture, measured in terms of CVM, and the deployment of SDMs, "deployment" referring to method support, method use, and method impact. The survey was targeted to IT departments in South Africa. They received completed IT manager questionnaires from 73 organizations and completed IS developer questionnaires from 234 developers from 71 organizations. The total number of organizations was 80 and the number of responses from organizations with both IS developer and IT manager responses was 64.

Recognizing that large organizations tend to develop a number of subcultures (Gregory 1983; Smircich 1983), Iivari and Huisman (2007) analyzed organizational culture of IT departments, since they can be expected to be most closely associated with the behavior of IS developers and the deployment of SDMs. Furthermore, they focused on the cultural perceptions of one occupational community (Van Maanen and Barley 1984), IS developers. The reason for this focus was to avoid associating culture with the IT managers' view of the desirable culture to be imposed on the IT department. IT managers' views of organizational culture may represent an organizational ideology that they exercise in their normative control over IS developers (Kunda 1992). This ideology may differ radically from the organizational culture perceived by IS developers.

In the case of SDM deployment, Iivari and Huisman (2007) studied both IS developers' and IT managers' perceptions. One reason for this is the possible common method bias brought by a research design in which the same respondents (i.e. IS developers) assess both organizational and SDM deployment. This research design allowed inter-group analysis in which organizational culture is assessed by IS developers and deployment by IT managers.

Descriptive data analysis showed that the their data were dominated by the classical structured and information modelling approaches and phased process models, characterised by sequential phases such as feasibility study, requirements analysis, design, implementation and installation (Huisman 2000), whereas more modern approaches such as object-orientation and agile methods were not well represented. Only Rapid Application Development represented the lighter and less bureaucratic ways of developing systems.

To test the effect of individual culture orientations, Iivari and Huisman (2007) used regression analysis, using seven measures of SDM deployment as the dependent variable and the four indicators of organizational culture as the independent variables. One striking finding was the positive relationship between the hierarchical culture orientation and SDM deployment in the case of IS developers: the more hierarchical a culture was perceived to be by IS developers, the more support SDMs was perceived to provide and the more they were used. The developmental culture was also found to have a positive association with SDM deployment, but not systematically. Quite interestingly, the more rational the culture orientation, the more critical IT managers were with regard to SDM support and impact. This was intriguing, since Huisman and Iivari (2006) found IT managers to have more positive perceptions of SDM deployment than IS developers.

To explain these empirical findings, Iivari and Huisman (2007) proposed a theoretical model depicted in Figure 10.2, which essentially views SDMs as norm systems (Lyytinen 1986). The model makes a distinction between propositions and hypotheses based on their generality. Propositions are more general, whereas hypotheses are more bounded in time and space.[6] Hypotheses confined to tradi-

---

[6]Even though influenced by Dubin (1978) our use of the terms "proposition" and "hypothesis" differs from his. For him propositions exist between theoretical constructs and hypotheses be-

tional methods and agile methods (see Tables 10.1-10.3 below) illustrate the significance of boundaries in our case.

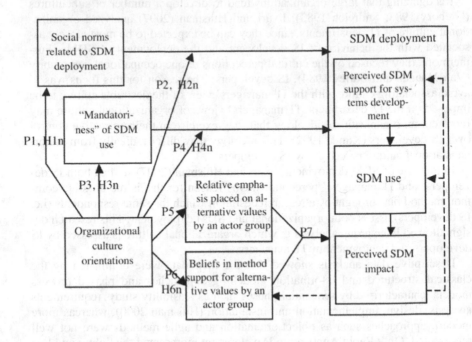

Fig. 10.2 The theoretical model (adapted from Iivari and Huisman 2007)

The following three sections will contrast agile methods with traditional methods discussing Propositions P1 and P2 in Section 10.3.2, Propositions P3 and P4 in Section 10.3.3, and finally Propositions P5 – P7 in Section 10.3.4. Although we agree with Conboy (2009) that the concept of "agility" in the context of SDMs is ambiguous, we simply interpret agile methods to form a set of methods coherent enough to be considered a systems development approach of its own (in the sense of Iivari et al. 1998). By traditional methods we mean model/documentation-oriented methods that apply a sequential phased process model akin to the linear waterfall model.[7] Contrary to Iivari and Huisman (2007) we do not limit the focus on in-house IT departments only, but our interest lies in any software development

---

tween operational variables. According to Dubin (1978) it would be more appropriate to talk about "laws of interaction" and "propositions". We are hesitant, however, to talk about "laws" in the context of behavioral sciences.

[7]Contrasting agile methods with traditional methods as opposites leaves out intermediate positions such as spiral models (Boehm 1988; Iivari 1990), which combine modeling with prototyping, are highly iterative (at least the version by Iivari 1990), and consequently imply a process mode of planning as a contrast to the blueprint mode of planning (Faludi 1973).

organizations. Therefore, instead of IS developers we speak about software developers. We also have non-safety critical software in mind rather than safety-critical software.

10.3.2 Agile Methods as Social Norms and Their Use

Social norms in Figure 10.2 cover SDMs as norm systems (Lyytinen 1987) and norms about their use (e.g. subjective norms in Fishbein and Ajzen 1975). Agile methods are often characterized as less prescriptive than more traditional ones (Tolfo and Wazlawick 2008). One can distinguish two aspects in the prescriptiveness – the degree of formalization of systems development implied by the method (see Proposition 1) and its mandatoriness (see Proposition P3). The degree of formalization implied a SDM can be conceptualized as the sum of concreteness (Abrahamsson et al. 2003) of the social norms embedded in the method. Mandatoriness to be discussed in Section 10.3.3 describes the extent to which the social norms embedded in the SDM are made mandatory in the organization. The distinction between the degree of formalization and mandatoriness is significant, since agile methods tend to be formalized to a lesser extent than traditional methods and therefore are lighter (Boehm and Turner 2005; Erickson et al. 2005), but the mandatoriness of principles and techniques of agile methods may be equally high as in the case of traditional methods (Parsons et al. 2007).

Table 10.1 suggests a number of hypotheses related to Propositions P1 and P2, contrasting agile methods with traditional ones. The major attention will be paid to hypotheses associated with agile methods in the following discussion. Hypotheses associated with the traditional methods (column 2) are argued in more detail in Iivari and Huisman (2007)[8].

Hypothesis H11 is a direct consequence of the hierarchical culture orientation that emphasizes following regulations and routinization (Denison an Spreitzer 1991). Hypothesis H12 concerns all SDMs equally. Recognizing that SDM methods may differ in their heaviness, we suggest that there is an inverted u-shaped relationship between the degree of formalization implied by a method and perceived method support for systems development and consequently with method use. The reasoning is that if the method is close to empty, i.e. includes quite few social norms at an abstract level, it does not provide much support for the systems development and consequently will not be used. On the other hand, we recognize that a method may grow too heavy, too complex to understand and to use, and therefore – although possibly including useful knowledge – may remain unused. The question is where is the peak of the inverted u-shaped curve.

---

[8]Compared with Iivari and Huisman (2007) Hypotheses H21 and H31 have been added and the wording of some hypotheses is also modified slightly.

Table 10.1 Propositions P1 and P2 with associated hypotheses

Propositions	Hypotheses (adapted from Iivari and Huisman 2007)	Hypotheses (inspired by agile methods)
P1 Organizational culture orientations affect social norms related to SMD use.	H11 The hierarchical culture orientation increases the degree of formalization of systems development.	Note that a high developmental culture orientation implies a lower hierarchical culture orientation.
		H12 There is an inverted u-shaped relationship between the degree of formalization implied by a SDM and the perceived method support for systems development and consequently with method use.
P2 Organizational culture orientations affect the extent to which social norms concerning SMD use influence actual method use.	H21 The hierarchical culture orientation affects positively the extent to which social norms concerning systems development influences the real systems development practice i.e. method use.	H22 The developmental culture orientation affects the inverted u-shaped relationship referred to in H12, moving its maximum value to the left.
		H23 The group culture orientation affects positively the extent to which the degree of formalization implied by an agile method influences real systems development practice i.e. method use

Hypothesis H21 claims that – independently of the degree of formalization – the hierarchical culture orientation affects positively the extent to which social norms concerning method use influence actual method use. Hypothesis H22 on the other hand suggests that the developmental culture orientation affects the inverted u-shaped relationship between the degree of formalization implied by a SDM and the perceived method support and consequently with method use (see Hypothesis H12) so that the inverted u-shaped curve achieves its maximum value sooner. The idea is that people in organizations with a strong development culture are less tolerant to heavy methods. Note that since the strong developmental orientation implies lower hierarchical orientation, organizations with a strong developmental culture tend to have lower formalization of systems development (see Hypothesis H11) and as a consequence lighter methods.

Hypotheses discussed above have been independent of the nature of methods – whether traditional or agile. Hypothesis H23 on the contrary concerns only agile methods. Much of the literature on agile methods concludes that they are highly people-oriented, implying an agile culture of minimal hierarchy, self-organization, equity, empowerment, commitment, responsibility, participation, learning and continuous improvement, consensus, respect, compromises, trust, honesty, openness, communication (Siakas and Siakas 2007, Suscheck and Ford 2008, Tolfo et al. 2009). These characteristics reflect the group culture in the Competing Values Model. Although altogether they sound idealistic, it is interesting to test to what extent the group culture orientation really facilitates agile method use as expressed in Hypothesis H23.

10.3.3 Mandatoriness of Agile Methods and Their Use

Mandatoriness describes the extent to which the social norms embedded in the SDM are made mandatory in the organization. It can be contrasted with "voluntariness" (Moore and Benbasat 1991), which is a more subjective view of the extent to which SDM use is perceived as voluntary. Table 10.2 suggests three hypotheses related the mandatoriness of SDMs.

Table 10.2 Propositions P3 and P4 with associated hypotheses

Propositions	Hypotheses (adapted from Iivari and Huisman 2007)	Hypotheses (inspired by agile methods)
P3 Organizational culture orientations affect the extent to which SDMs are made mandatory.	H31 The hierarchical culture orientation affects positively the extent to which SDMs are made mandatory	Note that a high developmental culture orientation implies a lower hierarchical culture orientation
P4 Organizational culture orientations affect the extent to which "mandatoriness" of SDM use influences actual method use.	H41 The hierarchical culture orientation affects positively the extent to which "mandatoriness" of SDM use influences actual method use.	H42 The development culture orientation affects negatively the extent to which "mandatoriness" of SDM use influences actual method use

Hypothesis H31 proposes that the hierarchical culture orientation tends to increase the degree of mandatoriness of SDMs and Hypothesis H41 claims that the strength of the hierarchical culture affects the extent to which mandatory methods are used. Although there is no prior research on the relationship between mandatoriness and SDM deployment, the negative association between voluntariness and the acceptance of SDMs and related software process innovations (Iivari 1996; Riemenschneider et al. 2002; Green et al. 2004) partially support H41, which claims that this is especially so in organizations with a strong hierarchical culture.

Hypothesis H42 assumes that the developmental culture orientation has a negative effect on the degree to which "mandatoriness" of method use influences actual method use. There is a long research tradition on method adaptation or tailoring to the fit the project (e.g. Basili and Rombach 1987; Harmsen et al. 1994), and recently the issue has been raised in the context of agile methods (Aydin et al. 2005; Fitzgerald et al. 2006; Parsons et al. 2007; Sharp and Robinson 2008; Cao et al. 2009; Sharp et al. 2009). Hypothesis H42 does not address exactly this, but the question of to what extent the mandatoriness of the method - tailored or not – is followed, the assumption being that the higher developmental culture is, the more method use comprises method improvisation.[9] Method improvisation means that the method is not read, interpreted and followed literally, but its various principles, models and techniques may be adapted, modified, changed, skipped, substituted, combined possibly in an innovative way on the fly.[10]

10.3.4 Alternative Values and Agile Method Use

Iivari and Huisman (2007) concluded that propositions P1-P4 with their related hypotheses are not effective in explaining the critical attitude of IT managers towards SDM deployment in organizations with a strong rational culture. To explain this they introduced values and actors' beliefs into the SDM support for alternative values in Figure 10.2. Based on CVM Proposition P5 suggests that organizational culture orientations affect the relative emphasis put on alternative values by different actor groups:

- hierarchical culture orientation: control, stability and efficiency through the following of regulations
- group culture orientation: underlining development of human potential and member commitment
- developmental culture orientation: growth, resource acquisition, creativity and adaptation to the external environment
- traditional culture orientation: productivity, efficiency and goal achievement

Proposition P5 allows for the fact that not all actor groups (e.g. managers and developers) necessarily emphasize the alternative values equally, even though they may share the same organizational subculture. Despite the difference in the absolute emphases on different values, P5 assumes that the direction of the influence of the culture will be consistent between the groups: the stronger the culture orientation, the stronger the emphasis on the values of that orientation in each actor group.

At the same time, the culture orientations may also have an impact on the actor groups' beliefs in the SDM support for alternative values (Proposition P6). Inspired by their two most striking empirical findings, Iivari and Huisman (2007) proposed Hypothesis H61 and Hypotheses H62, pointing out that these two hypotheses are specific to traditional SDMs (Table 10.3).

---

[9]Improvisation in the context IS development and software engineering has been of increasing interest during the last years (Dybå 2000; Bansler and Havn 2004).

[10]The idea of method improvisation has some similarity with dynamic method adaptation in Aydin et al. (2005), but they regard the project manager as the key actor of the dynamic adaptation. Hypothesis H42 concerns IT managers, project managers and ordinary software developers equally. Suscheck and Ford (2008) discuss jazz improvisation in the context SCRUM, but they do not really address method improvisation.

Table 10.3 Proposition P6 with associated hypotheses

Propositions	Hypotheses (adapted from Iivari and Huisman 2007)	Hypotheses (inspired by agile methods)
P6 Organizational culture orientations affect the beliefs in SMD support for alternative values.	H61 The hierarchical culture orientation has a positive impact on software developers' beliefs in <u>traditional method</u> support for the values of the hierarchical culture. H62 The rational culture orientation has a negative impact on IT managers' beliefs in <u>traditional method</u> for the values of the rational culture.	H63a The hierarchical culture orientation has a positive impact on IT managers' and software developers' beliefs in <u>agile method</u> support for the values of the hierarchical culture H63b The hierarchical culture orientation has a negative impact on IT managers' and software developers' beliefs in <u>agile method</u> support for the values of the hierarchical culture when compared with <u>traditional methods</u>. H64 The hierarchical culture orientation has a negative impact on IT managers' and software developers' beliefs in <u>agile method</u> support for the values of the rational culture when compared with <u>traditional methods</u>. H65a There is an inverted u-shaped relationship between the rational culture orientation and IT managers' and software developers' beliefs in <u>agile method</u> support for the values of the rational culture. H65b The rational culture orientation has a positive impact on IT managers' and software developers' beliefs in <u>agile method</u> support for the values of the rational culture when compared with <u>traditional methods</u>. H66a There is an inverted u-shaped relationship between the group culture orientation and IT managers and software developers' beliefs in <u>agile method</u> support for the values of the group culture. H66b The group culture orientation has a positive impact on IT managers and software developers' beliefs in <u>agile method</u> support for the values of the group culture when compared with <u>traditional methods</u>. H67a There is an inverted u-shaped relationship between the developmental culture orientation and IT developers' and software developers' beliefs in <u>agile method</u> support for the values of the developmental culture. H67b The developmental culture orientation has a positive impact on IT developers' and software developers' beliefs in <u>agile method</u> support for the values of the developmental culture when compared with <u>traditional methods</u>.

When considering hypotheses related to Proposition P6, one should be explicit about the anchor to which one compares the methods in question. The anchor may be totally *ad hoc* development in the case of traditional methods. Now when there is a transition going on from traditional methods to agile ones, the former may provide a natural anchor in the agile case. One should note, however, that there are increasingly software development organizations that do not have any experience with traditional methods. In their case *ad hoc* development would be a natural anchor.

Table 10.3 includes a number of hypotheses concerning both cases. Hypotheses H63a and H65a-H67a concern agile methods, *ad hoc* development as the anchor. Hypothesis H63a claims, that when compared with *ad hoc* development, also agile methods imply more discipline, although they are claimed to work at the edge of chaos or close to it (Wang and Vidgen 2007; Kautz and Zumpe 2008). Hypotheses H65a-H67a suggest that there is an inverted u-shaped association between the culture orientations and IT managers and software developers' beliefs in agile method support for the values of the respective culture orientation, i.e. after some point on the culture orientation dimension the respondents see agile methods to provide less and less support for the values in question. There are at least three explanations for this. First, as pointed out above, agile methods aim at balancing values of different culture orientations. Second, according to the CVM there are contradictions between the culture orientations – especially between diagonally opposing ones (hierarchical vs. developmental and group vs. rational). Third, when a culture orientation gets higher the expectations of the support also grow higher, and when high enough the support will be perceived to be lower.

Hypotheses H63b and H65b-H67b compare agile and traditional methods. Hypothesis H63b argues that the hierarchical culture orientation has a negative impact on IT managers' and software developers' beliefs in *agile method* support for control, stability and efficiency through following regulations, when compared with traditional methods. Together H63a and H63b suggest that the lack of discipline is not an absolute property of agile methods and that it is related to the hierarchical culture orientation. This allows the possibility that in organizations with a weak developmental culture and a low hierarchical culture people may perceive agile methods to imply more discipline than traditional ones, the latter appearing more or less crazy to them.

Hypotheses H65b-H67b claim that except in the case of hierarchical culture each culture orientation has a positive impact on IT managers' and software developers' beliefs in agile method support for the corresponding values, when compared with traditional methods. One should note here that these three hypotheses do not claim that the agile methods support better the values of development, group and rational cultures, even though they may well do so. They only state that a stronger culture orientation in each of these three cases favors agile methods, when compared with traditional ones. We believe that it is especially so in the case of development and group culture orientations. In our view Hypothesis H65b is most questionable among the three, whether the assumed disappointment in agile methods in organizations with a strong rational culture orientation (see Hypothesis H65a) starts to exceed the corresponding disappointment with traditional methods.

In addition to "intra-cultural" hypotheses, which have the same culture orientation on both sides of the hypothesis (Hypotheses H63a, H63b, H65a-H67a, H65b-H67b), one could state "cross-cultural" hypotheses, illustrated by Hypothesis H64 in Table 10.3. It claims that the hierarchical orientation has a negative impact on IT managers' beliefs on agile method support for the values of the rational culture, when compared with traditional methods. Together with Hypothesis H63b it assumes that in highly hierarchical organizations respondents believe that traditional methods do not only support order and discipline, but also productivity, efficiency and goal achievement better than agile methods.

Proposition 7 suggests that the relative emphasis placed on alternative values by actor groups and their beliefs in SDM support for these alternative values influence SDM deployment in an interactive manner (see Figure 10.2). This implies that if an actor group (IT managers, for example) places strong emphasis on certain values (e.g. productivity and efficiency) and see SDMs as supporting these values, this promotes method deployment. If, on the other hand, they see that SDMs support these negatively, this will have a negative influence on method deployment.

10.4 Conclusion

The relationship between organizational culture and the deployment of agile systems development is a rich and interesting issue. One reason is the richness of the concept of "organizational culture" and the variety of ways it may be related with the deployment of agile methods. After a review of the literature on organizational culture and the deployment of SDMs, Table 10.1 proposed thirteen new hypotheses inspired by the agile methods. The number of hypotheses is to a great extent explained by the four dimensions of organizational culture identified in the CVM and by the fact that agile methods are contrasted with *ad hoc* development and with traditional methods.

The hypotheses have quite interesting implications. First, not surprisingly they are consistent with the current understanding that agile methods are most incompatible with hierarchical culture orientation (Hypotheses H63b and H64), although they also imply more discipline than *ad hoc* development (Hypothesis H63a). Furthermore, assuming that agile methods are adopted in an organization with relatively strong hierarchical culture, Hypothesis H11 would predict that they will be formalized further by combining complementary features of different agile methods, for example, such as XP and Scrum (Fitzgerald et al. 2006) and agile modeling. This makes these combined models heavier and as a consequence they may start to loose some of their agility.

Quite interestingly, Hypotheses H31, H41 and H42 suggest that there may a paradox between the hierarchical culture and developmental culture, if the goal is faithful enactment of methods. Less mandatory methods may be more effectively enacted in organizations with a strong hierarchical culture orientation than in organizations with a strong developmental culture orientation, because the desired behavior will be followed more faithfully in the former case (Hypothesis H41) than in the latter case where we expect more method improvisation (Hypothesis H42).

Hypotheses H63a, H65a-H67a suggest that, when compared with *ad hoc* development, each culture orientation favors agile methods but only up to some point in the case of rational, group, and development culture orientations. Furthermore, one can conjecture that more formalized the agile method becomes (Hypothesis H11), the sooner it will be considered dysfunctional in organizations with strong developmental culture (Hypothesis H22).

Tables 10.1-10.3 also contrasted agile methods with traditional methods, interpreting the latter to be modeling/documentation-oriented methods that follow sequential phased process. We hypothesized that each culture orientation, except the hierarchical one, favors agile methods, but as pointed out above that does not imply that agile methods are better ones, even though they may well be.

The major limitation of the present paper is the conception of organizational culture implied by the CVM and the focus of culture as a set of measurable independent variables. As pointed out in Section 10.2, organizational culture and related context can be interpreted to include aspects such as basic assumptions and beliefs, attitudes, values, norms, morals, models of behaviour, customs, rituals, practices, habits, specific languages, ideas and symbols, heroes, art, artifacts, knowledge and technology, with varying degrees of awareness by the cultural members. The CVM focused only on values among this variety.

Despite this limitation the present paper opens an avenue for interesting future research. After operationalization of the relevant variables Figure 10.2 with associated hypotheses (Tables 10.1-10.3) is ready for empirical testing. Although the model looks fairly complex, it is still testable using quantitative confirmatory methods, which seem most appropriate in its case. We wish to be able to proceed to the empirical validation of the model as soon as possible.

References

Abrahamsson, P., Conboy, K. and Wang, X. (2009) 'Lots done, more to do': the current state of agile systems development research, *European Journal of Information Systems*, Vol. 18, pp. 281-284

Abrahamsson, P., Warsta, J., Siponen, M. and Ronkainen, J. (2003). New directions on agile methods: A comparative analysis, in *Proceedings of the 25th International Conference on Software Engineering (ICSE'03)*, IEEE Computer Society, Washington, DC, pp. 244-254

Allaire, Y. and and Firsirotu, M.E. (1984). Theories of organizational culture, *Organization Studies*, Vol. 5, No. 3, pp. 193-226

Aydin, M.N., Harmsen, F., van Slooten, K. and Stegwee, R.A. (2005). On the adaptation of agile information systems development method, *Journal of Database Management*, Vol. 16, No. 4, pp. 24-40

Bansler, J.P. and Havn, E.C. (2004). Improvisation in information systems development, *Information Systems Research: Relevant Theory and Informed Practice*, Springer, Boston, pp. 631-646

Basili, V. and Rombach, H. (1987). Tailoring the software process to project goals and environments, in *Proceedings of the 9th International Conference on Software Engineering, IEEE*, pp. 345-357

Boehm, B. (1988). A spiral model of software development and enhancement, *Computer*, Vol. 21, pp. 61-72

Boehm, B. and Turner, R. (2005). Management challenges to implementing agile processes in traditional development organization, *IEEE Software*, Vol. 32, No. 5, pp. 30-39

Burns, T. and Stalker, G.M. (1986). *The Management of Innovation*, Tavistock, London, 1961

Cameron, K.S. (). Effectiveness as paradox: Consensus and conflict in conceptions of organizational effectiveness, *Management Science*, vol. 32, No. 5, pp. 539-553

Cao, L., Mohan, K., Xu, P. and Ramesh, B. (2009). A framework for adapting agile development methodologies, *European Journal of Information Systems*, Vol. 18, pp. 332-343

Chan F.K.Y. and Thong, J.Y.L. (2009). Acceptance of agile methodologies: A critical review and conceptual framework, *Decision Support Systems*, Vol. 46, pp. 803-814

Chow, T. and Cao, D.-B. (2008). A survey of critical success factors in agile software projects, *The Journal of Systems and Software*, Vol. 81, pp. 961-971

Cockburn, A. and Highsmith, J. (2001). Agile software development: The people factor, *Computer*, Vol. 34, No. 11, 131-133

Conboy, K. (2009). Agility from first principles: Reconstructing the concept of agility in information systems development, *Information Systems Research*, Vol. 20, No. 3, pp. 329-354

Cusumano, M. A., and Shelby, R. W. (1995). *Microsoft Secrets: How the Worlds Most Powerful Software Company Creates Technology, Shapes Markets and Manages People*, The Free Press, New York.

Czarniawska-Joerges, B. (1992). *Exploring Complex Organizations: A Cultural Perspective*, SAGE Publicaations, Newbury Park, CA.

Denison, D.R. and Spreitzer, G.M. (1991). Organizational culture and organizational development: A competing values approach, in Woodman, R.W. and Pasmore, W.A (eds.), *Research In Organizational Change and Development*, Volume 5, JAI Press Inc, Greenwich, CT, pp. 1-21

Dubin, R. (1969). *Theory Building*, The Free Press, New York.

Dybå, T. (2000). Improvisation in small software organizations, *IEEE Software*, Vo. 17, No. 5, pp. 82-87

Dybå, T. and Dingsøyr, T. (2008). Empirical studies of agile software development: A systematic review, *Information and Software Technology*, Vol. 50, pp. 833-859

Erickson J., Lyytinen, K. and Siau, K. (2005). Agile modeling, agile software development, and extreme programming: The state of research, *Journal of Database Management*, Vol. 16, No. 4, pp. 88-100

Faludi, A. (1973). *Planning Theory*, Pergamon Press, Oxford.

Fitzgerald, B., Hartnett, G. and Conboy, K. (2006). Customising agile methods to software practices at Interl Shannon, *European Journal of Information Systems*, Vol. 15, No. 2, pp. 200-213

Fishbein, M. and Ajzen, I. (1975). *Belief, Attitude, Intention and Behavior: An Introduction to Theory and Research*, Addison-Wesley, Reading, MA.

Gagliardi, P. (1986). The creation and change of organizational cultures: a conceptual framework, *Organization Studies*, Vol. 7, No. 2, pp. 117-134

Gallivan, M. and Srite, M. (2005). Information technology and culture: Identifying fragmentary and holistic perspectives of culture. *Information and Organization*, Vol. 15, pp. 295-338.

Green, G.C., Collins, R.W. and Hevner, A.R. (2004). Perceived control and diffusion of software process innovations, *Journal of High Technology Management Research*, Vol. 15, No. 1, pp. 123-144

Gregory, K.L. (1983). Native-view paradigms: Multiple cultures and culture conflicts in organizations, *Administrative Science Quarterly*, Vol. 28, No. 3, , pp. 359-376

Hardgrave, B.C. and Johnson, R.A. (2003). Toward an information systems development acceptance model: The case of object-oriented systems development, *IEEE Transactions on Engineering Management*, Vol. 50, No. 3, pp. 322-336

Harmsen, F., Brinkkemper, S and Oie, H. (1994). Situational method engineering for information systems projects, in Olle, T.W. and Verrijn Stuart, A.A. (eds.), *Methods and Associated Tools for Information Systems Life-Cycle*, North-Holland, Amsterdam, pp. 169-194

Hofstede, G. (1991). *Culture and Organizations. Software of the Mind*. McGraw-Hill, London.

Hofstede, G. (2001). *Culture's Consequences. Comparing Values, Behaviors, Institutions, and Organizations across Nations*. 2nd Edition. Sage Publications Inc, Thousand Oaks.

Hofstede, G., Neuijen, B., Ohayv, D.D. and Sanders, G. (1990). Measuring organizational cultures: A qualitative and quantitative study across twenty cases, *Administrative Science Quarterly*, Vol. 35, No. 2, pp. 286-316

Hossain, E., Babar, M.A. an Paik, H.-Y. (2009). Using Scrum in global software development: A systematic literature review, in *2009 Fourth IEEE International Conference on Global Software Engineering*, IEEE Computer Society, Washington, DC, pp. 175-184

Huisman, H.M. (2000). *The deployment of systems development methodologies: A South African experience*, Ph.D dissertation, Potchefstroom University for CHE, Potchefstroom, South Africa.

Huisman, M. and Iivari, J. (2006). Deployment of systems development methodologies: Perceptual congruence between IS managers and systems developers, *Information & Management*, Vol. 43, No. 1, pp. 29-49

Iivari J. (1990). Hierarchical spiral model for information system and software development, Part 2: de- sign process, *Information and Software Technology*, Vol. 32, No. 7, pp. 450-458

Iivari, J. (1996). Why are CASE tools not used?, *Communications of the ACM*, Vol. 39, No. 10, pp. 94-103

Iivari, J., Hirschheim, R. and Klein, H.K. (2000-2001). A dynamic framework for classifying information systems development methodologies and approaches, *Journal of Management Information Systems*, Vol. 17, No. 3, pp. 179-218

Iivari, J. and Huisman, M. (2007). The relationship between organisational culture and the deployment of systems development methodologies, *MIS Quarterly*, Vol. 31, No. 1, pp. 35-58

Iivari, N. (2006). 'Representing the User' in Software Development – A Cultural Analysis of Usability Work in the Product Development Context, *Interacting with Computers*, Vol. 18, No. 4, pp. 635-664

Kappos, A. and Rivard, S. (2008). A Three-Perspective Model of Culture, Information Systems, and Their Development and Use. *MIS Quarterly*, Vol. 32, No. 3, pp. 601-634.

Kautz K. and Zumpe, S. (2008). Just enough structure at the edge of chaos: Agile information system development in practice, in Abrahamsson, P. et al. (eds.), *XP 2008*, LNBIP 9, Springer-Verlag, Berlin, pp. 137-146

Keesing R. and Strathern, A. (1998). *Cultural Anthropology. A Contemporary Perspective,* 3rd Edition, Harcourt Brave College Publishers, Fort Worth.

Kroeber, A. and Kluckhohn, C. (1952). *Culture: a critical review of the concepts and definitions*, Harvard University Press, Cambridge.

Kunda, G. (1992). *Control and Commitment in a High-Tech Corporation*, Temple University Press, Phiadelphia, PA.

Leidner, D.E. and Kayworth, T. (2006). Review: A review of culture in information systems research: Toward a theory of information technology culture conflict, *MIS Quarterly*, Vol. 30, No, 2, pp. 357-399

Lyytinen, K. (1986). *Information Systems Development as Social Action: Framework and Critical Implications*, Jyväskylä Studies in Computer Science, Economics and Statistics, No. 8.

Moore, G.C. and Benbasat, I. (1991). Development of an instrument to measure the perceptions of adopting an information technology innovation, *Information Systems Research*, Vol. 2, No. 3, , pp. 192-222

Nerur, S., Mahapatra, R. and Mangalaraj, G. (2005). Challenges of migrating to agile method-ologies, *Communications of the ACM*, Vol. 48, No. 5, pp. 73-78

Overby, E., Bharadwaj, A. and Sambamurthy, V. (2006). Enterprise agility and the enabling role of information technology, *European Journal of Information Systems*, Vol. 15, No. 2, pp. 120-131

Parsons, D., Ryu, H. and Lal, R. (2007). The impact of methods and techniques on outcomes from agile software development projects, in McMaster, T., Wastell, D., Ferneley, E. and DeGross, J. (eds.), *Organizational Dynamics of Technology-Based Innovation: Diversifying the Research Agenda*, Springer, Boston, MA, pp. 235-249

Quinn, R.E. and Kimberly, J.R., Paradox, planning, and perseverance: Guidelines for managerial practice, in Kimberly, J.R. and Quinn, R.E. (eds.) (1984). *New Futures: The Challenge of Managing Organizational Transitions*, Dow Jones-Irwin, Homewood, IL, pp. 295-313

Quinn, R.E. and Rohrbaugh, J. (1983). A spatial model of effectiveness criteria: Towards a com-peting values approach to organizational analysis, *Management Science*, Vol. 29, No. 3, pp. 363-377

Riemenschneider, C.K., Hardgrave, B.C. and Davis, F.D. (2002). Explaining software developer acceptance of methodologies: A comparison of five theoretical models, *IEEE Transactions on Software Engineering*, Vol. 28, No. 12, pp. 1135-1145

Robinson, H. and Sharp, H. (2005). Organizational culture and XP: three case studies, *Proceed-ings of the Agile Development Conference (ADC-05)*.

Schein, E.H. (). *Organizational Culture and Leadership*, Jossey-Bass, San Francisco, CA, 1985

Sharp, H. and Robinson, H. (2004). An Ethnographic Study of XP Practice, *Empirical Software Engineering*, Vol. 9, pp. 353-375

Sharp, H. and Robinson, H. (2008). Collaboration and co-ordination an mature eXtreme pro-gramming teams, *International Journal of Human-Computer Studies*, Vol. 66, pp. 506-518

Sharp, H., Robinson, H. and Petre, M. (2009). The role of physical artefacts in agile software de-velopment: Two complementary perspectives, *Interacting with Computers*, Vol. 21, pp. 108-116

Sherehiy, B., Karwowski, W. and Layer, J.K. (2007). A review on enterprise agility: Concepts, frameworks, and attributes, *International Journal of Industrial Ergonomics*, Vol. 37, pp. 445-460

Siakas, K.V. and Siakas, E. (2007). The agile professional culture: A source of agile quality, *Software Process Improvement and Practice*, Vol. 12, pp. 597-610

Smircich, L. (1983). Concepts of culture and organizational analysis, *Administrative Science Quarterly*, Vol. 28, No. 3, pp. 339-358

Strode, D.E., Huff, S.L. and Tretiakov, A. (2009). The Impact of Organizational Culture on Ag-ile Method Use, *Proceedings of the 42nd Hawaii International Conference on System Sci-ences*, IEEE.

Suscheck, C. and Ford, R. (2008). Jazz improvisation as a learning metaphor for the Scrum soft-ware development methodology, *Software Process Improvement and Practice*, Vol. 13, pp. 439-450

Tolfo, C. and Wazlawick, R.S. (2008). The influence of organizational culture on the adoption of extreme programming, *The Journal of Systems and Software*, Vol. 81, pp. 1955-1967

Tolfo, C. and Wazlawick, R.S., Gomes Ferreira, M.G., and Forcellini, F.A. (2009). Agile meth-ods and organizational culture: Reflections about cultural levels, *Software Process Improve-ment and Practice*, (in press)

Turk, D., France, R. and Rumpe, B. (2005). Assumptions underlying agile software-development processes, *Journal of Database Management*, Vol. 16, No. 4, pp. 62-87

Van Maanen, J. and Barley, S.R. (1984). Occupational communities: Culture and control in or-ganizations, in *Research in Organizational Behavior*, Vol. 6, JAI Press, Inc, p. 287-365

Van Oosterhout, M., Waarts, E. and van Hillegersberg, J., V. (2006). Change factors requiring agility and implicatiobs for IT, *European Journal of Information Systems*, Vol. 15, No. 2, pp. 132-145

Vijayasarathy, L. and Turk, D. (2008). Agile software development: A survey of early adopters, *Journal of Information Technology Management*, Vol. XIX, No. 2, pp. 1-8

Wang, X., Vidgen, R. (2007). Order and Chaos in Software Development: A comparison of two software development teams in a major company, in *Proceedings of the 15th European Confreence on Information Systems*, St. Gallen, Switzerland.

Author Biographies

Juhani Iivari is a professor in Information Systems at the University of Oulu, Finland. He received his Ph.D. degrees from the University of Oulu in 1983. He is a Senior Editor of *MIS Quarterly* and serves in editorial boards of four other IS journals. His research has broadly focused on theoretical foundations of information systems, design science research in information systems, information systems development methodologies and approaches, organizational analysis, implementation and acceptance of information systems, and the quality of information systems. He has published in a number of journals conference proceedings

Netta Iivari received her doctoral degree in information systems from University of Oulu in 2006. She also has a master's degree in cultural anthropology from University of Jyväskylä. She currently holds the position of a post doctoral research fellow from the Academy of Finland. She was appointed as an adjunct professor in the Department of Information Processing Science, University of Oulu in 2009 with the field of 'user-centered, participative information systems design'. Her research is strongly influenced by interpretive and critical research traditions. Her long lasting research interests are related to the empirical, interpretive examinations of participation of different kinds of stakeholder groups in defining, developing, shaping and framing information systems. Her empirical investigations have mainly been carried out in new IS contexts: in packaged software and open source software development contexts and related to solutions targeted at children. Currently, she is specifically interested in participatory design with children and in user participation in open source software development. She has published related to these matters in several IS conferences and journals.

11 Future Research in Agile Systems Development: Applying Open Innovation Principles Within the Agile Organisation

Kieran Conboy, Lorraine Morgan

Abstract: A particular strength of agile approaches is that they move away from 'introverted' development and intimately involve the customer in all areas of development, supposedly leading to the development of a more innovative and hence more valuable information system. However, we argue that a single customer representative is too narrow a focus to adopt and that involvement of stakeholders beyond the software development itself is still often quite weak and in some cases non-existent. In response, we argue that current thinking regarding innovation in agile development needs to be extended to include multiple stakeholders outside the business unit. This paper explores the intra-organisational applicability and implications of open innovation in agile systems development. Additionally, it argues for a different perspective of project management that includes collaboration and knowledge-sharing with other business units, customers, partners, and other relevant stakeholders pertinent to the business success of an organisation, thus embracing open innovation principles.

11.1 Introduction

The last 10 years or so has seen the emergence of a number of agile systems development (ASD) methods, such as XP (Beck, 1999) and Scrum (Schwaber & Beedle 2002). These methods have been well received by those in ISD and there is strong anecdotal evidence to suggest that awareness and indeed use of these methods is highly prevalent across the community. However, some reports have heavily criticised what agile research exists (e.g. Dybå and Dingsøyr 2008; Abrahamsson et al. 2009; Conboy 2009). These reports accuse the current body of agile method research of lacking rigor, cumulative tradition and sufficient theoretical grounding. They even point to the ambiguity as to what constitutes 'agility', stating that it "now means so many things to so many people, it has lost a lot of its meaning" (Conboy 2009).

A particular strength of agile approaches is that they move away from 'introverted' development where the team building the system is detached from the customer. Instead, agile approaches continually involve the customer in the development process, supposedly leading to the development of a more innovative and

T. Dingsøyr et al. (eds.), *Agile Software Development*,
DOI 10.1007/978-3-642-12575-1_11, © Springer-Verlag Berlin Heidelberg 2010

hence more valuable information system (Beck 1999; Schwaber & Beedle 2002). However, while the customer plays an essential part in the agile process, this practice could be extended to include multiple stakeholders and even other organisations. We propose that it is useful to consider how the agile innovation process can benefit from becoming more 'open', e.g., by opening up the boundaries of a systems development entity to include other stakeholders besides the customer. For example, it has been suggested that companies must increasingly work with each other to enhance their agility in adapting to market developments and developing new products/services cheaper and faster (Tapscott and Williams 2005).

As far as we are aware, no research has focused on the role of other stakeholders in agile development besides the customer. Nor has research looked at how principles of open innovation could complement an agile approach, despite the commonalities between the two models, particularly its emphasis on the value of people and communications. In addition, there is no research that we know of that investigates the implications of a more open approach for project management. Furthermore, there is no research that examines the development of appropriate and effective project management practices to support high quality open innovation in agile information systems development. Thus, exploring the notion of open innovation and its applicability and implications in a multiple project environment that employ agile methods is timely.

The remainder of the paper is structured as follows. The next section presents the current state of research on innovation in agile development. Next, some contemporary views on innovation are described. A conceptual framework to discuss future research is then put forth, followed by some conclusions.

11.2 Innovation in Agile Development – The Current State of Research

Innovation and creativity have been advocated as a core part of Information Systems Development (ISD) for many years (Brooks 1987; Elam and Mead 1987; Cougar 1990; Sampler and Galleta 1991; Lobert and Dologite 1994; Gallivan 2003; Carayannis and Coleman 2005). According to Sternberg and Lubart (1999), creativity is the ability to produce work that is considered novel, appropriate and adaptive. Indeed Cougar (1990) believed that creative activities should play a pivotal role "in all aspects of IT development, from requirements definition through program design". Three reasons have been proposed for this. Firstly, "technology is evolving on a daily basis and we can continually look for new ways to utilise resources". Secondly, "most simple systems have already been developed and the challenging ones are still ahead". Finally, "many information systems are old, not meeting existing demand, and will soon become obsolete" (Lobert and Dologite 1994). In addition researchers such as Gallivan (2003) highlight the importance of creative developers, and Brooks (1987) even contends that the critical problems in

ISD may not be addressed by ISD methods per se, but rather by how those methods facilitate creativity and improvisation. The importance of creativity has also been highlighted and the support towards creativity claimed within the agile method movement (Highsmith and Cockburn 2001; Cockburn and Highsmith 2001; Highsmith 2002; Highsmith 2002a; Highsmith 2004). Agile advocates believe that "creativity, not voluminous written rules, is the only way to manage complex software development problems" (Highsmith and Cockburn 2001). Cockburn and Highsmith (2001) also claim that "agile methodologies deal with unpredictability by relying on people and their creativity rather than on processes". Additionally, it has been contended that "agile approaches are best employed to explore new ground and to power teams for which innovation and creativity are paramount" (Highsmith 2002a). The literature also illustrates the fact that the requirement for creativity has been highlighted in discussions of specific agile methods, such as eXtreme Programming (XP), one of the most popular agile methods (Highsmith 2002a; Crispin and House 2003; Benediktsson et al. 2004). Highsmith (2002a) observers that "although XP contains certain disciplined practices, its intent is to foster creativity and communication". Indeed, Benediktsson et al. (2004) claim that "given the benefits of XP in terms of creativity, value delivery and higher satisfaction levels, it is not surprising that many managers and developers have adopted such practices".

Despite these claims, however, there is a lack of understanding of what constitutes creativity and innovation in software development in general and to what extent agile methods actually facilitate these processes.

11.3 Contemporary Thinking on Innovation – Open Innovation

Innovation is now viewed as the lifeblood of organizations that want to survive and prosper in a marketplace that is global in nature and intensely competitive. However, this particular stance on the importance of innovation did not always exist. Traditionally, the innovation process has taken a linear approach, the expectation being that investment in research and development will provide organisations with a competitive advantage (Kane and Ragsdell 2003). In addition, conventional approaches to innovation assumed that it was the experts 'within' the company that invented and designed innovative new products to meet customer needs and organisations rarely looked outside for new ideas or inventions (Tapscott and Williams 2005). As Hamel and Prahalad (1990) pointed out, "organizations often tend to be hidebound and so orthodox ridden, "that the only way to innovate is to put a few bright people in a dark room, poor in some money, and hope that something wonderful will happen" (p. 66). This 'Silicon Valley' approach resulted in innovation being an isolated activity where growth depended on the inventive capacity of individuals and small teams (Hamel and Prahalad 1990). Thus, this very approach in which organisations generate, develop and commercialise their own ideas belong to the closed model of innovation (Fasnacht 2009).

Closed innovation is a view that successful innovation requires control and that firms need to be strongly self-reliant because of uncertainty with quality, availability and capability of others' ideas (Chesbrough 2003). Traditionally, new business development processes and the marketing of new products took place within the firm boundaries and exclusively with internal resources. Within the closed model, the innovation process is characterised by firms that invest in their own R&D, employing smart and talented people in order to outperform their competitors in new product and service development. In addition, after producing a stream of new ideas and inventions, firms must defend their intellectual property thoroughly against the competition (Dahlander and Gann 2007). Changes in society and industry, however, have led to an increased availability and mobility of knowledge workers and the development of new financial structures like venture capitalism. Indeed, Gassmann and Enkel (2004) propose that shorter innovation cycles, industrial research and the rising costs of development, in addition to a lack of resources are motives that are changing companies' innovation strategies towards a more open direction (Gassman and Enkel 2004).

It has been argued that a paradigm shift is taking place in how companies commercialise knowledge, resulting in the boundaries of a firm eroding. This has been characterised as a move towards 'Open Innovation', a paradigm viewed as the antithesis of the traditional model of innovation where research and development activities lead to internally developed products that were then distributed by the firm (Chesbrough et al. 2006). A general theme underling open innovation is that firms cannot continue to look inward in their innovation processes, isolating themselves from possible partners, collaborators and competitors. In other words, open innovation invites firms to open up their boundaries to achieve a flexible and agile environment. The term 'open innovation' has been defined by West and Gallagher (2006, p.82) "as systematically encouraging and exploring a wide range of internal and external sources for innovation opportunities, consciously integrating that exploration with firms capabilities and resources and broadly exploiting those opportunities through multiple channels". In addition, Laursen and Salter (2006) focused on external search breadth and external search depth for different types of innovation in a large-scale sample of UK manufacturing firms. These authors defined openness as "the number of different sources of external knowledge that each firm draws upon in its innovative activities" (2004, p.1204). In contrast to the linear closed model of innovation, the open innovation approach suggests that firms develop processes to ensure a flow of ideas across its boundaries because not all smart people work for the organisation and there is an increasing geographical dispersion of knowledge (Dahlander and Gann 2007). Thus, ideal business search outside their own companies for the best ideas, seeking input from other companies, which include competitors, as well as from customers, suppliers and vendors.

11.4 Project Management in An Open Agile Environment

In an agile development environment, the project manager's role is greatly changed, and is more akin to that of a facilitator or coordinator (Alleman 2002; Lindstrom & Jeffries 2004; Nerur et al. 2005). In agile projects, the organisation or team structure is "organic and flexible", as opposed to traditional structures which are "mechanistic, bureaucratic and formalized" (Nerur et al. 2005); the method is there not as a prescription, but something to be continuously tailored and moulded by the team (Fitzgerald et al. 2006; Conboy and Fitzgerald 2009); the project is completed through a series of iterations, each often as short as a few working days (Fowler & Highsmith 2001; Fitzgerald et al. 2006), resulting in more frequent, short-term development; budgeting is more fluid and short term (Conboy 2010), and software is valued over documentation (Fowler & Highsmith 2001). Significantly, the customer plays a more continuous and embedded role, and thus is intrinsically involved in most project management decisions (Beck 2000; Griffin 2001; Farell et al. 2002; Beck & Andres 2004). Moreover, developers are not confined to a specific specialised role and are encouraged to self-organise, interchanging and blending roles (Nerur et al. 2005) and become involved in project management issues that may fall outside their traditional skill areas.

However, the very concept of incorporating open innovation principles may prove challenging for an agile project manager. As well as coping with managing in such a fluid, short-term environment, dealing with multiple projects and external entities adds further challenges and risk of unexpected outcomes. However, mechanisms for scanning the project landscape need to be incorporated into project management practices in agile organisations and project managers need to be aware that an IS project is no longer a local matter that can be treated as a closed innovation isolated from the rest of the organisation. After all, it has been found that project boundaries are pliable and negotiable and a project should be seen in light of other projects within an organisation. Indeed, knowledge in and about projects should be exchanged and individual projects should scan the open space of the organisation for other projects that constitute potential collaboration (Elbanna 2008). Thus, taking an open innovation route may present many additional benefits for an agile environment.

11.5 Conceptual Framework to Guide Future Research

For our theoretical base, we propose a framework drawn from three central open innovation archetypes proposed by Gassmann and Enkel (2004). These include: (1) the outside-in process; (2) the inside-out process; and (3) the coupled process. This framework provides a useful lens to examine the applicability of open innovation in a multiple-project agile environment and the challenges and implications of such an approach for project management. Open innovation can be analysed at a number of levels, which include the intra-organisational and inter-organisaional networking level (Chesbrough et al. 2006). However most existing research on the phenomenon of open innovation focuses on inter-organisational aspects. In contrast, the implications that open innnovation has *within* an organisation and in particular the fact that it affects different parts of an organisation differently are largely neglected in the current literature (Alexy and Henkel 2009). While there exists much research about intra-organisational level networking in general to stimulate innovation (e.g., Tsai and Ghoshal 1998; Foss and Pedersen 2002; Lagerstrom and Andersson 2003), this type of networking has not been analysed explicitly within the open innovation context (Vanhaverbeke 2006). In particular, there is no research that we know of that addresses intra-organisational networking in an agile project environment. In order to address this, we have tailored Gassmann and Enkel's framework to include innovation that occurs outside the boundaries of a business unit rather than outside a firm per se.

11.5.1 The Outside-in Process

Companies that decide on an outside-in process as a core open innovation approach choose to cooperate with suppliers, customers third parties etc. and integrate the external knowledge gained. This can be achieved by investing in global knowledge creation, applying innovation across industries, customer and supplier integration and purchasing intellectual property. IBM has been cited by Gassmann and Enkel (2004) as one company that invests substantially in contact with customers and other external knowledge sources while CISCO is another that invests in young start-up companies in order to monitor their attractiveness and innovativeness. According to Gassmann and Enkel (2004), if firms possess the necessary competencies and capabilities, they can successfully integrate internal company resources with the critical resources of other members such as customers, suppliers etc, by extending new product development across organizational boundaries. As the focus of this research in on open innovation at the intra-organisational level, an outside-in open innovation approach will refer to the integration of external knowledge and resources gained from multiple stakeholders outside the business unit.

11.5.1 The Inside-out Process

This process focuses on the externalising of company knowledge and innovation in order to bring ideas to market faster. This approach includes licensing IP or multiplying technology by transferring ideas to other companies. Additionally, focussing on an inside-out proces by commercialising ideas to different industries can increase a company's revenue base substantially. For example, companies like Novartis, Pfizer and Roche are well recognised for developing substances that were originally aimed at treating one ailment but became better known when used for others. One example of this is Viagra, initially developed to control blood pressure but became more successful as a sexual aid (Gassman and Enkel 2004). Outsourcing has been recognized as one mechanism that can also be used to channel knowledge and ideas to the external environment. The benefits of outsourcing include gaining access to new areas of complementary knowledge, managing capacity problems which allows for more flexibility, reduced time-to-market, sharing of costs and concentration of core competencies It has been found that companies that choose an inside-out process are mainly research-driven companies like IBM, Pfizer or Novartis. Such companies aim to decrease their fixed costs of R&D and share the risks by outsourcing part of their development process (Gassmann and Enkel 2004). In the context of this study, an inside-out process refers to leveraging and transferring knowledge to stakeholders outside the boundaries of a business unit and gaining certain advantages by letting ideas flow to the outside.

11.5.3 The Coupled Process

This open innovation approach combines the outside-in (gaining external knowledge) with the inside-out process (to bring ideas to market). In order to accomplish both, these companies collaborate and cooperate with other companies (e.g. strategic alliances, joint ventures), suppliers and customers, as well as universities and research institutes.

Alliances with complementary partners can lead to the occurrence of cooperative innovation processes, e.g. Canon and HP joined forces to develop printers while Boeing developed the Boeing 777 with companies in seven different countries. To collaborate and cooperate successfully, a give and take of knowledge approach is crucial. Benefits of such an approach include an intensive exchange of knowledge and a mutual learning process (Gassmann and Enkel 2004). In this research, a coupled process will also refer to a combination of outside-in and inside-out as specified for this study. In particular, how business units cooperate and interact with other business units in intra-organisational networks will be explored.

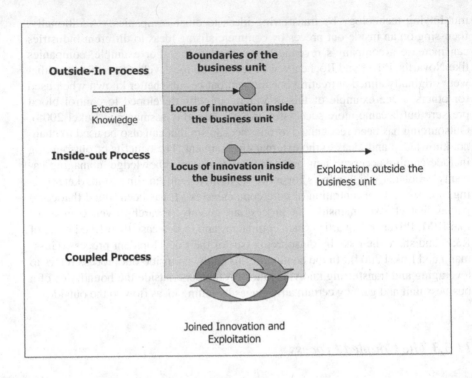

Fig. 11.1. Adapted Open Innovation Framework: Applying Intra-Organisatoinal Innovation Principles in Agile Software Development

11.6 Conclusion and Implications for Future Research

This chapter explores the intra-organisational applicability and implications of open innovation in agile systems development. Additionally, it argues for a different perspective of project management that includes collaboration and knowledge-sharing with other business units, customers, partners, and other relevant stakeholders pertinent to the business success of an organisation, thus embracing open innovation principles.

In terms of future research it raises a number of significant questions that could be addressed. There are many far-reaching, multi-disciplinary questions, but some of the fundamental key ones could simply seek to examine the current state of innovative collaboration between the agile team and other stakeholders outside that business unit. This analysis should go well beyond the well-established on-site customer practice that usually involves one representative, often with a very focused and myopic role within that client organization. Researchers could examine the extent to which various intra-organisational stakeholders are typically involved in the agile development process, and how they contribute to the innovation process on these projects. Research could also examine the current barriers to open innovation that exist in agile development and what steps 'best practice' teams are using, if any, to overcome these barriers.

The conceptual framework proposed earlier also raises some interesting research questions. In terms of 'outside-in' open innovation, how should teams choose which suppliers, customers and third parties to collaborate with? This has not been the focus of any agile development research as far as we are aware. More importantly from an agile perspective given the tight and continuous interaction between all involved, how should they choose people to represent each party, and what are the characteristics of these representatives? Furthermore in an outside-in process, integration of the external knowledge gained is vital, but this can be quite challenging in an agile environment where knowledge transfer is almost exclusively tacit. Indeed, knowledge creation and generation, applying innovation across the organization and customer and supplier integration can be difficult to achieve in such an environment. The 'inside-out' open innovation process also throws up some relevant questions. Deciding to change the locus of knowledge-sharing by transferring ideas to stakeholders outside the business unit may prove challenging. Again this is exacerbated in an agile environment where explicit documentation and transfer of knowledge is usually greatly reduced. Similar to the outside-in approach, a successful inside-out approach may be contingent on the team's knowledge transfer capabilities and selection of appropriate stakeholders and their willingness and ability to engage and cooperate with the team. In relation to the 'coupled process' approach, how teams develop complementary internal value networks to create and gain external knowledge and ideas is a significant question. Where the coupled approach is enabled by a internal ecosystem or value network, there are more questions as to how the network is coordinated and maintained. Additionally, it is crucial to understand how governance is shared across the internal network and how conflict is managed if it arises. Again, agile development if particularly difficult in this case where the traditional, formal, bureaucratic role of the project manager is diminished to that of a coach. This may work well on a small co-located team within a business unit, but may be very problematic when scaled up.

Other research areas beyond the conceptual framework include the question of how an organization can successfully manage the transition to a more open form of agile innovation is one that will be addressed. In addition, who will drive and who will resist the implementation of open innovation practices in an agile environment is another interesting arena. As the agile philosophy focuses on people and their creativity, we expect that individual attitude and acceptance will almost certainly be a prerequisite for the successful implementation of open innovation practices by the firm in question. Additionally, one could examine the capabilities and requirements needed for open innovation practices to be successful. The role of the project manager can also be explored. Introducing open innovation practices in an organisation implies change and is likely to result in uncertainty, risk and a great need for better coordination, which in turn may increase the current workload of a project manager. Indeed, identifying and engaging stakeholders in an intra-organisational network is one such challenge for the project manager. Thus, further research in this area would be beneficial in providing an insight into the role of the project manager in facilitating open innovation in a systems development environment, particularly focusing on the benefits, challenges and best practices of open innovation.

Acknowledgements

This work is supported in part by Science Foundation Ireland grant 03/CE2/1303_1 to Lero – the Irish Software Engineering Research Centre.

References

Abrahamsson, P., Conboy, K. and Wang, X. (2009). "Lots Done, More To Do: The Current State of Agile Systems Development Research," *European Journal of Information Systems*, 18, pp. 1-7.

Alleman, G. (2002). "Agile Project Management Methods for IT Projects." In the *Story of Managing Projects: A Global, Cross-Disciplinary Collection of Perspectives*, Greenwood Press, Berkeley, CA.

Beck, K. (1999). *Extreme Programming Explained*, Addison-Wesley.

Beck, K. (2000). *Extreme Programming Explained: Embrace Change*. Addison-Wesley, Reading, Mass.

Beck, K. and Andres, C. (2004). *Extreme Programming Explained* (2nd Ed). Addison Wesley, Reading, Mass.

Benbasat, I., Goldstein, D.K. and Mead, M. (1987). "The Case Research Strategy in Studies of Information Systems." *MIS Quarterly*, 11(3), pp. 369-386.

Brooks, Frederick P. (1997). No Silver Bullet: Essence and Accidents of Software Engineering. Reprinted in the 1995 edition of *The Mythical Man-Month*.

Chesbrough, H. (2006). *Open Business Models: How to Thrive in the New Innovation Landscape*, Boston, MA: Harvard Business School Press.

Chesbrough H. (2004). "Managing open innovation." *Research & Technology Management*, (47:1), pp. 23-26.

Chesbrough, H. (2003). *Open Innovation: The New Imperative for Creating and Profiting from Technology*, Boston, MA: Harvard Business School Press.

Chesbrough, H., Vanhaverbeke, W. and West, J. (2006). *Open Innovation: Researching a New Paradigm*, Oxford University Press: New York.

Conboy, K. & Fitzgerald, B. (2009). "Method and Developer Characteristics for Effective Agile Method Tailoring: A Study of XP Expert Opinion." *The Transactions on Software Engineering and Methodology (TOSEM)*.

Conboy, K. (2009). "Agility From First Principles: Reconstructing The Concept of Agility in Information Systems Development." *Information Systems Research*, 20(3), pp. 329-354

Conboy, K. (2010). "Project Failure En Mass: A Study of Budgetary Control in Systems Development Projects." *European Journal of Information Systems*, In Press.

Dahlander, L. (2004). Appropriating Returns from Open Innovation Processes: A Multiple Case Study of Small Firms in Open Source Software, 2004, Available at: http://opensource.mit.edu/papers/dahlander.pdf.

Dahlander, L. and Gann, D. (2007). "How Open is Innovation? " *DRUID Summer Conference 2007 on Appropriability, Proximity, Routines and Innovation*, Copenhagen.

Dybå, T. & Dingsøyr, T. (2008). "Empirical Studies of Agile Software Development: A Systematic Review." *Information and Software Technology*, 50, 833-859.

Elbanna, A. (2008). "Open Innovation and the Erosion of the Traditional Information Systems Project's Boundaries". *Proceedings of the International Federation for Information Processing (IFIP 8.6) on Open IT-Based Innovation: Moving Towards Cooperative IT Transfer and Knowledge Diffusion*, eds. León, G., Bernardos, A., Casar, J., Kautz, K., and DeGross, J. (Boston: Springer), pp. 423-439.

Farell, C., Narang, R. Kapitan, S. and Webber, H. (2002). "Towards an effective onsite customer practice. " In *Proceedings of the Third International Conference on Extreme Programming and Agile Processes in Software Engineering*, Alghero, Sardina, Italy (Succi, G. and Marchesi, M. Eds), pp. 52-55.

Fasnacht, D. (2009). *Open Innovation in the Financial Services: Growing Through Openness, Flexibility and Customer Integration*. Springer, Berlin.

Fitzgerald, B., Hartnett, G. & Conboy, K. (2006). "Customising Agile Methods to Software Practices." *European Journal of Information Systems*, 15, pp. 197-210.

Foss, N.and Pedersen, T. (2002). "Transferring Knowledge in MNCs: The Roles of Sources of Subsidiary Knowledge and Organisational Context." *Journal of International Management*, 8, pp. 1-19.

Fowler, M. and Highsmith, J. (2001). "The Agile Manifesto." *Software Development*, 9(8), pp. 28-32.

Gassmann, O. and Enkel, E. (2004). Towards a Theory of Open Innovation: Three core process archetypes. Available at: http://www.alexandria.unisg.ch/Publikationen/274.

Glaser, B.G. (1992). *Basics of grounded theory analysis: Emergence vs. Forcing.* Mill Valley, CA: Sociology Press.

Griffin, L. (2001). "A Customer Experience: Implementing XP." In *XP Universe Raleigh*, NC, July 23rd-25th (Wells, D. Ed), pp. 195-200.

Hamel, G. and Prahalad, C.K. (1989). "Strategic Intent." *Harvard Business Review*, May-June.

Kane, H.C.M. and Ragsdell, G. (2003). "How Might Models of Innovation Inform the Management of Knowledge." *KMSS Proceedings*.

Lagerstrom, K. and Andersson, M. (2003). "Creating and Sharing Knowledge within a Transnational Team - The Development of a Global Business System." Journal of World Business, 38(2), pp. 84-95.

Lindstrom, L. and Jeffries, R. (2004). "Extreme Programming and Agile Software Development Methodologies." *Information Systems Management*, 21(3) pp. 41-52.

Miles, M. and Huberman, A. (1999). *Qualitative Data Analysis*. Sage, London.

Nerur, S., Mahapatra, R. and Mangalara, G. (2005). "Challenges of Migrating to Agile Methodologies." *Communication of he ACM*, 48(5), pp. 72-78.

Oppenheim, A. (1992). *Questionnaire Design, Interviewing and Attitude Measurement*. Continuum, New York.

Potter, J. (1999). Discourse Analysis as a Way of Analysing Naturally Occuring Talk. *In Qualitative Research, Theory, Method and Practice* (Silvermann, D., Ed.), Sage Publications, London, pp. 144-160.

Rubin, H. and Rubin, I. (2005). *Qualitative Interviewing: The Art of Hearing Data*. Sage, Thousand Oaks, CA.

Schwaber, K. and Beedle, M. (2002). *Agile software development with SCRUM*, Prentice Hall.

Stake, R.E. (2000). "Case studies." In *Handbook of Qualitative Research* (in Denzin, N.K., Lincoln, Y.S. Eds), Sage Publications, Thousand Oaks, pp. 435-454.

Stapleton, L. (2008). "Ethical decision making in technology development: a case study of participation in a large-scale information systems development project." *AI and Society*, 22(3), pp. 405-429

Strauss, A. and Corbin, J. (1990). *Basics of Qualitative Research: Grounded Theory Procedures and Techniques*. 1990, Sage Publications, Newbury Park, CA.

Strauss, A. and Corbin, J. (1998). *Basics of Qualitative Research: Grounded Theory Procedures and Techniques (2nd Ed)*, Sage Publications, Newbury Park, CA.

Tapscott, D. and Williams, A. (2005). Realising the Power of Innovation Webs, *Optimizemag.com*, December (http://www.cioindex.com/nm/articlefiles/2776-Optimize_InnovationWebs.pdf.

Trauth, E. and O'Connor, M. (1991). "A study of the interaction between information technology and society: An illustration of combined qualitative research methods." In Nissen, H.E., Klein, H.K. and Hirschheim, R. (Eds) *Information Systems Research: Contemporary Approaches and Emergent Traditions*, 131-144. Amsterdam: North-Holland.

Tsai, W. and Ghoshal,, S. (1998). "Social Capital and Value Creation: The Role of Intrafirm Networks." *Academy of Management Journal*, 41(4), pp. 464-76.

Vanhaverbeke, W. (2006). "The Interorganisational Context of Open Innovation. " In *Open Innovation: Researching a New Paradigm*, Chesbrough, H., Vanhaverbeke, W. and West, J., Eds., Oxford University Press: London.

Wengraf, T. (2001). *Qualitative research interviewing: biographic narrative and semi-structured method*, London: Sage Publications.

West, J. and Gallagher, S. (2006). "Challenges of open innovation: the paradox of firm investment in open-source software." *R&D Management*, (36:3), pp. 319-331.

West, J. and Gallagher, S. (2006). "Patterns of Open Innovation in Open Source Software." In *Open Innovation: Researching a New Paradigm*, Chesbrough, H., Vanhaverbeke, W. and West, J., Eds, Oxford University Press.

Author Biographies

Kieran Conboy is a lecturer in information systems at the National University of Ireland Galway. His research focuses on agile systems development approaches as well as agility across other disciplines. Kieran is currently involved in numerous national and international projects in this area, and has worked with many companies on their agile initiatives including Intel, Microsoft, Accenture, HP, and Fidelity Investments. Kieran has chaired related conferences including the European Conference in Information Systems (Galway 2008) the XP and Agile Development Conference (Limerick 2008) and also has chairing roles at XP2009 and XP2010. Some of his research has been published in various leading journals and conferences such as Information Systems Research, the European Journal of Information Systems, the International Conference in Information Systems (ICIS), the European Conference in Information Systems (ECIS), IFIP 8.6 and the XP200n conference series. He is also associate editor of the European Journal of Information Systems. Prior to joining NUI Galway, Kieran was a management consultant with Accenture, where he worked on a variety of projects across Europe and the US.

Lorraine Morgan works as a researcher with Lero, the Irish Software Engineering Research Centre at the University of Limerick. Her research focuses on agile methods and open innovation, open business models, value networks and open source software. In addition, some of her research has been published in journals and conferences such as Database for Advances in Information Systems, European Conference of Information Systems (ECIS), International Federation for Information Processing (IFIP) Working Conference 8.6 and 8.2 and the International Open Source Systems Conference.

Index

T. Dingsøyr et al. (eds.), *Agile Software Development*,
DOI 10.1007/978-3-642-12575-1, © Springer-Verlag Berlin Heidelberg 2010